Monica Larner and
John Howell

*Buying a property*

# ITALY

**CADOGAN**guides

# Contents

## Acknowledgements

**Monica Larner** would like to thank Rupert Wheeler of Navigator Guides for putting this project together and the many people who helped ink the following pages. Special thanks goes to my family, Stevan, Christine and Michael Larner, for planting a vineyard and grafting me to the vine.

**Navigator Guides** and **Cadogan Guides** would like to thank Gabriella Cursoli for her help with updating and research.

# About the authors

**Monica Larner** resides in Rome and has divided her time between Italy and France for the past 15 years. She has written several books about her adopted homes, including *Living, Studying, and Working in Italy* (Henry Holt), *In Love in Italy* (Universe) and *Working and Living France* (Cadogan Guides). She is the Italian correspondent for *Wine Enthusiast* magazine and writes about wine, food and travel for many other publications. She is also completing her training as a *sommelier*. When not in Europe, she can be found with pruning shears in hand at Larner Vineyard in California's Santa Ynez Valley.

**John Howell** established John Howell & Co in Sheffield in 1979 and by 1997 it had become one of the largest and most respected law firms in the north of England, employing over 100 lawyers. On moving to London in 1995, John Howell has gone on to specialise in providing legal advice to clients buying property in France, Spain, Italy and Portugal.

**Cadogan Guides**
2nd Floor
233 High Holborn
London WC1V 7DN
info@cadoganguides.co.uk
www.cadoganguides.com

**The Globe Pequot Press**
246 Goose Lane, PO Box 480, Guilford,
Connecticut 06437–0480

Cover photographs: (front) © Mathew Lodge/Alamy; (back) © Ben Ramos/Alamy, Misha Gordon/Alamy
Maps © Cadogan Guides, drawn by Maidenhead Cartographic Services
Cover design: Sarah Rianhard-Gardner
Editor: Linda McQueen
Proofreader: Susannah Wight
Indexing: Isobel McLean

Produced by **Navigator Guides**
www.navigatorguides.com

Printed in Finland by WS Bookwell
A catalogue record for this book is available from the British Library
ISBN 10: 1-86011-178-5
ISBN 13: 978-1-86011-178-5

The author and publishers have made every effort to ensure the accuracy of the information in this book at the time of going to press. However, they cannot accept any responsibility for any loss, injury or inconvenience resulting from the use of information contained in this guide.

Please help us to keep this guide up to date. We have done our best to ensure that the information in it is correct at the time of going to press. But places are constantly changing, and rules and regulations fluctuate. We would be delighted to receive any comments concerning existing entries or omissions. Authors of the best letters will receive a copy of the Cadogan Guide of their choice.

# Introduction

Italy is an easy sell. The breathtaking natural beauty, spanning black volcanic beaches and glacier-carved lakes, a dizzying anthology of artistic treasures, excellent food and wine and a populace prone to spontaneous *trattoria* singalongs have universal appeal. The *dolce vita*, or 'sweet life', is not a cliché, it's a proud national anthem. Many visitors come to Italy on holiday and leave haunted by the feeling that they've seen their personal paradise. Some return and commit to Italy in the most emphatic way possible: they purchase a tiny piece of it.

Precisely because Italy sells itself, the aim of this book is quite other. More than a guide, *Buying a Property: Italy* is a companion. Packed with essential information – ranging from logistical considerations to fiscal implications – this book directs the buyer, step by step, on their investment abroad. A section of colour photographs combined with lively text will whet your appetite, we hope, for your new life abroad.

The book includes a detailed regional breakdown of the *bel paese*, intended to help you choose, for example, between the comforts of Florence's extensive English-speaking expatriate network and the remote, rustic south where Baroque palaces can still be picked up at bargain prices. It addresses the needs of buyers searching for a summer home or a retirement lifestyle, of those employed in Italy and those looking for a sound investment opportunity. Thinking about converting a 15th-century Umbrian farmhouse into a bed-and-breakfast? The legal chapter will tell you how. Need to know where to find English-language schools for your children? A chapter on settling in describes the intricacies of life in a new country. Want to build a swimming pool overlooking your olive grove? The dos and don'ts of home improvement and restoration, and how they vary from region to region, are detailed. Concerned about crime? Basic Italian street smarts are covered, to help you avoid becoming an unknowing target.

Throughout the book are personal anecdotes from seasoned experts who have already bought property in Italy and have long since settled into their Italian life. Their stories – sometimes humorous, sometimes less so – have been selected to highlight common pitfalls and misunderstandings. They also communicate just how rewarding buying a home in Italy can be, in owners' own convinced words. In general, the book is structured to supply all the information you need, accompany you through bureaucratic procedures and expose basic cultural curiosities. More importantly, it should nudge you along so that you ask the right questions and make the right decisions.

If you're already sold on Italy, let us accompany you on your journey to buy your very own piece of it.

# First Steps and Reasons for Buying

02

This book was conceived, structured and written with one goal in mind: to explain clearly how to buy a house in Italy. But before we can begin to tackle our assignment, you must complete a task of your own. Call it soul-searching, acting on instinct, following a personal epiphany, a momentary lapse of reason – whatever you like. When investing abroad, especially in a country that evokes such personal reactions among its visitors as Italy does, the 'why' must precede the 'how'. For this reason, this first section revolves around two questions only you can answer – the first: 'Why Italy?'; the second: 'Why buy?'

Most likely you already know the answers to those questions. But if you are still mulling over whether or not to buy property in Italy, this section should help you make a decision. For those beyond reconsideration, the second half of this chapter details visas, permits and other necessary paperwork. When you embark on your adventure, you need to start a paper trail that will ultimately become the foundation of your *vita italiana*.

# Why Italy?

In his book *The Italians*, journalist Luigi Barzini asks of foreigners who settle in his country 'what mysterious emptiness in their souls is filled merely standing on Italian soil?' . If you interpret Barzini's words to mean that he considers Italy an uniquely upbeat place, and the rest of the world less so, you're probably on the right track. If he seems to imply that some move to Italy to run away from something back home, that may also be the case. Only we foreigners are in a position to know; as a native Italian, Barzini could never fully comprehend the spell his country casts on its visitors. Volumes have been written over centuries by expatriate poets and authors trying to capture the essence of Italy's magic, and every soulful metaphor has been elaborated for this purpose. No matter how you deconstruct this unique fascination, one common theme almost always emerges: Italy makes people happy.

Foreigners come to Italy to find love, freedom, artistic expression or to escape less fortunate conditions back home. Those looking to improve their physical health can feast on fresh ingredients at any *trattoria* while soaking in the sunshine. Those looking for human contact will find it in spades on a train, in the *piazza* or at the local snack bar. Italy is a miracle cure for most ailments and a prescription for feeling good. Sounds like a bunch of clichés? Perhaps. But most of the clichés are born from truths. Consider the following stereotypes.

## Solar over Lunar

Since ancient times the people of this elongated peninsula have been governed by the sun. Smiles and laughter are more forthcoming, and being an extrovert or having a bubbly disposition are prized personal traits. Sunshine makes grapes sweeter and vegetables darker and colours the local diet. Warmth also heats libidos and relationships. On the other hand, when the sun does not shine, this careful balance of elements is off kilter. Prolonged exposure to cold and rain would do untold damage to the Italian persona.

## Quality over Quantity

This is another truism, especially in the retail world. An elegant woman prefers to drop several hundred euros on a single item rather than fill her closet. A businessman will purchase one pair of hand-stitched leather shoes and polish them regularly rather than buy replacements. Quality is the only criterion considered in cooking. Deciding what to eat has little to do with cravings; it has to do with what produce is in season and is available at the local market that morning.

## Small over Big

Everything seems petite in Italy – cars, streets, parking places, houses, kitchens and your water heater capacity. The country is so tightly packed that you can travel to Naples from Rome in just a few hours and cross dozens of cultural borders along the way. Head 100 kilometres out in any direction and you're likely to land in a new world with different dialects, cultures and cuisines. Wander across the *piazza* and you're likely to run into a long-lost friend.

## Slow over Fast

Italians love life in the slow lane. A Sunday lunch is a full day's occupation. Coffee- and cigarette-breaks at the office are not an exercise in brevity. If they were measured in mere minutes, they would not be a break at all. Dinner wouldn't taste as good if you gathered all the ingredients at the local convenience store. The perfect meal entails finding the best bread store, walking over to the best butcher then backtracking to the best pastry shop. Even during the most hectic days, most find a quiet moment to read the newspaper.

## Fast over Slow

But Italians love life in the fast lane just as much. Speed demons dominate the roads and expertly edge slower vehicles out of their way. Wisecracks and humour are exchanged like rapid fire and Italians have an uncanny swiftness when it comes to 'getting with the programme'. They know how not to stand in a queue and yet be the first in the line. Love at first sight is faster than the speed of light.

If you are as unmoved by those stereotypes as Italians are tired of hearing that their country is one of pizza-dough-throwing, *mandolino*-playing, moustache-twirling playboys singing '*O Sole Mio*' with a red-chequered tablecloth around their waist, then consider these more tangible reasons to call Italy home.

First and foremost is **quality of life**. All other considerations – ranging from beautiful surroundings, good geography, better weather, good food and wine, healthy living and cheaper prices – fall under this heading. Without a doubt, quality of life is what sets Italy above the rest. Investing in the country doesn't just mean buying a new home, it means acquiring a new lifestyle to go with it.

People with a penchant for **aesthetics** will have all their senses satisfied. The borders of the peninsula enclose stunning natural beauty – from Alpine meadows and glacier lakes to sand dunes and volcanic islands. With more than 7,600km of coastline, Italy satisfies sun-worshippers, and with its snow-capped peaks it is also a winter paradise. Eyes, ears and tastebuds will also be energised by what mankind has added to the surroundings. By most accounts, Italy houses half of the world's artistic treasures. There are too many monuments, museums, churches and other treasures to explore in ten lifetimes.

Beauty and healthy living brought English Romantic poets like Keats and Shelley. Both moved to Italy to escape tuberculosis and the damp of home, and both found their final resting place in Rome. Millions of other romantics have followed in their footsteps to enjoy a mild **climate** where citrus and olive trees flourish. Italy's elongated shape reads like an inverted thermometer, with heat-waves in the south and freezes in the north. The further you move in either direction, the more extreme the readings within the range of the so-called Mediterranean climate. Geography and climate have produced a **cuisine** celebrated for being low in fat and cholesterol. Olive oil replaces butter, and fresh vegetables, meat and fish are boiled, stewed, fried and grilled in infinite combinations. Even wine has been celebrated as a healthy food since doctors discovered that a glass or two is good for the human heart. A French food critic once brushed off Italian cooking as too simplistic; he said that it was all based on a combination of two things: flour and tomato. An Italian colleague had a quick reply: 'That's exactly where its genius lies.'

**Price** is also an important factor when making the move. While the 2002 currency switchover from lire to euros made Italy's cost of living rise – if not double – it still remains slightly below that of England and most northern European countries. Metropolitan centres like Milan and Rome are priced similarly to sister cities in France and England, but Italy is, generally speaking, cheaper. Prices vary enormously between the prosperous northern and central regions of Italy, and the relatively poor south. A three-course meal with wine at a sophisticated Milan restaurant might cost €80 per person. A similar restaurant in Rome could be €10 less. Meanwhile, an all-fish bonanza in Palermo with white wine, and spaghetti coloured with black squid ink followed by fried shrimp and calamari, costs about €40 a head.

Despite the euro, French and Germans habitually cross over the Italian border at weekends to buy olive oil and other household items. Italians complain that greengrocers have doubled prices since the début of the euro currency, but meat and vegetables still cost less compared with neighbouring countries. On the other hand, heavily taxed goods like luxury items may cost more in Italy. You are probably better off purchasing your Gucci luggage or your Bulgari diamond bracelet in a London or New York boutique. Sadly, the infamous days of cheap wine have almost disappeared. Up until a few years ago, you could purchase a litre of wine for less than what you'd pay for a bottle of mineral water. Wine prices have increased dramatically and, if you insist on the cheap plonk, you won't forgive yourself the next morning. But still, wine is overall cheaper than elsewhere in Europe.

As a non-Italian-tax-paying foreigner, your cost of living could be more appealing. As one of the most taxed nations in the world, Italians lose up to 45 per cent of their income to fiscal authorities. You are probably better off continuing to pay taxes in your country of origin where rates are lower. But watch out for that sneaky exchange rate. As the euro entered circulation, both the British pound and the US dollar gained 15 per cent in value thanks to a weak euro exchange. More recently, however, the dollar took a tumble strengthening the euro by 30 per cent. Who knows what could happen next.

The fact that Italy and the UK share many similarities is another reason to make Italy your second home. In fact, no two European nations match each other as well in terms of size, population and economic power. Italy may be a little bigger, but the English only slightly outnumber the Italians. Italy relies more on industry, while the UK is almost fully a service-based economy.

Despite that, both nations share similar gross domestic products and per capita outputs.

# Why Buy?

Once you've answered 'Why Italy?', the next question is 'Why Buy?'. Spending longer holidays there may satisfy your appetite for Italy. Or, you could dip your toes in the water with a short-term rental in Rome or in a cottage by the lakes in Lombardy. Buying a house will certainly propel you into a whole other level of intimacy with Italy and the Italians. And, during that process, you will undergo a personal transformation. You will become a little more *italiano* and a little less *straniero* (foreigner).

There are two main reasons why foreigners buy property in Italy, and they are often intertwined. The first is because they are in the market for a holiday home, and the second is because they are looking for a sound investment. Following that, other motivations get drawn into the mix. For example, some simply want to live in Italy, or open a business. Others identify with Italian family values and choose to raise their own children there. Others come on the strength of a second wind during their retirement years.

No matter what your reasons, buying a house in Italy has never been easier. Call it 'globalisation' of the property market, general economic prosperity makes having and maintaining a home abroad a realistic dream. The Internet means that working from home is as feasible on the island of Stromboli as it is in

London. A united Europe facilitates travel and smoothes many of the bureaucratic obstacles. And budget airlines have made it possible to fly to Italy several times a month without breaking the bank. So as you become a little more *italiano*, you also become a little more *cittadino del mondo* (citizen of the world).

## A Second Home

Italy is paradise for second-home-seekers. There is no shortage of beautiful properties or beautiful locations. Most of the peninsula is easily accessible through improved transport hubs and newly added regional airports. Waves of artistic and architectural movements over centuries speak to all tastes, from rustic to refined. Most importantly, locals and foreigners cohabit without a glitch. They've been doing it for so long that cultural assimilation is virtually painless today. Among European nations, Italy is certainly among the most welcoming of foreign home-owners.

Very many Italians own a second home. Once regarded as a status symbol, an extra home by the sea for the *ferragosto* summer holiday or in the mountains for the *settimana bianca* winter ski break is now the norm. One reason is because Italians traditionally shy away from the stock market and less tangible assets, preferring instead to invest in bricks and mortar. Another is because most employment contracts allow for four weeks, if not more, of paid holiday each year. Northern European workers might squeeze in a sequence of mini-breaks over a stretch of long weekends, but Italian employees can settle into their second home for a full month each year. After prolonged rest and recuperation they go back to the cities *en masse* and work for another three months before the winter break. And, whereas we might travel far and wide to a new corner of the planet each year, Italians tend to replay the exact same summer holiday year after year. Hence, in the long run, it is cheaper for them to buy than to rent. There are whole communities of second-home-owners who have grown up and grown old together exclusively during summer months. Rather than meeting at school or university, many lifelong pals are linked because their families owned summer homes on the same beach.

According to Italy's contractors' lobby, Confedilizia, 26 per cent of home-owners have a second home. More than a third of wealthy northerners have a getaway property somewhere else in the country, although only 12 per cent of people living in Sardinia and Sicily – islands where vacation homes are coveted – have a holiday home. Two-thirds of second homes are not in the province where their owners reside normally, and only one in five is in the same municipality.

## Investment

The volatile euro might be an embarrassment for the European Central Bank, but not for estate agents and their clients. Favourable exchange rates are fuelling a buying binge. Since its 1999 début, the euro first fell over 15 per cent against the British pound and over 20 per cent against the US dollar, then rose again to recover much of its value (June 2005). Canny foreign investors will thus have seen the value of their home in Italy increase not just in local value, but also – and even more – when measured against their own currency. With the euro likely to strengthen further, buying property in Italy is an investment with the potential to yield further gains on currency rates alone.

Traditionally, those who wanted to speculate in the market faced housing prices that rose only 5 per cent each year – not much for a quick cash turn-around. But since the introduction of the euro, Italian property prices have skyrocketed beyond anyone's wildest imagination. People who purchased property only three years ago are reporting 30–50 per cent gains on their property, especially in big cities like Rome. Foreign interest in Tuscany, especially the area south of Florence known as 'Chiantishire', has so inflated the market that most restored farmhouses are unattainable. Now they are bought and sold by pop and movie stars and the élite of the business world. The same is true of seaside property on the island of Sardinia. Ironically, until recently islanders considered the beaches and rocky coastline useless because it was no good for sheep-herding. Savvy foreign investors with little interest in sheep saw new potential and turned Sardinia into one of the most exclusive resorts on the planet. A similar phenomenon happened in Umbria, considered the anti-Tuscany because its prices were so much lower than its neighbour. Today, the anti-Umbria area for home-seekers to explore is the Marches (Le Marche). It's also happening in the Veneto, Emilia-Romagna, the northern part of Lazio, Abruzzo and the northeastern corner of Sicily. It's no surprise that people with the fore-sight to buy decades ago in places like Tuscany, the Amalfi Coast, Portofino, Lombardy's lake region or Venice are sitting on goldmines today.

What is a surprise is that not all tasty morsels of Italian territory have been gobbled up. For example, extremely good deals can be had in the deep south. Puglia, or the 'heel' of Italy, has been unfairly labelled a backwater. But 15-room Baroque palaces that sell for as little as €700,000 are quickly attracting the attention of investors from England, Germany and America bent on converting them into hotels and conference centres. The whole eastern flank of central Italy, including Le Marche, Abruzzo and Molise, is saturated with crumbling castles and hilltop towers. Unfortunately, the area is also earthquake-prone, but, as engineering techniques improve, prices will undoubtedly rise. Remember, these places have already stood for hundreds of years. There are entire ghost towns in Calabria that can be had for pocket change. Of course, that doesn't include restoration costs, but local labour in the south is cheaper than elsewhere.

What makes the south even more attractive to investors is that the Italian government offers a generous series of tax breaks and subsidies for those who buy in undeveloped areas. The EU sometimes kicks in with funding too. For example, if you own a crumbling farmhouse in Sicily, state money will cover almost all the restoration costs if you pledge to convert the property into a business, such as a bed-and-breakfast. Funding is made available for those who create jobs in areas with soaring unemployment rates.

There are strings attached, as with everything. What makes the south unattractive to investors is poor infrastructure, poor services and organised crime.

# Living in Italy

Rather than wanting a second home or an investment property, some buy simply because they wish to live permanently in the country. In this case, their Italian home is their primary residence and all the smaller tributaries of life – from family to friends to profession – flow into and become one river that is dictated by local currents. To take this waterway allegory one step further, they opt to become part of Italy's 'mainstream'.

There are countless reasons for this, but the primary ones are starting a business, self-employment, raising a family and retirement. What follows is a broad sociological overview of each, although all are discussed in detail and from a practical point of view elsewhere in this book.

## Starting a Business

The backbone of the Italian economy is not blue-chip companies, like Fiat and Pirelli, but small 'mamma and papa' businesses. In fact, the vast majority of Italian businesses have fewer than 15 employees, and many rely on a labour force that shares a common surname. Fathers and sons go into business together, as do mothers and daughters, sisters and brothers and uncles and cousins. When not in the family, other businesses are shared between friends or a small group of close associates. There are so many small businesses, especially in the affluent north, that Italy's entire economy, employment structure and tax base cannot survive without them. For this reason, Italy is a decidedly pro-small-business environment.

Another reason is that small 'niche' operations have put Italy on the map of the world's best products. A family-run company in the Veneto region makes ski boot buckles considered the best on the slopes by Olympic athletes. Another makes components for spectacle rims that are used by the most exclusive fashion firms. A tie-maker in Naples hand-stitches fabric to produce the celebrated Marinelli cravat worn as a badge of success by the nation's top politicians and entertainers. A suitcase- and trunk-making business founded in 1913 by the Prada family has become a world-recognised emblem of Italian ingenuity. A man named Giorgio Armani built his fashion empire by

## Case Study: A Dream Come True

Chris Larkman's tale of buying an apartment in the heart of the Eternal City starts with what can only be described as an act of Divine Intervention. A former Roman Catholic priest who studied at the English College in Rome for almost a decade in the 1960s, Larkman went on to leave the priesthood, marry and have four children. Throughout those life changes, he could not shake his love for Rome. In particular, he could not shake the image of a tiny courtyard called Arco degli Acetari, draped with flowers, embedded with Roman artefacts and just steps away from Campo de' Fiori. He found a poster of this picturesque corner and brought it home to England. Years later, when he decided to look for an investment property in Rome, he knew the only snag would be convincing his wife, Clare. 'She pointed to the poster and said, "If you find somewhere like that, I'm with you",' he recalls. 'We did Internet research and got some numbers. The first one we called was for an apartment in Arco degli Acetari. We flew to Rome, saw the apartment on Monday and had signed the contract by Wednesday.'

The property is unusual because it is below ground, but that explains the bargain price – a mere €115,000 when others of the same size in this neighbourhood go for three or four times that. Chris took equity from his house in England and bought the apartment in October 2001, with plans to let it to help pay off the 15-year mortgage. Eight trips to Rome and €12,000 in renovation later, it was ready for tenants. 'We decided to rent on a weekly basis because, with the advent of budget airlines, taking short breaks in Italy has become a very attractive option.' His first tenants arrived on 15 March 2002, and the apartment was immediately booked right through to November.

'The experience has been a dream come true, but there is one thing that haunts me,' Chris says. 'From the apartment I can hear the very same clock tower of my college that I heard every quarter-hour for seven years while I studied for the priesthood.'

hand and now fights off an army of investors courting him with multimillion-euro figures. Faced with a saturated Italian market, Barilla now feeds more pasta to foreign countries than any other. Enzo Ferrari, an engineer from the town of Modena with a need for speed, hand-assembled his first auburn-coloured racer that gave birth to a long line of Formula One championship winners. The list goes on.

Whatever your business concept, you will find an environment that caters to and nurtures the entrepreneur. The trick is to start off with an idea that doesn't already exist in Italy or is better than ones that do. Many foreigners import business ideas from home. For example, an American woman inaugurated Italy's first one-hour photography development laboratory in the early 1980s. A group of Britons opened English-language bookstores that are frequented by foreigners and English-starved Italians alike. Other foreigners have made their mark on local gastronomy by introducing the concepts of the salad bar, the Sunday brunch, take-away Chinese food and, of course, the Irish pub. Alternatively, start a business servicing the needs of local businesses that lack English language skills or other skills that you can provide.

# Self-employment

Some foreigners prefer to take a permanent vacation from the office by working for themselves in an idyllic setting. If you can make enough money, self-employment in Italy is an incredibly rewarding experience. Writers and artists dream of freelancing in Italy the same way that astronauts dream of going to the moon and archaeologists dream of exploring undiscovered sites. For many self-employed professionals in Italy, once you make it there, why go anywhere else?

Of course, there's that little issue of money. It is not easy to be self-employed in a country with an already high unemployment rate, and all freelancers know the difficulties of surviving from cheque to cheque only too well. Because of its vast artistic heritage, Italy does bode well for writers and artists. If you are handy with a paintbrush and palette, you could avoid the 'starving artist' trap by using your skills on the countless art restorations under way throughout the peninsula. There is work to be had, from retouching frescoes in a rural church to peeling the grime off marble monuments in Rome. In down-times, wordsmiths can attract a fair amount of work through translation, public relations and teaching English as a second language. Self-employed professionals also do well in two other fields: tourism and technology. Italy hosts one of the world's biggest number of tourists. Freelance graphic designers, web-page architects or anyone else with a firm grasp of major English-language software (such as Photoshop or Quark XPress) and of the Italian language can find freelance work in Italy if they are determined to. Of course the high cost of living in Italy means personal determination is the most important factor when considering self-employment.

# Educating and Raising Children

One of Italy's most admired virtues is the importance its society places on the family nucleus. The family blood-bond forms the fabric that holds the entire culture together. A newborn is cuddled by aunts, uncles and grandparents, not to mention parents, to the point of ecstasy. These tiny citizens respond by brandishing bigger smiles and widening their eyes to win adult hearts and an overdose of affection. Italian infants can be seen with €300 sunglasses in the summer and personalised *après-ski* boots in the winter. It is not uncommon to see pierced and tattooed teenagers shopping for undergarments with their grey-haired grandparents. Even pensioners still refer to their parents as *mamma* and *papa*. And Italians of all ages abide by a cardinal rule: never, ever insult someone's mother.

Because the concept of family is so sacred, foreigners find Italy, by and large, a fantastic place to raise offspring. There's no doubt that it is. Schools are staffed with exceptionally caring teachers, and neighbours and friends are quick to step in with car-pooling or babysitting. Everyone surrounding a child, from priest to nearby shopkeeper, plays a role in its upbringing. Italian women have children later in life (the average age of a woman in the north giving birth to her first child is her very late 20s) and they are having fewer children. Babies are a very precious gift indeed. There are few teenage pregnancies and some of the woes linked to adolescent life – such as drug abuse – are tempered only because parents and society keep a much closer eye. Like anywhere else there are bad seeds but, in general, this is a country extremely focused on providing for the next generation.

But there is a dark side to these deep blood-bonds. One example may be found somewhere among the obscure and muddled cultural pressures that forced the Mafia into existence. Although Italy's Mafia is a very complex and unique phenomenon, it has something to do with the fact that citizens in the most remote parts of the peninsula felt abandoned by the state and turned to the support and protection of the 'family' instead. Even today, there are poor neighbourhoods where public electricity and water utilities have failed to set up services. Illegal providers saw an untapped market and now those residents have heat and running water. Rather than paying the state for those services, they pay the local Mafia. It's not too hard to see how mistrust of outsiders is deformed into dependency on insiders.

There is another, perhaps sillier example of Italian family values gone too far. It is known as *mammismo* and is an increasingly embarrassing and debated issue in popular culture. *Mammismo* is best defined as the inability of Italian youth to let go of their mother's apron strings. A lack of affordable housing is the main reason young adults opt to live under their parents' roof. But there is a growing suspicion that many prefer the comforts of home to personal independence. What is disconcerting is that sometimes these *mammoni* are not young at all. A 30-something corporate lawyer in Rome with a hefty monthly stipend from his firm still prefers to live at home where his mother cooks his meals and irons his shirts. Indeed, he is proud to be a *mammone*. In this case, the lawyer in question actually rented a bachelor pad with a rooftop terrace and a stunning view of St Peter's Basilica. After only a few months of struggling with the settings on his washing machine and doing dishes, he gave up and moved back in with his parents.

According to official statistics, 70 per cent of 29-year-old men live with their parents, and the number of 38-year-old men living at home has grown from 20 to 27 per cent over the past five years. Only half as many women stay at home,

### Mammoni

Advocates of the notion that offspring should eventually leave the nest should consider the following: in mid-2002, Italy's highest appeals court ordered a father to continue paying €1,500 a month in child support to his 29-year-old son. The son, who has a law degree, several job offers and a €250,000 trust fund, was sued by his father, who claimed he was 'fed up' with having to support his adult son. But the court did not side with the father from Naples. Judges ruled that the son was entitled to reject employment that he deemed 'inappropriate to his specific training, habits, attitudes and interests'. The Italian constitution establishes that parents have the duty of supporting their children and making sure they get an education. But the constitution does not indicate when parents' obligations might end. Civil law states that it is up to the child to determine when he or she has achieved economic independence. Many courts enforce the idea that economic independence is reached when the offspring reaches the same standard of living as his or her parents. People who marry in Italy vow to support their children until they are able to achieve their own goals and aspirations. But the omission of a cut-off age determining when enough is enough gives offspring the final say.

There is hope for parents, however. In a contrasting case three years before, Italy's highest court ruled to reduce a 35-year-old man's 'maintenance' allowance paid by his parents. In this case, the judges said the young adult was partly to blame since he had failed to earn a medical degree in 15 years of study!

although their numbers are also on the rise. Italians with university degrees are 30 per cent more likely than those without degrees to live with the folks.

# Retirement

For many foreigners, Italy is a prize enjoyed at the end of a lifetime of hard work spent elsewhere. A pension from England can easily be paid in Italy to ensure that your golden years are what they are supposed to be. Italy's health care system is accessible to all EU pensioners who reside in the country and to other EU citizens who pay a modest annual contribution. Slow years are easy years in Italy and, with an ever-ageing population, retirees will find plenty of communities to live in and people with whom they share common interests.

As a foreign pensioner, you are shielded from a huge problem Italians of the same age are just beginning to ponder. With its fiscal health threatened by a demographic time bomb, Italy's government is struggling to fund the pensions of the future. The welfare state doled out generous pensions and continues to do so. But, in another 30 years, Italy will face a certain financial crisis thanks to the ageing baby-boom generation, the rising number of pensioners and the shrinking number of workers. Eventually, Italy's state pension system must face either sharply cutting benefits or making people work longer, or both. On current trends, by 2040 the Italians will spend nearly 20 per cent of GDP on providing pensions – as opposed to 5 per cent in the UK. Until a legal loophole was closed, women with state jobs could retire with as little as 15 years on the job. Some retirees live on pensions that pay more than their jobs did. Gradual reforms are being made to reduce the burden of retirement benefits that now cost 15 per cent of GDP a year. For one, the retirement age was raised to 65, effective from January 2001. And recently approved tax breaks should encourage private pension funds and the so-called pay-as-you-go system. Italy's pension plan was set up when life expectancy was much lower. Now people live longer and the old scheme must pay out for longer than expected. In the United Kingdom, 18.7 per cent of the population will be over 65 in 2015 and employees now pay 10 per cent of earnings, with 12.2 per cent of earnings paid by the employer. In Italy, 21.1 per cent of the population will be over 65 in 2015, with

## Case Study: Retiring to Rome

Craig and Evie Robertson have lived in some of the world's most glamorous cities, including Paris, Rome, Milan and New York, but when it came to finding a place for retirement, they knew that Rome would be home. To be fair, this couple from Scotland knew the dos and don'ts of Italian real estate because they have owned a home near Orvieto for some 14 years. But even that did not fully prepare them for buying an apartment in Rome.

'We saw the pleasant things about the place immediately; the unpleasant things came afterwards,' Robertson says of their fifth-floor walk-up apartment near the capital's landmark Castel Sant'Angelo. 'We had to install double-glazed windows because there is a lot of noise, and we put in a new kitchen and bathroom.' They lovingly restored the apartment, fitting mahogany doors and removing the colour-coordinated upholstery that the previous owner had blanketed over everything including panelled walls. Even with the improvements completed, they don't reject the idea of selling. 'I'm still sprightly,' says the 62-year-old, 'but there may come a day when carrying 12 bottles of mineral water up five flights just won't do.' That said, they are happy in their new home because they are surrounded by friends and a familiar ambience that they find quite comforting.

With two properties in Italy, the Robertsons have learned a few important lessons. The first is to find a good *notaio* (notary – an official licensed by the state to investigate the property before the deal is closed). They were almost stuck with a €4 million bill when they discovered that part of their land in Umbria had been mortgaged by a former owner. If you buy in the city, make sure you speak with the condominium administrator to check you don't inherit back bills, Craig says. And don't be surprised if you are advised to under-declare up to half the value of the property for tax reasons: 'Some things are just part of life in Italy,' he says with a knowing chuckle.

### Are Italians Near Extinction?

Every once in a while media reports, charting troublesome demographic trends, conclude that in the not-so-distant future the entire race will be wiped clean off the planet. Italy often swings in and out of a purgatory-like state known as 'zero birth rate'. In other words, in most years, more Italians die than are born. Alarmists calculate that Italians will be extinct in the next few hundred years. Here's what Istat, the nation's statistics institute, says: by the year 2010, one out of every five Italians will be over the age of 65. The overall population will grow from 57.7 million to 58.5 million, after which the demographic curve will drop dramatically to 52 million in 2050. The long-term outlook indicates that Italy's population will shrink by as much as 5.5 million people within the next 50 years.

A short-term growth in population is being attributed to an increase in immigrants. An average 111,000 foreigners each year take up residence in Italy, totalling more than one million people by the end of this decade. By 2010, immigrants will represent 4.1 per cent of the total population (still lower than most European nations). As more immigrants arrive, the number of actual Italians is falling because of ageing and a decline in fertility rates. In 2010, the average Italian woman will give birth to 1.4 babies nationwide and that number diminishes to 1.1 for women in the north.

For every 100 Italians under the age of 14 now there are 125 people over the age of 65. In 10 years, the latter figure will skyrocket to 146. That demographic shift is due to an increase in life expectancy. In fact, within 10 years, 5.9 million Italians will be over the age of 75 compared with 4.5 million now. By 2050 deaths will outnumber births by 500,000 per year.

employee contributions now covering 8.9 to 9.9 per cent of earnings and employers covering 23.8 per cent. Sadly for future generations, pension reform is slow in coming as political and ideological pressures have frightened off recent governments from making real changes.

# Visas and Permits

It is almost possible to understand Italy's maniacal attention to paperwork and red tape if you consider the Latin proverb 'verba volant, scripta manent' ('spoken words fly away; written ones remain'). So many written words exist in Italy in the forms of laws, bureaucracy and administration that seemingly infinite government corridors are lined with volumes of data on its citizens that has yet to be computerised. Romans at odds with politicians can affix letters of lament to the Pasquino statue near Piazza Navona. Although frustrations have been vented in this manner for hundreds of years, it remains unproven that elected officials actually take notice. Today's scholars can scrutinise legal directives chiselled in marble dating from the ancient Romans. In Modena, the city's antique standard for weights and measures is carved in the cathedral wall. There is even a round, shallow cavity in the church wall where 15th-century housewives could mould cheese to produce the correct measurements for government-certified *ricotta* cheese.

Life in Italy means accepting, and living with, bureaucracy. The best way to do that is to avoid prolonged contact and resist becoming obsessed with it. Too many foreign residents spend cocktail hour chronicling their latest permit-renewal adventure. The stories are amusing at first, but become dreadfully boring for those who have lived in Italy long enough to know better. Rest assured that everybody, Italian and foreigner alike, has had less-than-pleasant tangles with red tape. Another word to the wise: when in Rome, do as the Romans. Being too fiscal can backfire as the more you seek contact with bureaucracy, the more it will seek you. For example, as you will learn below, EU nationals who enter Italy to find a job have three months in which to apply for a *permesso di soggiorno*. But if your passport has not been stamped on entry (which is the norm under the Schengen Convention for travel between member nations), authorities have no way of knowing when the three-month-period kicked off. In effect, the enforcement of those 'three months' would be difficult for authorities to implement and so many foreigners ignore the requirement. Learn basic Italian law and you will discover that there is more built-in 'flexibility' than in other countries.

Depending on whether or not you are an EU citizen, it might be necessary to start your personal paper trail in your home country with a visa application to enter Italy. Once in the country, you have the option to follow up with a stay permit and, ultimately, residency. Foreigners who can prove they have lived in Italy for many years may acquire citizenship. There are no special visas or permits needed for buying or owning property in Italy, although working there is another matter.

# Visas

Holders of a **valid British passport** and **Irish nationals** do not need a visa to enter Italy. Once in Italy they can stay for up to **90 days**; however, their passport must be valid when returning from Italy. If they intend to stay more than three months, they must apply for a **stay permit** (*permesso di soggiorno*) for living, working or studying in Italy (although many students rarely bother).

The same holds true for all member countries of the **European Union**, in addition to Andorra, Argentina, Australia, Bolivia, Brazil, Brunei, Bulgaria, Canada, Chile, Costa Rica, Croatia, Ecuador, El Salvador, Guatemala, Holy See, Honduras, Hong Kong (special passport), Israel, Japan, Macao (special passport), Malaysia, Mexico, Monaco, New Zealand, Nicaragua, Panama, Paraguay, Romania, San

Marino, Singapore, South Korea, Switzerland, United States of America, Uruguay, Venezuela.

If you are a citizen of a nation not included in the above list, you require a **Schengen Visa** to enter any Schengen member state for a period of up to three months. Schengen counties, so far pending enlargement, include Italy, Austria, Belgium, Denmark, Finland, France, Germany, Greece, Iceland, Luxembourg, the Netherlands, Norway, Portugal, Spain and Sweden.

For additional information, contact the Italian Embassy in England (**www.embitaly.org.uk; emblondon@embitaly.org.uk**). The Italian Embassy also runs a 24-hour information hotline (**t** 0906 550 8984). The various addresses for Italy's embassy and consulates in England are listed at the end of this book, although you will find useful phone numbers and web addresses included with the text below.

People who do need a visa to visit Italy include **foreign residents in the United Kingdom**. In this case, you must be a resident in the UK at the time of application. Your permit, issued by the Home Office, must be either indefinite or valid for at least six months beyond the expiration date of your requested visa to Italy. If you are currently staying in the UK with a stamped leave of entry in your passport issued at the port of entry for a period of six months or less, the Italian Consulate is not in a position to grant you a visa. You are required to request the visa in your 'home' country.

## Where to Apply

To apply for a visa, you should make an appointment at one of the following Italian consular offices.

- If you live in **Scotland or Northern Ireland**, you should apply for a visa at the Italian Consulate General in Edinburgh (**t** (0131) 226 3631).

- If you live in **Cheshire, Cleveland, Cumbria, Derby, Durham, Humberside, Lancashire, Leicester, Lincolnshire, Greater Manchester, Merseyside, Northumberland, Nottinghamshire, Staffordshire, Shropshire, Tyne and Wear, Yorkshire, Clwyd, Gwynedd, Powys (districts of Montgomery and Radnor) or the Isle of Man**, you should apply for your visa at the Italian Consulate in Manchester (**t** (0161) 236 9024).

- If you live in **Bedfordshire, Cambridgeshire, Norfolk, Northamptonshire, Suffolk or the northern part of Buckinghamshire**, you should apply for your visa at the Italian Vice Consulate in Bedford (**t** (01234) 356647).

- If you live in **Avon, Berkshire, Buckinghamshire, Channel Islands, Cornwall, Devon, Dorset, Dyfed, Essex, Gloucestershire, Glamorgan, Gwent, Hampshire, Hereford and Worcester, Hertfordshire, the Isle of White, Kent, London, Oxfordshire, Powys (Brecknock District), Somerset, Surrey, Sussex, Warwickshire, West Midlands or Wiltshire**, you should apply to the Visa

Section of the Italian Consulate General in London (**t** (020) 7235 9371). Appointments can be made by telephoning (Mon–Fri 3–4.30) or by e-mail (**itconlond_visti@btconnect.com**). You can go in person to make an appointment during office hours (Mon–Fri 9–12). Once the appointment has been arranged, applicants are required to submit their application using the form that can be downloaded from the website (**www.embitaly.org.uk**).

## Special Considerations

• Applications are by appointment only.

• You should book the appointment well in advance of your departure date (approximately three to four weeks). Delays are common especially during holiday periods (summer, Easter, and Christmas).

• Remember that making an appointment does not guarantee receipt of a visa.

• Visa applications by mail are not accepted.

• Italian consular authorities in England are not in a position to issue visas on the same day that an application is filed.

• Minors under 18 years of age travelling on their own must produce a declaration (an affidavit, duly authorised) from parents or legal guardians allowing them to travel and appointing a person to be responsible for them in Italy.

• The cost of a visa depends on its type and on the length of its validity, and is subject to change with the rate of exchange of the British pound. Visas are issued free of charge to the spouse and dependants of EU nationals (proof of relationship is required).

• The Italian Embassy warns that visa information may change without prior notice.

The visa process might seem confusing, but it is really very simple. To summarise: the great majority of us can hop on a plane and go to Italy without a visa whenever we'd like and meander about for three months. If you fall in the group that does need a visa to enter Italy, it is important that you start the paperwork in your home country and well in advance of your departure date. If you want to work in Italy or set up in business there, you should seek advice from a specialist lawyer before you apply for a visa.

## Types of Visas

Luckily, the number of visas available has recently been reduced and simplified. All signatories of the Schengen Convention issue a new type of visa called the **Schengen Visa**. (Again, Schengen counties include Italy, Austria, Belgium,

Denmark, Finland, France, Germany, Greece, Iceland, Luxembourg, the Netherlands, Norway, Portugal, Spain and Sweden.)

This uniform visa, issued by an embassy or consulate from one of the above countries, allows the holder to move freely in all those countries. To obtain a Schengen Visa you must hold a passport or travel document from a nation that is recognised by all Schengen member states and is valid for at least three months beyond the validity of the visa. If you hold a passport that is only recognised by certain Schengen states, the validity of your visa will be limited to those states. If your passport is due to expire, get it replaced before you apply.

If you plan to visit only one Schengen country, you must apply for the visa at the embassy or consulate of that country. If you intend to visit more than one Schengen country, you should apply for a visa at the embassy or consulate of the country that is your main destination. If you wish to visit several Schengen countries without a main destination, apply for the visa at the embassy or consulate of the first country of entry.

A Schengen Visa is not appropriate if you plan on staying in a Schengen member state, including Italy, for more than three months or wish to take up employment or establish a business, trade or profession.

There are three types of Schengen visas, which are described below.

## Airport Transit Visa

Foreign nationals from the following countries require the Airport Transit Visa: Afghanistan, Bangladesh, Congo (Democratic Republic of), Eritrea, Ethiopia, Ghana, Iran, Iraq, Nigeria, Pakistan, Senegal, Somalia and Sri Lanka.

This allows the applicant to transit through a Schengen member state without leaving the international transit area of the airport. To obtain this visa you will need the following:

> • **a passport or official travel document, valid for at least three months beyond the validity of the requested visa, with a blank page on which to affix the visa sticker.**

> • **one application form, fully completed and signed by the applicant, with one passport-size photo.**

> • **an airline ticket.**

> • **a visa for your destination country, if one is required.**

## Transit Visa

This allows the applicant to pass through the territory of one or more Schengen states and has a validity of five days with up to two entries. To obtain this visa you will need the following:

> • **a passport or official travel document, valid for at least three months beyond the validity of the requested visa, with a blank page on which to affix the visa sticker.**

- one application form, fully completed and signed by the applicant, with one passport-size photo.
- a valid residence permit issued in the UK.
- transport documentation, such as an airline or railway ticket, or, if you are driving, you will need to submit the registration document and proof of legal ownership of the vehicle and your driving licence.
- a visa for your destination country, if required.
- evidence that you have sufficient funds to cover the cost of your intended stay. Credit cards and cash are not accepted as proof of means.

## Short-stay Entry Visa

This is good for visits up to three months, six months or longer and is issued according to the purpose of the visit. They include the following:

*Tourism*

For this visa, you will need:

- a passport or official travel document valid for at least three months beyond the validity of the requested visa, with a blank page on which to affix the visa sticker.
- one application form, fully completed and signed by the applicant, with one passport-size photo.
- a valid residence permit issued in the UK.
- proof of travel arrangements (evidence of accommodation such as hotel reservations, or a letter of invitation from the Italian citizen who invited you as well as a photocopy of his or her passport).
- evidence that you have sufficient funds to cover the cost of your stay; credit cards and cash are not accepted as proof of financial means.
- evidence of occupation/student status. This should be an original letter from your employer, solicitor or a chamber of commerce.

*Business*

For this visa, you will need the following:

- a passport or official travel document valid for at least three months beyond the validity of the requested visa, with a blank page on which to affix the visa sticker.
- one application form, fully completed and signed by the applicant, with one passport-size photo.
- a valid residence permit issued in the UK.
- proof of the purpose of your visit. This proof should be in the form of an official work or professional presentation letter, addressed to the Italian Consulate General, explaining in detail the nature and dates of your trip to

Italy. People who are self-employed should provide a letter from their accountant, solicitor, company secretary, bank manager or local Chamber of Commerce. Applicants should also arrange for an invitation to be faxed from the Italian company or firm you are doing business with, if this is the case. It should be faxed directly to the Italian Consulate General in London (**t** (020) 7823 1609), 48 hours prior to the application submission. The fax should specify the date of your visit and the nature of your business.

• depending on individual circumstances, additional documents may be required.

*Study*

For this visa, you will need the following:

• a passport or official travel document valid for at least three months beyond the validity of the requested visa, with a blank page on which to affix the visa sticker.

• one application form, fully completed and signed by the applicant, with one passport-size photo.

• a valid residence permit issued in the UK.

• a letter (original plus a copy) from the Italian university, confirming acceptance of the application, which includes details on the course (duration, programme of study, and so on).

• a statement (original plus a copy) from the UK university.

• proof of medical insurance for the entire period of stay.

• proof of financial means to cover the cost of the intended stay.

Holders of Schengen Visas are still subject to immigration control and are not guaranteed entry into Italy or any of the Schengen member countries, even if they hold a valid visa.

# Stay Permits

Once past the visa phase, you should apply for a stay permit (*permesso di soggiorno* or sometimes called *carta di soggiorno*) if you intend to stay in Italy longer than three months. Unlike the visa, which is determined before your arrival, the *permesso di soggiorno* is acquired once you are already in the country. Under EU law, EU nationals are automatically permitted to stay in Italy indefinitely, but must register and therefore must still apply for a *permesso*.

To apply for one, you must go to the foreigners' office (*ufficio stranieri*) of your local *questura* (*see* p.25). Technically this must be done within eight days of your arrival (as the whole process can take up to three months). Although it caters to immigrants, **www.stranieriinitalia.it** (with readable English-language translations) is an excellent and intelligent source of additional information.

## Types of Permit

There are various kinds of permits (including those for political and religious refugees) but the most common are the following:

### Permesso di Soggiorno per Turismo

This lasts three months and can be renewed for an additional three. In theory, anyone not lodging in a hotel is also supposed to apply, although this rarely occurs. This permit is most useful for non-EU residents who would like to stay up to 90 days and do not intend to work in Italy.

### Permesso di Soggiorno per Ricongiungimento Familiare

This permit is for the spouse, minor children or dependent parents of foreigners married to Italians. It is given when family members from overseas come to join those already in Italy.

### Permesso di Soggiorno per Coesione Familiare

This is for the foreign spouse or minor children of an Italian citizen, who have moved to Italy together.

### Permesso di Soggiorno per Studio

This is for students on university exchange programmes. In many cases it requires a study visa already stamped in your passport on entry to Italy.

### Permesso di Soggiorno per Dimora

This is for those who wish to live in Italy and who do not intend to work or study there. You should request this one if you plan to retire in Italy.

### Permesso di Soggiorno per Lavoro

This is for foreigners who have a contract to work in Italy and, in many cases, it requires a work visa before it is issued. Most companies will take care of the paperwork on behalf of their employees. If not, you must solicit approval of your company's work petition from the appropriate authorities. The permit is good for either two years, five years or as long as your job in Italy lasts.

### Permesso di Soggiorno per Lavoro Autonomo/Indipendente

This is for independent or freelance workers and is the hardest type of permit to get.

## Applying for a Permit

The above permits are valid for different lengths of time and some are not renewable, depending on factors including your nationality. Most EU nationals receive permits good for five years. To apply for a *permesso di soggiorno* you must go to the *ufficio stranieri* of the local *questura* with the following:

• **your passport (bring a photocopy of the page with your photo) and the applicable visa if necessary.**

- an application for the *permesso* (a blue or green form available at the *questura*).

- a *marca da bollo* tax stamp for €10 (be sure to check the price at the time of application).

- three passport-size photos.

- the expired *permesso di soggiorno*, plus four photocopies, if you have come for a renewal; you should start the renewal process at least one month before the permit's expiration date.

- depending on the type of permit requested, you may also be asked to supply your birth certificate, marriage certificate, or proof of financial means. Students are usually asked for proof of health insurance coverage. You will be required to authenticate or notarise some documents.

Remember that if you intend to apply for an Italian **residency card** (*see* pp.26–7) you will need to have a valid *permesso di soggiorno*. Be careful if you have a *permesso di soggiorno per turismo* as this has limited renewal options and can't be used as a basis for residency.

If you **leave Italy** for more than three months and your *permesso di soggiorno* was only good for two years, you may have a hard time renewing it. Likewise, if you remain outside Italy for more than half of the duration of your *permesso di soggiorno*, it technically can't be renewed. (Exceptions are made if you leave because of a serious emergency or to fulfil military service requirements in your home country.) Because of the Schengen Convention, however, Italian authorities have no way of knowing how long you've been out of the country unless you tell them.

If you are a **foreign correspondent** in Italy for any major media outlet you enjoy special privileges when it comes to the *permesso di soggiorno*. Once you are accepted to the Stampa Estera (Foreign Press Association) Italy's Foreign Ministry will automatically grant you a stay permit. To take this route, your editor-in-chief must prepare three letters on your company's letterhead stating that you are a foreign correspondent and you must supply ten published articles to back up the claim. The letters must be addressed to the Foreign Ministry, the Stampa Estera and your country's embassy respectively. Bring all three to the press officer of your embassy and he or she will take care of the rest (including forwarding your information to the Foreign Ministry). All you have to do is pick up the *permesso di soggiorno* at your local *questura* when it is ready. The Foreign Ministry will arrange permit renewals as well.

## Administrative Departments in Italy

When your paperwork is in order, stamped, notarised and authenticated, you'll need to know where to file it. Italy is home to three monuments to bureaucracy.

These are the *questura*, the *comune* and the *anagrafe*. Even cigarette kiosks, as you will learn, are a part of the institutional landscape.

## The *Questura*

This is the main police headquarters in any Italian city and is where foreigners get their *permesso di soggiorno* (stay permit) and Italians are issued passports. It is also where you can file a police report (*denuncia*) in the case of accident, burglary or any other crime. You'll find that spending time at the *questura* is about as enjoyable as driving nails into your ears. On entry, you will be greeted with a scene reminiscent of the *Titanic* moments before the ship sank. Rarely do signs indicate which of the maddening queues before you is the one you should join, and trying to find someone to ask for directions is pointless. As a result, a visit to the *questura* is usually an exercise in both futility and repetition (especially since it is only open during restricted hours in the morning).

## The *Comune*

This is the municipality where you live. Each *comune* has its own governing administration including a mayor (*sindaco*). Its history goes back to when Italy was divided into thousands of tiny city-states that all despised each other. These warring communities were so intent on asserting their differences that many developed individual currencies, weights and measures, standards and laws. A *comune* can be divided into smaller parcels called *circoscrizioni*. For example, the city of Rome is one *comune* with 20 *circoscrizioni*. If you buy property or move from one *comune* to another, you need to pay a visit to its central office to register your presence.

## The *Anagrafe*

If the above offices are appendages of Italian bureaucracy, this is the nerve centre. Packed with dusty files and archives, this is the bureau of vital statistics, or census office. Each *comune* has one. Also known as the Ufficio di Stato Civile, it is responsible for safeguarding and collecting demographic data including deaths, births, marriages and for issuing related documentation. There's even an *anagrafe canina* for your four-legged friends. Come here if you are in the market for an identification card (*carta d'identità*), birth certificate (*certificato di nascita*), a death certificate (*certificato di morte*), marriage certificate (*certificato di matrimonio*), residency certificate (*certificato di residenza),* criminal record document (*certificato di carichi pendenti* or *casellario giudiziario*), certificate of citizenship (*certificato di cittadinanza*) or family status document (*stato di famiglia*).

## Tabacchi

Even non-smokers should become familiar with the *tabacchi*, or state-licensed cigarette shops. They are always marked with a big, black 'T' outside and are where you once purchased salt and quinine for treating malaria, among other curiosities. Today you can purchase bus and metro tickets as well as lottery cards here, but one of its most important functions is as distributor of the **marca da bollo**. This is a tax stamp that comes in different denominations (from €5 upwards) and is required when you file official documents, including ones related to property. Sometimes the tax stamp is incorporated into a piece of pre-stamped paper known as *carta bollata*.

# Italian Residency

If you find renewing your *permesso di soggiorno* exhausting, you should consider applying for Italian residency. But there's much more to it than convenience. With residency, you gain almost all the privileges of citizenship, except the right to vote. Even that is slated to change soon, although many foreigners consider it a bigger privilege *not* to partake in the Italian electoral process. With a residency card (*residenza*) you may enter and leave Italy as you please without a visa or permit, carry out any legal work activity, and make use of all public administration services including healthcare (*Unità Sanitaria Locale*). In addition, you can get an Italian identity card and driver's permit, register a car, sign up for many home utilities, and send your children to public schools. With residency, the only reason you can be expelled from the country is if you are found to be a threat to public order or national security, or if you are found in violation of anti-Mafia laws.

The drawback is that having Italian residency makes it much harder to avoid Italian taxes.

Residency guarantees an undetermined length of stay for you, your spouse and dependent children if you can prove the following:

- **You have lived in Italy for five years.**
- **You have a stay permit that allows an undetermined number of renewals.**
- **You earn enough income to provide for yourself and your family.**
- **You have not been caught committing a crime and have not been convicted of a criminal act.**

To apply for residency, you must bring your passport and your *permesso di soggiorno* to the *anagrafe* of your local *comune* and fill out a *dichiarazione di residenza* form. You might also need a consular declaration (*dichiarazione consolare*) from your country's embassy in Italy stating your personal data.

The tricky part is that you will need to supply a 'suitable' address with your paperwork, because applying for residency usually entails a surprise visit from police officers (within three months of your application) to confirm that you live where you say you do. Because the address you supply is your official residence, most landlords do not want their tenants to list their address. Indeed, a glance at classified ads for homes to let will reveal numerous requests for 'non-residents only'. If you own property and would like to let for income, you too should consider renting exclusively to non-residents. If you let to a resident, you will have a much harder time getting your tenant out if they fail to pay the rent; Italian property laws greatly favour the tenant over the owner and this fact should not be underestimated.

The residency process takes up to six months and you will be issued a temporary residency card while you wait. When residence is granted, you will receive notification by mail to pick up your residency card at the *anagrafe*. Residency must also be renewed. That doesn't mean it expires *per se* but you should request 'authentication' of your residency card every ten years.

Minors under 14 years of age are automatically included on parents' residency cards. After the age of 14, a child is issued his or her own residency card, which is valid until age 18 and can be renewed.

## Italian Citizenship

If you're goal is full immersion, you should consider citizenship. Italy recognises dual citizenship (*doppia cittadinanza*), so it is possible to hold both an Italian passport and a British one, an Australian one, an American one, or one for whichever country you originated from. Anyone with dual citizenship must travel to and from Italy with his or her Italian passport. Young men should be aware that they could be called to arms as an Italian citizen.

Italian citizenship is automatically given to the following:

- **A child of an Italian mother or father.**
- **A child born in Italy to unknown or stateless parents.**
- **A child born in Italy to non-Italian parents, as long as they are from a country where the law does not impose adopting the citizenship of the parents.**
- **A child of unknown parents found in Italy without proof of other citizenship.**

If you do not qualify for automatic citizenship, you may acquire it if you fall into one of the following five categories:

- **One of your parents, or one of your grandparents, are or were citizens at birth.**
- **You were born in Italy and have resided in the country legally without interruptions until the age of 18 and you declare your intention to acquire Italian citizenship within one year of reaching 18.**

• **You marry an Italian citizen. You must be the spouse of an Italian citizen and have resided legally in Italy for at least six months or have been married for three years. You will not be considered if there has been a legal divorce or annulment, or if you are in the process of separating. If you have a criminal record, you probably won't get far either.**

• **You are naturalised. This is a bit more complicated and usually means you can prove that you have lived in Italy for some time. For example, EU citizens must live in Italy for at least four years before acquiring citizenship. Naturalisation is also considered if you have worked for the Italian state for at least five years, or if you are a non-EU citizen and have lived legally in Italy for at least ten years.**

• **You are the minor son or daughter of someone who has acquired or re-acquired citizenship and you live with one of your parents at the time that he or she is granted or re-granted citizenship.**

Although each case differs, you will be required to provide a truckload of documents in exchange for citizenship. And be very patient. The process can take months, if not a whole year. The application (an official declaration of your intention to acquire citizenship) must be presented (with five copies, and the original must have a *marca da bollo*) to either the Ministry of the Interior (*Ministero degli Interni*), or to your local *comune*, or to an Italian embassy abroad. You will need your birth certificate; your residency permit (if required); proof of how long you have lived in Italy; marriage certificates; a family status certificate; proof that you don't have a criminal record; your parents' or grandparents' citizenship (if required); your spouse's citizenship (if required); and, in some cases, a copy of your tax returns. All photocopies of documents presented in lieu of originals must be notarised.

# Tax-related Paperwork

Italy has two additional documents that you should consider acquiring. The first, a tax identification number, is extremely important if you want to invest in property, sell or rent or even set up an e-mail account. The second is only necessary if you are self-employed or owner of a small business in Italy. They are the *codice fiscale* and the *partita IVA*.

## Codice Fiscale

The *codice fiscale* is a tax identification number required of all individuals – foreign and Italian – engaged in financial transactions. While it does not permit a foreigner to be employed, it is necessary for getting paid legally, for either fully contracted work or when starting your own business. It is also necessary if you invest in property (or sign any type of contract, including house rental or sale), buy a car, open a bank account, pay taxes, buy shares in an Italian company, apply for a professional licence, register with the Italian Chamber of Commerce (Camera di Commercio), or set up an e-mail account with an Italian Internet service provider. With your tax number, you can also enrol in Italy's national health service. Issued by the Internal Revenue Office of the Ministry of Finance, the *codice fiscale* is mandatory for Italian citizens and strongly recommended for residents and *permesso di soggiorno* holders. Each number is alphanumeric, meaning that it combines a sequence of letters from your name and numbers from your date of birth.

Getting one is easy and free of charge and, better yet, having one does not mean you will automatically be liable for Italian taxes. In order to get one, you must go to the Ufficio delle Imposte Dirette or Anagrafe Tributaria of your *comune* with a valid identification card or passport. Technically, foreigners should also bring their valid *permesso di soggiorno*, although most foreigners report that they were never asked to show it. (Even those without a *permesso di soggiorno* should try to get one.) If your civil status changes, through marriage or divorce, you have up to six months to report it to the Ufficio delle Imposte Dirette. Any changes in your name will upset the string of data that makes up your alphanumeric identification. Not reporting changes can result in a fine.

## Partita IVA

The *partita IVA*, on the other hand, is a value-added tax (VAT) number, with 'IVA' standing for *imposta sul valore aggiunto*. The *partita IVA* is required of all self-employed professionals, including freelancers and small-business owners. Individuals selling a service or product are required to charge the standard 20 per cent value-added tax, and this number ensures that the government can keep tabs on your financial transactions. *Partita IVA*-holders are required to keep their accounting on special stationery (*registri*), keep invoices and receipts in order, and file a special income tax return. Because the procedure is very complicated, most hire an accountant. It is also expensive since there is a hefty initial fee and annual renewal fees to keep the *partita IVA*. If you need one, bring your *codice fiscale*, your photo identification, and proof that you have paid the initial fee at your local post office, to the Ufficio Provincial IVA in your *comune* within 30 days of starting your professional activity. You will also be asked to leave your *registri* with the office for registration. When they are returned, you may issue official invoices for your services. If you terminate your activity, you have one month to cancel the *partita IVA*.

## Other Paperwork

There is one last little document that you may encounter that makes a nice metaphor for the end of this chapter. It is the *nulla osta* (which means 'no obstacle') certificate required for getting certain jobs and getting married. This is issued by the state and confirms that you are a generally upstanding citizen and all-round decent person. Once you have decided to own a home in Italy, and have scaled the tortuous paper trail described above, there is no obstacle to realising the next steps of your dream.

# Profiles of the Regions

Chances are that you have already fallen, irretrievably, for the charms of the *bel paese* – the 'beautiful country'. This section is intended to paint a miniature picture of each of Italy's 20 regions for those who want to supplement their own knowledge with more detailed descriptions of local flavour and character. From the northernmost Valle d'Aosta to Sicily in the deep south, facts relating to history, geography, transport, architecture, gastronomy and even local superstition have been collected here to give you a better idea of what it's like to actually live in each of Italy's regions. Do you crave the urban comforts of a restored penthouse in Milan's centre or are you ready to rough it in a country *trullo* in Puglia? If you are house-hunting, this section should help you to narrow your search.

The housing price guidelines – in euros per square metre – given in each region were supplied by the prestigious Bologna-based Nomisma real estate research unit at the beginning of 2005. For sample prices for a selection of properties, *see* pp.86–9.

# The North

Italy's upper third is comprised of Lombardy, the Veneto, Piedmont, Valle d'Aosta, Trentino-Alto Adige, Friuli-Venezia Giulia, Liguria and Emilia-Romagna. These eight regions represent a huge chunk of the country's economic wealth and its highest standard of living. Northern Italy offers across-the-board comforts, solid infrastructure and proximity to the rest of Europe.

## Lombardy

Lombardy is the Italian region that will remind you most of home, although that doesn't mean it is un-Italian by any stretch. Where mountains meet mirror-like water, Lombardy's **lakes** are of unparalleled beauty. In small cities such as **Mantua** and **Pavia**, bicycles outnumber – and outpace – motorised forms of transport. Fruit and vegetable vendors hawk their goods on market day, throwing in gossip and cooking tips for added value. However, this region also flaunts its functionality. Lombardy is well serviced by infrastructure connecting it to its northern neighbours. As home to banking and other industries, it is Italy's richest region. Its prosperity has attracted many foreigners, including immigrants from less developed parts of Italy and the world, to form a truly cosmopolitan corner. Urbanites from Milan – Italy's second-largest city – will greet you with 'Welcome to Europe, you've just left Italy', and nothing could make them prouder.

This landlocked region is bordered by the Alps to the north and flanked by Lago Maggiore and Lago di Garda. Two-thirds of Lombardy spreads across the agricultural plains of the Po river basin, Europe's biggest rice-growing region.

The mountains block the frost, allowing for lemon and olive groves and even palm trees on the lakes' rims. Italy's farming heartland is Lombardy's plains, or *pianura*, where fog and clover blanket the ground, sustaining a long dairy- and cattle-farming tradition.

Lombardy was part of Ancient Rome's Gallia Cisalpina and was a crossroads for nomadic tribes and invaders. It is named after the Lombards (or Longobards), a group of ruthless Germanic barbarians who settled here after picking at the bones of the mighty Roman Empire. The Lombards also had an appetite for the area's milder temperatures and eventually baptised it Mailand, meaning 'land of May'.

Located at a natural junction of trade routes connecting alpine passes to Tyrrhenian and Adriatic ports, and fitted with a complex web of canals supplied by the Po river, the city of **Milan** has always been a prize catch. It has seen French, Venetian, Spanish and Austrian invaders, all of whom have left their mark on local traditions, most notably its food.

Today, Milan is branded by two 'F's: finance and fashion. Some Milanese claim the number of banks headquartered in their city matches that of Rome's churches. They have the stock exchange and Rome has the Vatican. These sister cities are rivals and accomplices on countless levels. Rush hour in front of the city's emblematic Duomo looks like London or New York. Briefcase-toting businesspeople with folded newspapers under one arm and bagged lunches in

## Lombard Cuisine

Milan is also the stage for the nation's best culinary maestros. Sophisticated palates require sophisticated restaurants. Lombardy's dairy tradition has given birth to pungent Gorgonzola and spreadable Stracchino cheese, and many dishes are prepared with butter and cream, borrowing from the French, rather than olive oil. The Spanish left behind saffron, which was extracted from paella to create *risotto alla Milanese*. In much of Lombardy, rice dishes outnumber pasta ones and a train ride through the region reveals soggy rice paddies as far as the eye can see. Another namesake speciality, *cotoletta alla Milanese*, is a cousin of Austria's *Wiener schnitzel*. Culinary capitals Sondrio, Cremona, Brescia, Bergamo and Mantua all boast their own tasty treats, and the lakes yield fresh fish like sturgeon (and its grey caviar) and eel. The Valtellina is partial to polenta, or cornmeal, topped with meat or mushrooms. Northerners have collectively consumed so much polenta that southerners affectionately, and sometimes not so affectionately, mock them as *polentoni*.

Although Lombardy is surrounded by premier wine regions, only its Franciacorta and Oltrepo Pavese vineyards are consistently applauded. But Milan is home to a thriving *aperitivo* culture. Free food is doled out with *kir royales* and mint *caprioskas* each afternoon at bars across town. The king of cocktail hour is a Milan native: bitter-sweet Campari, packaged in its trademark triangular bottle.

the other hand hustle by. The *tramezzino*, or sandwich snack, was invented here to nourish time-impaired bankers. In Rome, excessive professional dedication is met with a raised eyebrow and seen as somehow unhealthy. In Milan, working late nights is a point of pride.

In the 1990s, Milan learned that too much money is not always a good thing. The city was dubbed Tangentopoli, or 'Bribesville', during an anti-corruption probe that put an entire class of businesspeople and politicians under criminal investigation. Before Operation Clean Hands, many brushed off nepotism, favouritism and kickbacks as simply part of the way things get done in Italy.

Milan made a quick comeback with a different home-grown symbol of money: Silvio Berlusconi. The former cruise-boat crooner turned media mogul has successfully clinched the prime minister's seat twice since Tangentopoli. Both times, Italy's richest man claimed to represent a sound business model that could be applied to government. Countless criminal investigations later – ranging from the bribing of judges to tax evasion involving Berlusconi's empire – not everyone sees things his way.

On the other hand, Milan's wealth and worldliness helped it develop a heightened sense of aesthetics. Its La Scala opera house is a music mecca and the most valued 'made in Italy' labels originate here. Milan *alta moda* put icons Giorgio Armani and Gianni Versace on the fashion map and, each year, the city hosts the Salone del Mobile dedicated to design. Milan's fashion and design contributions are as much a part of the Italian landscape as Vespa scooters, Ferrari or the Leaning Tower of Pisa.

Lombard life is good, then, but it does come at a price. A restored apartment in the centre of Milan costs up to €7,000 per square metre, making it the nation's most expensive real estate. Living in Brescia or Mantua costs one-third as much, and an outlying area costs a quarter. Second homes near the lakes or mountain skiing resorts can be pricey, too – up to €4,000 per square metre. The trade-off is that Lombardy guarantees comfort and quality. The high number of foreigners and businesses in a city of the likes of Milan assures urban benefits, such as professional and networking opportunities, not to mention an unrivalled social scene with art vernissages, fashion week parties and plenty of places to see and be seen.

## The Veneto

This is a land blessed by Venus. Romeo and Juliet stole kisses to cement their ill-fated love affair in **Verona**. Modern-day disciples pay them homage by engraving their own names, linked by hearts and plus signs, near Shakespeare's balcony (or at least the one that many like to think inspired him). Others under the spell of Eros or otherwise looking for a nuptial nudge visit Venice, the world's most popular honeymoon destination. No matter where you turn,

> ### Venetian Specialities
> Although locals sing its praises, not everyone loves Venetian cuisine. Onion is a constant theme, featuring in the preparation of *fegato alla Veneziana* (calves' liver simmered in butter and white wine), *sarde in saor* (sardines layered with fried onions, raisins and pine nuts) and *bigoli in salsa* (spaghetti-like pasta with anchovy and onion paste).

Cupid and his arsenal of love-spiked arrows are poised to make sure you fall in love with the Veneto.

The region is drenched in enchanting propositions. East of Verona lies **Vicenza** – a city celebrated as a temple to architecture. Villas and churches built by Palladio showcase how stone and mortar can be transformed into humanistic and classical expressions. Midway to Venice is **Padua** – home to one of Europe's oldest universities. Petrarch, Galileo and Dante all appeared on the student roster. The Renaissance also had its roots there. Giotto added renderings of shadow and depth to his fresco cycle in the Cappella degli Scrovegni, signalling one of the first uses of dimension in painting. Once content with its *radicchio* harvest, Treviso has blossomed into a prosperous centre, thanks to a local family dynasty named Benetton. **Bassano del Grappa** is, of course, not a bad place to sip *grappa*, while nearby **Maròstica** puts on a curious oversized chess match in which humans stand in for the pieces. The region's only eyesore is **Mestre**. Designed and developed as the Adriatic's most industry-friendly port, it has caused untold distress to its neighbour. Waves and shifts in underwater sand sparked by shipping traffic have eroded nearby Venice's foundations, sending it on a sinking trajectory that worsens with each passing year.

Regardless, the Lagoon City remains the region's undisputed highlight. Gondolas and the Bridge of Sighs have sunk deeper into our collective imagination of Italy than Venice itself will sink. It may not appear so, but Venice is a real city: Boat police issue traffic violations and hardware stores do exist. It's not easy to live here but, for those who do, Venice is a lifelong love affair.

Housing prices make Venice Italy's second most expensive city behind Milan. A canal-facing apartment can scrape the €8,000 per square metre mark, especially if it is located anywhere near the Grand Canal. The lowest end of the scale is €3,000 per square metre. Settling down elsewhere in the Veneto is more affordable. Prices in Verona, for example, range from €3,000 to €5,000 per square metre.

# Piedmont

Translated as 'at the foot of the mountains', Piedmont is the cradle of Italian liberty. Founding father Camillo Cavour and the Savoy royal family launched the Risorgimento here, which led to the unification of Italy in the late 1860s. When Vittorio Emanuele I was crowned king in 1574, Turin took the honour of being

## Piedmont Cuisine

One feature that is never questioned is Piedmont's gastronomic tradition. A list of its towns reads like an encyclopaedia of Italian wine. Barolo lent its name to what is, in most years, Italy's most expensive bottled export and the wine-based town of Barbaresco is just a short drive away. Sparkling Asti Spumante is made in Asti as its name implies. Nebbiolo – a grape named after the fog that blankets the nearby foothills – makes up Piedmont's prized red wines.

One of Turin's biggest events is the Salone del Gusto, sponsored by the Piedmont-based Slow Food organisation. During the food fair, a library of wine is unveiled and local specialties, such as Barolo-aged cheese, white truffles and hazelnut desserts, are proudly displayed and available for tasting.

the first capital of Italy. During the dynamic post-war years of Italy's economic boom, the city became the birthplace of Fiat and the nation's industrial identity took form. The Agnelli group founded the number one car-maker and controlled a lucrative portfolio that included publishing interests and Turin's beloved Juventus soccer team. In recent years, Piedmont has spearheaded yet another so-called revolution: the switch from 'old economy' to 'new economy'.

Piedmont is, without a doubt, Italy's most forward-looking region. The inventor of the MP3 file compression format, used to download and store music from the Internet, hails from these parts, and **Turin** was among the first to be fitted with fibre-optic cable for broadband Internet services. A line of high-tech companies squeezes into a corridor of land between Turin and **Ivrea** to the north (headquarters of the former typewriter-turned-telecoms giant Olivetti).

In 2006, Turin hosts the Winter Olympic Games. An ambitious public works campaign has scrubbed away dust and grime to beautify the city. New parking and public services have been put in place. In the Alps to the north and elsewhere in the region, skiing resorts have been modernised to host professional athletes and weekend snow-seekers alike.

But Turin is also a weird city. Followers of the occult believe it is a point of converging magical forces. An active underground music scene strums out sounds inspired by industry and archaic languages. Straddling the banks of the mighty Po river, this awkwardly beautiful city with its broad, sweeping avenues seems too big on Sundays and too small the rest of the week, when it is bustling with activity. Rendering it even more eclectic, two of its biggest attractions are the Shroud of Turin and the bizarre Mole Antonelliana tower, which stands so tall that it casts a cross-town shadow and seems very much out of place against Turin's low-lying imperial architecture. Not a 'city of art' in its own right, Turin showcases a museum dedicated to Egyptian art and the most complete Museum of Italian Cinema, located inside the Mole tower.

Expect moderate property prices in Piedmont. An upmarket loft apartment in Turin shouldn't run to more than €4,500 per square metre. Properties in smaller cities are up to one-third cheaper.

# Valle d'Aosta

Often overlooked because of its size, this tiny region packs a powerful punch. Crowned by Europe's highest peaks – Mont Blanc, the Matterhorn, Monte Rosa and Gran Paradiso – every tiny part opens on to views of alpine perfection. Of course, where there is snow, there are skiers. World-class resort towns such as **Courmayeur**, **Breuil Cervinia**, **St Vincent**, **Brusson** and **Pila** make Valle d'Aosta a true winter wonderland. Referred to as the 'Rome of the Alps', the region's capital city of **Aosta** is also the site of a semi-autonomous regional government. Because the local population and tax base is so small, Valle d'Aosta enjoys an administrative independence that removes it from the real Rome. It is a French- and Italian- speaking region where even the street signs are bilingual and where a French aftertaste will delight gourmands. Wild boar crêpes and mushroom-stuffed sausage can be washed down with floral white and red wines produced in some of the highest vineyards in Europe.

Throughout history, Valle d'Aosta served as a gateway through the wall of the Alps, which severs Europe from the Italian peninsula. The ancient Romans were not the first to understand the strategic significance of the region, but they left behind a network of trade routes and rest stations that are still used today. Aosta, for example, grew rich thanks to pilgrims and merchants passing through the region's main artery, the Dora Baltea valley. A stunning Roman amphitheatre sits at the centre of Aosta and, outside the city, is a 1st-century BC stone bridge. Following the same paths first carved by ancient mule-riding travellers, the Mont Blanc tunnel and the Great St Bernard tunnel service motorists with stacks of skis on their car roofs who zip across Italy's borders into France and Switzerland. So vital to the Italian infrastructure are these tunnels that even Sicilians felt the squeeze on trucked-in goods when the Mont Blanc tunnel, one of Europe's longest, was boarded up for three years until 2002, following a devastating fire.

Snow- and mountain-sports devotees will be tempted to buy a holiday home in the Valle d'Aosta. Deals can be had in the centre of the region along the Dora Baltea River, but property prices climb the closer you get to the ski resorts at the northern rim. A two-bedroom winter cottage, with wooden panelling and a picturesque slate roof, will cost about €3,000 to €4,000 per square metre.

# Trentino-Alto Adige

Geography has settled on Italy a crown fit for a queen. The jagged, snow-capped Dolomites reflect the rose colours of dawn and afternoon ambers as if they were made from precious stones. Legend says that this mountainous area was once dominated by a tribe of warrior women who surrendered their femininity and beauty to the landscape in exchange for immortality. Some say their restless spirits still lurk among the rocky peaks.

> ### Cuisine of the Alto Adige
> Dishes south of the Brenner Pass have heavy German overtones. Darker and tastier speck replaces prosciutto and menus offer *sauerkraut, knödel* (breadcrumb dumplings), pretzels and poppyseed cake. Quality wines (sparkling too) are made from chardonnay and pinot nero. Others include riesling, gewürztraminer and a native red grape called teroldego. A very appropriate *après-ski* beverage is a warm red wine sprinkled with cinnamon.

Trentino-Alto Adige is roughly split into two separate worlds, but the dividing line is not topography, it is cultural. Trentino pledges allegiance to Italy, whereas Alto Adige – otherwise known as Süd Tirol – maintains an all-Austrian soul. Both enjoy measures of regional autonomy, but Süd Tirol is, in many ways, a nation apart. In its capital city, **Bolzano**, or Bolzen, the central streets are lined with painted chalets and cheerful beer halls, many of which make their own brews. Almost 70 per cent of the local population converses in German, leaving a small Italian-speaking minority.

All find a common language in the surrounding beauty. Verdant valleys radiate outwards from the cities of **Trento** and Bolzano like the spokes of a bicycle wheel. Nearby are two of Europe's best skiing resorts: **Madonna di Campiglio** and **Cortina d'Ampezzo** (technically in the Veneto territory), which hosted the 1956 Winter Olympic Games. Like a high-altitude Beverly Hills, Cortina has chic shopping and exclusive luxury spas. If you are seeking chill with a thrill, sporting options span the spectrum. There is downhill skiing, cross-country skiing, luge, bobsled, skating, bigfooting, ski-jumping, snowboarding and every other conceivable snow-based sport.

With the exception of Cortina, houses here are relatively affordable. A handsome *maso* – a typical wooden house, built on a rock foundation with shingled roofing – can be purchased for as little as €2,500 per square metre. A few rare specimens of the *tàbia* also come on to the market. These are ancient hay barns that are now being converted into winter holiday homes. But don't even think of buying vineyard land in Trentino. The region is Italy's most expensive and an hectare of trellised vineyard can fetch as much as €800,000.

# Friuli-Venezia Giulia

A wooden cross at the summit of the Montasio peak marks Italy's northeast corner. With a spin of the foot, a climber can peer down at the territories of Italy, Austria and Slovenia. It is at this tiny spot that Europe's three main cultures – Saxon, Slavic and Latin – collide. Only a few kilometres away, a stream runs along a continental divide. Half its water trickles down to the Adriatic and the other half to the Black Sea.

Despite its vantage point, Friuli-Venezia Giulia is a curious and untouched place. The rugged Alpi Giulie have made the area north of **Tolmezzo** rather

> ### *Friuli Food*
> At the dinner table, Friuli is most noted for its world-class white wine, including indigenous Tocai Friulano. The alluvial plains also produce an extremely rare dessert wine from a grape called picolit. Because the varietal is afflicted by difficulty to pollinate, only a tiny number of grapes on a cluster come to maturity. Those specimens are plucked off by hand and dried on hay mats.
>
> Poorer parts of the region cook herbs and grass to eat. A spinach-tasting herb called *sclopit* (after the sound its seedpods make when popped) is stuffed into ravioli-like *cjarsons*. White asparagus is another spring speciality.

impenetrable and a breeding ground to strange superstitions and strange traditions. In ancient times, travelling salesmen known as *kramârs* (an archaic German word for 'closet') filled their knapsacks with lightweight spices from Venice for export to northern markets. They left behind half-garbled tales of elves and fairies from faraway lands. The power of conservation in these isolated parts has also allowed for Ladino – a language that is directly descended from Latin – still to be used today. Even the footprints of celebrated mountaineers, such as the valiant Alpini brigade, have remained imprisoned in ice and frozen mud since the First World War.

The Tagliamento river, as its Italian name (meaning 'to cut') implies, splices the southern part of the region in two. One of Italy's most precious jewels, the city of **Udine**, lies on the east, with **Pordenone** to the west. Snug up against the Slovenia border are **Gorizia**, with its awkward Eastern European feel, and perhaps Italy's most intellectual city: **Trieste**.

In Carnia, delicate lilies-of-the-valley waft in the breeze. Alpine fields pillow rudimentary homes, built of rock to keep out humidity and with overhead barns for hay storage. Goblins called *Sbilf* are believed to roam the forests. Nearby, in the Valcanale north of Carnia, old timers hold that San Niccolò has the power to achieve world harmony. During a pre-Christmas festival, this Santa Claus precursor is dressed in a familiar red suit and paraded through Tarvisio amid blazing bonfires.

Few foreigners venture, much less live, outside of Trieste and Gorizia. Udine attracts more attention because it has repeatedly been voted best place to live in Italian polls. A restored home sells for €2,000 to €3,000 per square metre.

# Liguria

Sandwiched between a brilliant blue stretch of coastline and the Maritime Alps and Apennines, this elongated region is usually associated with *pesto*, flowers, the San Remo music festival and seaside summer holidays. Dotted with beach towns – **San Remo, Alassio, Finale Ligure**, the **Cinque Terre, Portofino, Portovenere** – Liguria is the obvious summer destination for northern Italians.

## Ligurian Cuisine

Ligurian fare is known as *la cucina profumata*, or 'fragrant food'. Fresh fish is a central ingredient, but the region's most prized culinary creation is pesto. Named after the mortar and pestle used to grind garlic, pine nuts, olive oil, cheese and basil, this tasty green sauce has a long shelf-life, which made it very appealing for sailors on a long sea voyage. South-facing slopes along the shoreline make Liguria ideal for sun-thirsty basil, but roses, mimosa and other flowers also thrive here, as the thousands of greenhouses above Ventimiglia demonstrate. Other edible goodies include *farinata*, or chickpea flatbread, and oven-baked focaccia.

August nights thump with techno beats and traffic can be intense along via Aurelia, the region's asphalt backbone. Genoa, Liguria's biggest city, is so long and thin (27km long and just 3km wide) that commuters opt for the toll road, or *superstrada*, to get from one neighbourhood to the next. The Cinque Terre are five fishing villages perched on sea-facing cliffs that were once only accessible by boat or foot. All in all, the region's lack of elbow-room makes you wonder how it can play host so well to so many guests.

**Genoa**'s history is stacked in layers and rarely in neat lines: medieval bell towers bump up against ancient walls and cupolas cast shadows on condos. The ancient maritime power once competed against the might of Venice, Amalfi and Pisa. Today, like Naples or Marseille, it is an authentic port town where people from all corners of the planet mingle and anything goes. Herman Melville said Genoa was a city 'fortified by Satan and fortified against the Archangels'.

Nicknamed *La Superba*, Genoa had fallen on difficult times since the glorious year of 1492 when Christopher Columbus, the son of a local wool merchant, discovered the New World. Some 500 years later, thanks to an ambitious public works agenda, Genoa has had a facelift, although a blemish surfaced in 2001, when street violence staged at the G8 summit ended with the shooting death of a young protester. Cars were overturned and storefronts smashed, turning what was supposed to be a proud moment for Italy into a national shame.

Housing prices in Liguria touch both extremes. Apartments in Genoa range from €2,000 to €5,000 per square metre, but a seaside villa – for example, near posh Portofino – can run prices into the stratosphere.

# Emilia-Romagna

The flatlands in the southern plains of the Po River are the self-proclaimed winners of two of Italy's most coveted titles. Without a flinch, Emilia-Romagna claims to have Italy's best food and its most beautiful women.

Flat and large, the region extends from **Piacenza** to the Adriatic Sea and down to **San Marino**, the world's smallest republic. In between, along the ancient Via

Emilia, are countless cultural and gastronomic sites. A visit to the ham-and-cheese utopia of **Parma** is a case in point. The same goes for cheese challenger **Reggio Emilia**. **Modena**, on the other hand, speaks to a different kind of indulgence. Besides being the home of balsamic vinegar, the headquarters of Ferrari are just a few kilometres away. Formula One fans can peek over a fence to watch engineers test new models on the Maranello racing track. A lucky few have even spotted Ferrari champion Michael Schumacher darting around town in a beaten-up Fiat Cinquecento. **Faenza**, to the south, produces majolica, and Ferrara, to the north, was one of the first Italian cities to benefit from Renaissance notions of urban planning. **Ravenna** retains Byzantine mosaics that stimulated the concept of Western Christian art, while the **Adriatic Riviera** is home to Italy's very own sin city – **Rimini**. Sun- and sea-worshippers make the pilgrimage each year from faraway Nordic lands to experience Rimini's topless beach parties and all-you-can-drink beer bonanzas.

Film-making legend Federico Fellini was born and raised here, and cast his home town in the leading role in the nostalgic movie *Amarcord* (local dialect for 'I remember'). Luciano Pavarotti, Bernardo Bertolucci and Giuseppe Verdi join him as Emilia-Romagna natives.

The capital of the region is **Bologna**. Home to Europe's oldest university, the city is a platform for timeless liveliness and a laid-back atmosphere encouraged by chatty, knapsack-wearing students. Politics and war also helped shaped the city's ideology. With a few exceptions during its recent history, it has always been a so-called 'red' city. A stronghold of the Communist Party and socialist virtue, it withstood the brunt of fascist violence during the Second World War. Today, street signs still carry names such as Via Stalingrado, Viale Lenin and Via Yuri Gagarin.

It is often said that Emilia-Romagna offers Italy's best quality of life. People are friendly and well-fed and the lack of large-scale industrialisation lends it an easy-going pace. A place in downtown Bologna can fetch as much as €3,500 per square metre and about €1,000 less in Modena. There are beautiful rural properties and estates to be had, however, as the region is populated by a large aristocratic class that has invested heavily in architecture, gardening and their upkeep.

### Cuisine of Emilia-Romagna

Does Emilia-Romagna have Italy's best food? A steaming plate of hand-assembled tortellini (made from dough that is never left in direct sunlight), stuffed with prosciutto from Parma (hung to dry in the pine-scented breeze of the Magra Valley) and topped with freshly grated *parmigiano-reggiano* (aged in dark cellars for years until the cheese's crust can withstand and deflect an oncoming metal ball) might persuade you to agree. After a few glasses of the local white bubbly Lambrusco, you'll award Emilia-Romagna top scores across the board.

# The Centre

The middle third of Italy is home to the divas of Italian geography – Tuscany, Umbria and Lazio. Dreams of idyllic Italian life are more often than not conceived in these territories, and their star power outshines central Italy's other two regions. However, largely unexplored Abruzzo and the Marches promise to reward the avid and the anxious looking to restore an abandoned monastery or ancient tower without spending excessive amounts of money. Indeed, property sharpshooters have purchased entire hilltop ghost towns. Sadly, the days of similar deals in Tuscany ended decades ago.

## Tuscany

This is a land that preaches the gospel of the cliché. The lone cypress tree, the sunset-drenched farmhouse, the sensuous rolling hills materialise before your eyes like fresh revelations, no matter how many times those same images have been encountered in pictures. This land also inspires religious metaphors. Many have likened it to paradise on earth, and foreigners who settle under the Tuscan sun are 'pilgrims' seeking their personal promised land. Most would agree that the region's food, wine and artistic heritage are nothing short of heavenly. In Tuscany, the clichés are never tired – and you might never tire of them.

It's no surprise that one beautiful corner of Tuscany is dubbed 'Chiantishire' because of the many foreigners who have purchased properties there. Home-owners range from Sting to Russell Crowe, and Tony Blair regularly takes time off there. Florence plays temporary home to throngs of tourists and more foreign exchange students than any other city in the world.

Scratch deeper, though, and you'll find that paradoxically Tuscany is one of Italy's most inward-looking regions, a microcosm of the whole nation. Spurred on by relentless squabbling between its *comuni*, or local municipalities, that peaked between the 13th and 15th centuries, Tuscany grew in military might and political prestige. Its noble families and benefactors had the foresight to amass more art than any other part of the nation and, almost certainly, the world. Tuscany (thanks to native son Dante Alighieri) imposed its language on the rest of Italy, giving birth to modern Italian, and produced top-notch authors, philosophers, explorers and artists.

Still, Tuscany remains home to a unique brand of provincialism known as *campanilismo*. This is an intuitive sense of belonging to one's home town, symbolised by its *campanile*, or main church steeple. For example, a Siena native is first a *contradaiolo*, or member of a local neighbourhood, then a Sienese, then a Tuscan and only last of all an Italian.

It is not an exaggeration to say that Tuscans hate each other. **Florence** and Siena are notorious enemies and, to this day, they relish exchanging insults during football matches. Florence, historically the big bully, is generally despised and so is **Pisa**. A common proverb of the region warns that it's 'better to meet death at your door than a Pisan'.

Yet these highly contentious people have nurtured a biting sense of humour. Dante Alighieri had so many gripes to hurl at his peers that he turned them into prose and penned one of the world's greatest pieces of literature, the *Divine Comedy*. Largely working-class **Livorno**, founded as a penal colony, publishes a humorous magazine that spares no one. A tradition of *burle*, or teasing, is embodied in the comedic routines of Oscar-winner Roberto Benigni. This Tuscan son masks cunning sarcasm with a naïve playfulness that lets him get away with grabbing staid politicians between the legs or tugging at their toupees on national television.

Over 90 per cent of Tuscany's territory is mountainous – there are only slivers of flat land along the rivers and the coast. The grape-growing region of Chianti Classico offers the ultimate Tuscan dreamscape. A two-lane road, known as the *Chiantigiana* (route SS222), wiggles its way from Florence to Siena, cutting through picture-perfect **Greve in Chianti**, **Panzano** and **Castellina**. The area south of Siena is known for its lunar rock formations, called *crete*, that caress the land like the folds of a curtain. To the north lie the Alpi Apuane and, to the east, the Apennine peaks with skiing resorts, natural parks and hiking trails. The self-contained valleys of the **Garfagnana** and the **Lunigiana** are bizarre backrooms to Tuscany itself. They run into the city of **Lucca**, famous for its perfectly intact ramparts. Outsiders say that the Lucchesi are closed-minded, but those inside claim that the walls have preserved their unique spirit. The **Valtiberina**, which branches east of the bourgeois city of **Arezzo**, is often the backdrop in famous

## Tuscan Cuisine

Tuscan cuisine has evolved to become one of Italy's best. Many books have been written to pay tribute to its meat dishes, featuring rabbit, wild boar and pheasant. Other courses include *tagliatelle* and *pappardelle* (ribbon-like pastas), Tuscan white beans, *acqua cotta* (bread and cabbage in broth) and *pappa al pomodoro* (a porridge-like tomato soup, the sing-song name of which is a children's rhyme).

The king of Tuscan food is the Florentine T-bone steak, which was technically banned during the mad cow scare, although one activist butcher in Panzano made sure the succulent cut was never far away, some earthly pleasures, he argued, were worth the risk.

More missives have been published on Tuscany's ruby nectar. 'Super Tuscans', once served in hay-wrapped flasks, have evolved into award-winning DOC (denomination of controlled origin) vintages. Sangiovese is also pressed into Vino Nobile di Montepulciano and a sangiovese clone goes into Brunello di Montalcino (aged at least three years in oak).

paintings. More than one town says it was depicted by Leonardo da Vinci in the grassy knolls behind the Mona Lisa's head. The town of **Vinci** is evidently the birthplace of the Renaissance all-rounder. **Pistoia** and **Prato**, west of Florence, have developed into textile and economic powerhouses. To the south, the **Maremma** – with provincial capital **Grosseto** – was once a malaria-infested swampland. Today, it is a playground for the rich and famous who come for its five-star thermal spas and rustic-chic allure.

The backbone of Tuscany is the ancient Via Francigena that linked Canterbury to Rome. This trade route was heavily trafficked throughout the Middle Ages and spanned the entire length of the region, carving a corridor of commerce and communication that forever enriched it. Once a shabby trading post, **San Gimignano** acquired a Manhattan-like skyline when its *nouveau riche* inhabitants raced to build the tallest tower – of the original 72, only 13 remain. **Pontrémoli**, **Carrara** and especially **Siena** (with the biggest hospital to serve sick pilgrims along the route) grew rich. Medieval merchants carried exotic ingredients that were incorporated into the local cuisine, such as chocolate that Tuscans had never tasted before and now use in game meat-based dishes.

Tuscany is expensive. The demand for property is so high that many opt for dream homes in neighbouring regions. It is also more difficult to find a property that you can restore yourself there. Strict local regulations make it difficult to modernise and near impossible to add more rooms. A home in the centre of Florence or a rural farmhouse both start at about €4,000 per square metre although, as in other historically significant areas, most homes aren't listed by floorspace. Details such as mouldings and stone fireplaces increase the price up to €7,000.

## Umbria

Once in the shadow of its prodigious neighbour to the north, Umbria has come into its own as the anti-Tuscany. Its natural beauty is as worthy of paintings by Leonardo da Vinci and its layers of history are stacked just as tall. Yet, unlike rambunctious Tuscany, this is a quiet corner and an incredibly soulful and introspective world apart.

Umbria is Italy's greenest region and, curiously, the most geographically isolated. Unlike every other Italian region, it has no access to the sea or international borders. Sandwiched between Tuscany, the Marches and Lazio, Umbria was originally inhabited by a mysterious and peaceful race called the Umbrii. They assimilated with the Etruscans and later become one of the few tribes clever enough to embrace Roman rule, thus avoiding hatchets in the battlefield. The gentle temperament of the Umbrii helped them to outlive their aggressors and the region went on to produce a glut of religious celebrities. St Clare and St Benedict, the founder of monasticism, St Rita, patron of impossibilities, and

## Umbrian Cuisine

Umbrian fare is similar to that of neighbouring regions. There are *crostini* starters and an array of handmade pastas, often topped with black truffles. Umbrian bread, baked with or without salt, is unusual (some would liken it to cardboard). However, white wines from the Orvieto DOC are applauded and made in different styles, from sweet to dry.

St Valentine, icon of lovers, left their mark on Italy's 'green heart'. Most important of all, wrapped in sackcloth-like clothing, St Francis of Assisi (1182–1226) preached love of nature, chastity and spiritual enrichment by virtue of poverty from these hills. At the same time, Tuscans were busy clobbering each other or scheming to get rich from pilgrims. The importance of *il Poverello* (the 'little poor one') in the Catholic Church is unparalleled, and his shrine in Assisi is the country's second most important holy site after the Vatican.

The frescoed Basilica of St Francis in **Assisi** is recovering from deep scars following a 1997 earthquake. This was captured on live television and hearts sank as Giotto's 700-year-old brushstrokes disintegrated like the film at the bottom of a bottle of vinegar when shaken. Art restorers took years to piece together pigment fragments as small as dust particles.

Perched on a tall plateau, **Perugia** is the regional capital. Originally one of the 12 cities in the Etruscan federation, it grew in might and money and blossomed into a Renaissance *città d'arte*. Today, it is home to arguably the best Italian-language school for foreigners and its streets swarm with polyglot students. It has also gained worldwide praise for its chocolates and its annual July music festival. Jazz legends ranging from Chet Baker to Wynton Marsalis have made appearances at the Umbria Jazz Festival. Italian artists – including Romano Mussolini, son of *il Duce* – also top the bill. **Spoleto**, to the south, hosts Italy's most important performing arts event, the Festival dei Due Mondi. (In a proud footnote, small Spoleto succeeded in keeping Hannibal and his army of elephants at bay. Overconfident after his victorious ambush at Lago Trasimeno, in which he massacred 15,000 Roman soldiers, the black conqueror never made it past Spoleto's gate.) Other regional highlights are **Orvieto**, famous for its colourful ceramics, **Gubbio**, another majolica mainstay, and the countryside surrounding **Todi**.

Umbria's potential as a second home cannot be stressed enough. Many foreigners buy property here as an alternative to overpriced Tuscany. Its zoning laws and availability give more flexibility to those with an eye to restoring. But buyers should move fast. The secret has long been out, and a farmhouse near Todi already costs as much as one in Chianti. An apartment in central Perugia starts at €3,000 per square metre and a rural home can be twice that.

# The Marches

The only Italian region with a plural name, the Marches (Le Marche) was named after an ancient word for hinterland. A 'march' was a bordering province of the Roman Empire and is also the root of the word 'marquis.' Throughout history, the region's Adriatic ports and its position, smack in the middle of the peninsula, made it a tempting morsel for foreign interests. Despite invasions and political haggling that even saw its towns auctioned off like livestock at a country market, Le Marche has proudly safeguarded its positioning off the beaten track.

Le Marche is the current 'in' region among foreign property-seekers. As land prices peaked in Tuscany, buyers moved to Umbria. But as asking prices also rise in Umbria, attention is now focused on Le Marche where cheaper property alternatives are available and where there are plenty of old houses to be restored.

Only about 10,000 sq km in area, the Marches is characterised by *mare e monti*, or sea and mountains. The Sibillini Mountains border Umbria and the Apennines slope towards the Adriatic coast, turning to smooth ribbons of hills in some places and rocky gorges in others. Once one of the country's most densely forested areas, with oaks and sycamores, less than 20 per cent is woodland today. Luckily, a low population and lack of industry have helped preserve it as one of Italy's least polluted regions. The coast is lined with summer resort towns (often modern and unattractive) straddling broad sandy beaches.

The only city with a population exceeding 100,000 is **Ancona**. Named after the Greek word (*ancon*) for elbow because of the shape of its bay, it was one of the biggest Mediterranean harbours under Emperor Trajan. After heavy bombing during the Second World War, and an earthquake in 1972, not much remains. **Macerata** and **Ascoli Piceno** to the south both reflect Renaissance urban planning. In the 15th century, Macerata's skyline was shaped to reflect its hilly surroundings. **Pesaro**, on the coast to the north, is a well-kept summer secret and nearby **Fano** claims Italy's oldest carnival. Tourism offices promote **Castelfidardo**, near **Loreto**, as the birthplace of the accordion. The university town of **Urbino** to the north gave birth to another artistic legend – Raffaello Sanzio. Raphael's father, Giovanni Santi, also dabbled in oils; in one of his renditions of the Madonna and child, a young angel to the right of the throne is said to be a portrait of his then eight-year-old son.

---

## *Mare e Monte: Cuisine*

Even local cuisine marries *mare e monti*. Black truffles and mussels are paired in sauces for pasta. Other tasty treats include *porchetta* (whole suckling pig roasted on the spit), *stocco all'anconetana* (dried cod) and *stringozzi* (a type of hollow spaghetti). The region's wine list features whites. Once served in green amphora-shaped bottles, Verdicchio is quickly gaining in prestige.

Property bargain-hunters should seriously consider the Marches. Housing prices average €2,500 per square metre and rarely exceed €5,000. More interestingly, this is the only region in central Italy where hilltop castles and lone towers are still available as fixer-uppers. Unfortunately, as in Umbria, earthquakes are a drawback. The Bologna–Bari motorway makes Le Marche accessible.

# Lazio and Rome

Removing **Rome** from Lazio is like trying to imagine our planetary system without the sun. The monumental, glorious and gorgeous Eternal City spreads rays of brilliance so far that the rest of the region might seem like a vacuous abyss. Rome's architects and philosophers were faced with the most ambitious of human tasks: to build *Caput Mundi*, or the capital of the world. They succeeded.

The rest of Lazio gravitates towards Rome in the same way that dozens of ancient trade routes (the Vvia Cassia, Via Aurelia, Via Salaria and Via Appia) converge on to the Italian capital from all sides like the spokes of a bicycle wheel. The rest of the nation also gravitates towards Rome – although sometimes reluctantly. In the final minutes of Federico Fellini's wonderful film *Roma*, writer and long-time Rome resident Gore Vidal is interviewed seated at an outside *trattoria* in the bohemian Trastevere quarter. He reminds the audience that Rome is a city of illusion. It is the home of cinema, the Church and the government: all illusions, he says. That backhanded compliment is one aspect of understanding the deep resentment felt by many other regions that would prefer not to answer to the capital's authority. A northern separatist movement used the slogan '*Roma ladrona*' ('Rome the thief') to rouse popular support.

The truth of the matter is, most Romans couldn't care less. Rome's proud citizens are thick-skinned, loud, spirited, opinionated and often downright vulgar. One local resident has coined the term '*deformazione romana*' to describe the city's collective persona – his explanation is that too much Imperial blood still rushes through the city's veins. 'Roman deformation' could be translated as 'Felliniesque' by non-Italians. The movie director created Roman street scenes of voluptuous women with low-cut sweaters, sucking on snails or eating raw cloves of garlic, and a band of Vespa-riding youths who awaken a sleeping city with the brain-grating sound of their engines. However, these snippets of life are not just seen on celluloid. Everyone recognises the madman on Piazza Barberini who wears flowers on his head and entertains drivers struck in traffic with his nymph-like ballet routine. An old man on a pedal bike clears the path ahead of him by warning pedestrians to 'make way for the horseman without a horse'. A recent public safety poster campaign to deter tailgating showed a grizzly three-dimensional lion with sharpened teeth on the backside of public buses. Underneath were the words 'Get any Closer and

Die'. Seems excessive? Not when attempting to impose discipline on the unruly Romans.

Beyond Rome, the large region of Lazio spans from Tuscany to Campania and acts like a sponge stuck between the north and the south. Drive down the length of Lazio and watch rolling hills planted with olives morph into arid rocks dotted with cacti. Its upper provinces, surrounding Lago di Bolsena and Lazio's Maremma, have absorbed a Tuscan feel. Here the imprint of the ancient indigenous people, the Etruscans (who lent their name to Tuscany), is everywhere. At Lazio's southern edge, a distinctive Neapolitan flair is palpable. Huge vats of fresh *mozzarella di bufala* line the stone streets of **Sperlonga**: a white-washed village perched on a cliff above the blue sea. In the port of **Gaeta**, it is not uncommon to see three people riding a single scooter, and the local dialect has the 'ssh-ssh' melody heard in Campania. Much of the rest of the region, especially near **Latina**, was mosquito-infested swampland that Benito Mussolini drained in an incredibly ambitious public works campaign. Today, it is fertile farmland and leftover Fascist-style buildings are a tribute to his success. Closer to Rome, on its south side, are the **Castelli Romani** – a collection of small towns near the perimeter of a volcanic lake. Lazio's wine region is located here and, during the harvest festival, some towns let white wine gush from their public fountains as a way of celebrating the autumn event. Although the wine is praised in folk song, wine connoisseurs won't go near the stuff.

Rome attracts a peculiar race of expatriates who tend to settle down for the long haul. Milan, like many other northern cities, sees foreigners who buy homes as investments or because they work in Italy. They come and go and property generally has a higher turnover rate. In Rome, however, many buy homes and sit on them forever.

In the not too distant past, Roman property could be considered affordable. But in the last few years the prices have doubled and are now downright

## The Legend of Romulus and Remus

The roots of the Romans' proud and unruly behaviour can be traced back to the legend of the founding of their city. It starts when an old shepherd discovered a she-wolf with two human infants sucking on her milk. The man took the boys in and named them Romulus and Remus. As young adults, during a quest for revenge and reunion with their biological relatives, they founded a new city. Brotherly conflict first emerged when the two tried to agree on a name for their town. They decided that whoever could count the most birds overhead would have the final say. Romulus won and called it Roma, and he marked its perimeter at the Palatine Hill. However he took victory a step further and announced that no one could enter his town without his permission. More than a bit peeved, Remus defied the ban and jumped over the border. In a fury, Romulus pulled out a sword, killed his twin and pledged to destroy anyone who insulted the name of Rome.

> ### Roman Cuisine
> Ironically, Rome's culinary specialities come from a poor people's tradition in which fresh meat was not always available. In its place are commonly discarded animal parts, usually deep-fried or swamped in sauce. *Cervello fritto* (golf ball-sized fried patties of cows' brains), *trippa alla romana* (slices of cows' intestines smothered in tomato sauce) and *lingua di vitella in salsa piccante* (pickled lamb's tongue) are favourite meals. The region's most refined cuisine comes from Rome's Jewish ghetto. The *carciofo alla giudia*, artichoke crisply fried with its leaves open like a sunflower, is perhaps considered the single most delightful vegetable dish in Italy.

outrageous. Some speculate that the market is at least 25 per cent overpriced and there are signs that prices will not go down anytime in the near future. An apartment in the centre goes for as much as €8,000 per square metre. Older buildings, wood-beamed ceilings and terraces can add as much as €2,000 per square metre to these prices. As this book was being updated, a one-bedroom apartment (about 70 square metres) in Trastevere had been put on the market for €800,000. Ouch.

# Abruzzo

Although the dividing line between central and southern Italy is a fuzzy one, by most accounts it runs somewhere across Abruzzo. This sparsely populated region shares common links with both extremes of the peninsula, although historically it was linked to the kingdom of Naples. This gives it a south-facing slant, despite its proximity to Rome and location in central Italy. Bourbon rulers divided it into four municipalities, which is why the region is sometimes referred to in the plural as 'the Abruzzi'. After Italy's unification, Abruzzo and Molise – its southern neighbour – were lumped together as one. They were separated once more into two distinct regions in 1963.

Abruzzo's population numbers sink far below the national average. Its rough terrain and snowcapped peaks make it good for little else than herding. Extreme poverty until the 1960s spurred waves of immigration to the new world. Pop singer Madonna's ancestors hail from Abruzzo and many foreign visitors come back to study their genealogy. Happily, Abruzzo has turned one-third of its space into natural reserves in which flora and fauna are intact. A rare alpine poppy is found there and some 80 examples of the Marsica bear still roam, as do Apennine wolves, wild cats, Orsini vipers, golden eagles, spotted salamanders and a unique species of squirrel.

The region has two of the Apennines' tallest mountains – the Gran Sasso ('Big Rock') and Maiella. A long winter season provides Romans with a nearby snow retreat as the Abruzzo has the best skiing in central Italy. It even has its own tiny glacier. In addition, Abruzzo has 120km of coast and several noteworthy seaside

> ### *The Taste of Abruzzo*
> Local cuisine is based on grilled and roasted meats, especially lamb. Pungent *pecorino* cheese, smoky *scamorza* and pasta known as *maccheroni alla chitarra* are other delights. Coastal specialities include squid stuffed with anchovies, breadcrumbs and garlic. Pescara is the birthplace of the *confetti*, or sugar-coated almonds, given as a gift at Italian weddings.

resorts. The biggest city is **Pescara** – a particularly unattractive Adriatic port town named after the word *'pesce'* because of its bountiful fishing. Pescara's most famous son is poet and patriot Gabriele D'Annunzio. Other important urban centres are **Chieti**, **Teramo** and **L'Aquila**, near the Campo Felice and Campo di Giove ski resorts. More than 6,000 people perished in L'Aquila in a 1705 earthquake, although its Romanesque churches still stand.

Property prices are low (as little as €2,000 per square metre). Most old farms are divided into small plots and there are entire abandoned towns for sale – left empty because of emigration. Entrepreneurs have purchased some of these ghost towns and converted them into tourist villages. The area is well served by roads, including the Rome–L'Aquila motorway and the Rome–Pescara toll road, which traces the ancient Via Tiburina.

# The South and the Islands

Those with a taste for spice will definitely be enticed by the south. Colours seem more vibrant there, people laugh louder and snippets of life from a bygone era lie around every corner. Like a chilli pepper, though, there is a sharp aftertaste. Campania, Molise, Puglia, Basilicata, Calabria, Sicily and to a lesser extent Sardinia share similar problems. The past has seen too much corruption, mismanagement, unemployment, emigration and organised crime. Not many foreigners have invested in the *mezzogiorno* (or 'midday', as the south is collectively known), although there are promising signs that this is changing.

## Campania

If Milan is Italy's brain and Rome its heart, **Naples** is its soul. The capital of Campania is a city of artisans, musicians, neighbourhood festivals, fireworks, sea views and sumptuous food. Natives of this wild city proudly declare 'see Naples and die', the implication being that its beauty is enough to satisfy a life-long search for perfection. The postcard image of the bay of Naples, with Mount Vesuvius in the background is on display in almost every shop, restaurant and home. Even in the city's darkest corners – such as the Spanish Quarter and the streets that branch off the Spaccanapoli – *palazzo* doors left ajar reveal spectacular interior courtyards that are a world apart from the decaying exteriors.

The people of Campania feed off the sun for spiritual nourishment. Its inhabitants are among the most energetic, unruly, generous, upbeat, musically talented and funny in Italy. Their outlook remains rosy despite the fact that their quality of life has been crippled by high unemployment and the *camorra* – the local crime syndicate. All of this has contributed to another trait tagged to them: *furbizia*. Translated as 'street smarts', and surely some kind of survival instinct that evolved in response to centuries of foreign rule, it means that tourists (especially from northern Europe) have a hard time fitting in. When seatbelts became mandatory, someone designed a T-shirt with a black stripe across the chest. When the helmet law came into effect, police stopped those complying with it to ask why they were hiding their faces. With dubious democratic intent, clever counterfeiters have reproduced everything from euro banknotes to the exclusive Pirelli calendar. Comedian Totò embodied *furbizia* Naples-style in countless black and white movies. In one, he sweet-talks an American with deep pockets who is looking for pretty properties into buying Rome's Trevi Fountain from him.

Naples – or 'new city' in antiquity – offers the best day trips anywhere in Italy. The ancient Roman ruins of Pompeii and Herculaneum are a short drive away and the recently restored Greek temples at Paestum are south of Salerno.

If you see Naples and die, then heaven must be the **Amalfi Coast**. No other place has a pink that rivals the neon hues of bougainvillaea in **Ravello**. No yellow can match the glowing brilliance of a lemon basking in the **Positano** sun. No body of water has the same lapis lazuli tint as the sea that snuggles up to the cliffs at **Sorrento**. The kaleidoscopic effect of the Amalfi Coast spans 40km along a thin peninsula between the Bay of Naples and the Gulf of Salerno. Its backbone is the Amalfi Drive, or Via Smeraldo. Hairpin bends open on to coves with bobbing fishing boats, rocky cliffs and vertical villages, each with its own glazed church dome. The entire coastline is named after Amalfi, once a regional powerhouse. The former maritime republic dominated the coastline from the 9th to the 11th century and was a worthy rival to Pisa, Venice and Genoa.

Only the richest of the rich can afford a villa on the Amalfi Coast. This is the summertime playground of Italy's most powerful and, in the past, has hosted the likes of Greta Garbo and Jackie Kennedy. Even apartments in central Naples are more expensive than one would think – prices per square metre in a refurbished building range from €4,000 to €6,000.

### Good Simple Food

Campania's tastiest traditions start off with the simplest ingredients. *Mozzarella di bufala*, as large as a grapefruit, paired with cherry tomatoes and broad leaves of basil, is culinary perfection. Coffee is stronger in Campania, and its thick-crust pizza made in wood-burning ovens is considered the world's best. Although this is not a prominent wine region, a local white called Greco di Tufo is on its way to becoming Italy's trendiest beverage.

# Molise

Separated from Abruzzo half a century ago, this is Italy's youngest region and possibly its poorest. Molise's difficult mountainous terrain, limited sea access and diminutive size have kept it in isolation. Elderly women still make their own clothing, agriculture sums up the job market and farmers vehemently protect their patches of land. Artisans work on lace, cutlery and bronze, employing methods developed centuries ago. If you have ever been awoken by church bells in Italy, chances are they were made in Molise.

Yet this earthquake-prone land remains in an excellent state of conservation. UNESCO has chosen Molise for two of its four Italian biosphere locations where nature is studied and safeguarded. Forested mountains reveal ancient castles, some flanked with circular guard towers. There are plenty of Roman theatres, amphitheatres and the remains of a Palaeolithic settlement. Dating from 900,000 years ago, it is the oldest such find in Europe. Hikers will run across *tratturi* (pathways), used by local shepherds, dating back to the 2nd century BC. The region's two main cities are **Campobasso** and **Isernia**, rebuilt 12 times following earthquakes and wars.

Immigration from the Balkans during the 15th and 16th centuries has also left its mark. Inhabitants of isolated towns converse in archaic dialects of Albanian and Serbo-Croat, especially in the province of Campobasso. It is no exaggeration to say that people in one town can't understand those in the next. Local cuisine is spiced with chillies called *diavolini molisani* (little devils), and *porcini* wild mushrooms are available by the basketful after the autumn rains.

The adventurous buyer, willing to make do with Italy's lowest standard of living, can find houses for as low as €700 per square metre. However, these properties can be worth the effort and cost of restoration (local construction labour is cheap). There are farmhouses and monasteries, abandoned decades ago, that still have their original decorative details intact. This is a poorer architecture loved by those looking for a rustic second home.

# Puglia

When the Pugliesi say their land will 'cast a spell', they are not just mouthing tourist board keywords. They mean that Puglia is, literally, a magical place. Fish dishes are aphrodisiacs and the common cone houses, called *trulli*, are attributed with mystical powers . Millions of knotted olive trees, some planted 600 years ago, blanket the rust-tinted soil like legions of drab-suited soldiers. Some locals say that if you stare at the trunks long enough, miraculous images will appear.

A peninsula flanked by the Adriatic and Ionian, 'the land of two seas' was inhabited by the Greeks, Romans, Byzantines, Normans and Spanish. These days, this is where scores of ethnic Kurds, Albanians and even Chinese first set foot on

European soil. The ruthless Sacra Corona, Puglia's Mafia, works with Albanian criminal organisations to control the lucrative illegal trade in human beings and contraband cigarettes from the Balkans. Coastguard authorities patrol for immigrant-stuffed dinghies on the last leg of a dangerous journey.

But Puglia is also one of the most industrial and wealthy regions in the *mezzogiorno* and its hotchpotch of foreign influences (evident in the architecture, food and language) truly make the thin peninsula a most fascinating place. Life is not the easiest, but nevertheless forward-thinking foreigners are buying spectacular properties here – poised to leave their own tracks on Italy's 'heel'. Dubbed the 'Tuscany of the south', Puglia is the hottest new trend among foreigner property-buyers today.

Regional capital **Bari** flaunts the cultural richness and wear-and-tear of foreign invasions. Bari Vecchia, the old quarter, was unsafe a few years back, but has since been cleaned up. In quintessential southern style, many households are located on the ground floor, making pedestrian zones analogous to living rooms especially on hot summer evenings. The **Gargano**, a peninsula to the north (the 'spur' of the boot of Italy), is the birthplace of Padre Pio (the beatified

## Case Study: A Small Price for History

A sum that might buy you a medium-sized new car back home, in Puglia buys 8,400 sq m (over 90,000 sq ft) of house on a large plot of land just a few minutes' drive from the shimmering blue sea. 'We love Greece and this area reminds me so much of it,' says Elizabeth Shelton who, with her husband George, picked up the bargain property not far from the whitewashed hamlet of Ostuni in 2002. 'I guess you could say it's off the beaten track, but we didn't want to be anywhere else.'

This couple from Cambridge realised a dream to which hordes of foreigners aspire. They found a beautiful property for a fraction of the price they would have paid in Umbria or Tuscany, but the best part is that they bought an authentic *trullo*, one of the characteristic homes of this area of southern Italy. 'Yes, it has the little pointed thing on top and basically consists of one big *trullo* cone with three large rooms inside,' she says, affectionately describing her teepee-like summer retreat.

Now the Sheltons join the ranks of owners of the some of the world's most peculiar architecture. The *trulli* are ancient cone-shaped homes made of stone, many of which are painted with mysterious symbols and markings to ward off the evil eye. Love lore says that couples who spend a night in *trullo* will never be parted. Although the origins of the curious buildings are unknown, many liken them to primitive houses found in Turkey, Greece or the Middle East and it is possible their architectonic roots do in fact spread that far. 'My daughter knew of the area and suggested it but we never expected it to be as charming as it really is,' says one woman who enjoys long walks and collecting wild flowers near her new home. 'Charismatic – yes, that's the word.'

religious personality who grew in popularity also thanks to Italian television) and is a summer holiday mecca. Regional cities such as **Manfredonia**, **Manduria** and **Monopoli** ('main city') still carry Greek names. Between Foggia and Bari is the mysterious octagonal Castel del Monte, built by Emperor Frederick II in the 1240s and visible on the backside of Italy's one-cent euro coin.

The breathtaking beauty of the **Itria Valley** is another regional highlight. **Ostuni** sits in white-washed splendour on a hilltop and recalls the towns the Greece. Nearby **Martina Franca**, with kasbah-like streets, puts on an August music festival in which Dixieland bands play from overhead balconies. **Alberobello** is entirely made of *trulli*, the teepee-like stone buildings that have become a regional emblem. Thousands of the mysterious buildings sit in a tight little cluster there.

The **Salento** starts further south, in the provinces of Brindisi and Lecce. The Romans were the first to bring wealth by building a port in **Brindisi** and connecting it to Rome's Appian Way. A column near the harbour marks the end of the ancient trading road and the 'gateway to the Orient'. Framed by olive, fig and cherry groves, secondary roads south of Brindisi are wide enough for one-way traffic. Many are lined with prickly pears and stone walls painstakingly built by hand. The splendours of the Salentine Baroque can be admired in **Lecce**. Sculptors carved life into the pink limestone that adorns city monuments and erosion has added to their appeal – angels and flowers on the central Santa Croce church's façade have been chiselled down by sea salt carried inland by the winds.

In **Otranto**, a beautiful seaside town surrounded by ramparts, a road ends at the Adriatic and a signpost marked 'Albania' points to some undefined spot in the distance. Down the coast, crumbling ancient defence towers every few kilometres are reminders of the region's strategic importance. **Santa Maria Leuca**, at the very tip of the peninsula, represents a point of contact for the people of the Mediterranean basin, and powerful surf marks where the Adriatic and Ionian Seas meet. The ancients called it *finibus terrae*, or 'land's end.'

Moving over to the Ionian side of Puglia, the sea turns a lighter shade of blue and rocky bluffs are replaced with wide sand beaches. A barren stretch of land

## Puglia: Another Wonderful Culinary Tradition

Puglia's culinary tradition is deeply influenced by the sea. Raw *ricci*, or sea urchins, are cracked open like nuts and the animal's orange flesh scooped out with bread. Inland specialities include *burrata* – part of the mozzarella family with creamy milk enclosed within. *Orecchiette* are ear-shaped pasta, served with tomato sauce and salty ricotta cheese or sometimes *cicoria* (chicory). Mashed broad beans and doughnut-like bread crackers, called *taralli*, are washed down with red primitivo. This is an indigenous grape, grafts of which Californian winemakers smuggled out and renamed zinfandel.

extends north until the bustling sprawl of **Taranto**, home to the south's biggest shipyard. Unfinished homes on prime coastal land look like fleshless carcasses. The sad sights are monuments to somebody's grandiose vision, but many of these houses were built without permits and abandoned when the money ran out. The pearl of this side of Puglia is **Gallipoli** ('beautiful city'), built on an island connected by an isthmus. Thirty years of Saracen rule was enough to leave a strong Islamic imprint evident in the oriental circular city plan. Like a lifebelt, the city appears to float on water.

Puglia is full of special properties that are a fraction of the price of those in Tuscany or Umbria. Here you can get a 15th-century Salentine Baroque estate with eight bedrooms, acres of olive groves and a working olive mill for as little as €1 million. Some €200,000 can buy a cluster of restored *trulli* near Alberobello. Italians and foreigners are flocking here to turn these precious properties into hotels and holiday villages. Remodelling restrictions are less stringent, and local artisans are capable and hardworking.

# Basilicata

Sadly, where there are lists, there is a last place. Basilicata sits glumly at the bottom of the 'nicest places to live in Italy' league. Few would disagree, not even local inhabitants, most of whom have emigrated, making this Italy's most sparsely populated region. Now synonymous with abandonment and extreme poverty, the name 'Basilicata' actually suggests lofty, noble aspirations as it comes from *basilikos*, the Greek for 'governors and princes'. Prior to Roman conquest, the arch of Italy's boot was called Lucania (either from the Latin word for forests, *lucus*, or the Greek word for a forest-roaming wolf, *lykos*). To this day, its people are the Lucani.

Another sad thing to note is its condition. Once mostly marshes and woodlands, rampant deforestation has turned Basilicata into an arid wasteland with little agriculture. Gone are both the *lucus* and the *lykos*. Not many Lucani are left either – there are more outside Basilicata's borders than within them. Between 1981 and 1991, the national census shows that its population grew by only 342 individuals.

Despite access to the Ionian and Tyrrhenian seas, Basilicata has no major harbours. Of its main towns, **Potenza** is the richest because of its location on trade routes linking Naples to Puglia's Greece-facing ports. **Matera**, the only town of its size not currently connected to the Italian railroad system, is a poor and curious place. Until a few decades ago, its citizens lived in caves carved from *tufa*. The *sassi* housed families and beasts together and there are also entire churches inside stone holes. **Maratea** – a quaint and picturesque hilltop resort town on the Tyrrhenian sea – is the region's most fashionable getaway. It is also strikingly beautiful – a greyer version of the Amalfi Coast.

A peasant culture produced superstition and folklore, mostly linked to weddings and funerals. On her wedding day, a bride wore her entire dowry in the form of beads and lace, giving birth to the expression *sposa come si trova* ('the bride comes as she is'). Author Carlo Levi, exiled in Basilicata by the Fascists, describes wailing women at funerals scratching blood from their cheeks. His book, *Christ Stopped at Eboli*, turned Basilicata into a national scandal because it exposed an isolated, poverty-stricken community, cut off from the rest of a nation in the midst of Italy's post-war economic boom.

Local dishes make use of fish, meat and goat cheese and *lagana* (hand-rolled noodles). Olives, figs and strawberries grow here, as do grapes for wine, including the robust, ruby-coloured Aglianico del Vulture.

Property prices match those in Molise. Harsh conditions and organised crime do not make Basilicata appealing to foreign buyers.

# Calabria

Campania's sun is reflected in its inhabitants' sunny disposition. Calabria, on the other hand, is awash with golden rays, but even the sun has done little to warm a sombre atmosphere. Once the mighty and magnificent Magna Graecia, the most important of the Greek colonies around 750 BC, Calabria has since been cursed with earthquakes, wars, feuding landlords, disease, organised crime, poverty, oppression, mass emigration to richer places and immigration from poorer ones. Throughout it all, its people have learned to get by and survive. They are hardworking and earnest and, it has been said, the most obsessed with death of all the Italians.

In mythological times, Italy's 'toe' posed the biggest challenges to Odysseus on his long voyage home to Penelope. Scilla, at the entrance of the Straits of Messina, is where Scylla, daughter of Hecate, transformed into a sea monster and gobbled up crewmen. Sailors still claim to witness the '*Fata Morgana*' – a mirage in which land, an island or a city appears to float on empty sea. Today, there are tours that trace Homer's *Odyssey* through an all-Calabrian itinerary. However, the region's strongest tourist magnets are the Bronze di Riace. Discovered in 1972 in an ancient shipwreck, these twin statues were retrieved from their watery tomb and carefully restored. They are among the most precious artefacts from Greek antiquity in existence and are on display in Reggio di Calabria's archaeological museum.

Four Cs adorn Calabria's signposts: Cosenza, Crotone, Catanzaro and Reggio di Calabria. **Catanzaro** is a rather uninteresting regional capital, but **Cosenza** makes a good base from which to explore the Sila mountain plateau with its hiking paths and camping sites. (The tip of the toe is formed by another wooded highland named Aspromonte.) **Reggio di Calabria**, once a beautiful, sea-facing city, has little left to see after a 1908 earthquake levelled it. **Crotone**, once the most powerful of Greek cities, is now largely industrial. **Nocera Terinese** is worth a visit at Easter if you care to watch a parade of self-flagellating Calabresi.

Although there are castles flanked by forests, jasmine plantations and wide sand beaches for sale, earthquakes and organised crime, known locally as the *'Ndrangheta*, make Calabria an uncommon choice for foreigners. Summer homes cost about €2,000 per square metre or less.

# Sicily

The best way to first experience Sicily is by attending one of the many festivals honouring its patron saints. Each summer, **Palermo** holds *il festino*, billed as the biggest party in the Mediterranean, in homage to Santa Rosalia. It is a harvest festival and a political parade all rolled into one. Some 200,000 citizens cram around a wooden statue of the pretty saint pulled by eight bare-chested men drenched in perspiration. When the saint reaches the Quattro Canti intersection, the mayor climbs into view and makes the same proclamation each year: *'Viva Santa Rosalia'*. Dedicated to a Catholic matriarch, *il festino* is awash with pagan flavours.

Specifically, this is a celebration of the cult of woman, or a fertility rite, born on an arid island with mineral-rich soil where grapes ripen, almond trees blossom and olive trees burst with fruit to fuel much of the local economy. According to legend, Santa Rosalia retired to a hermetic existence on Mount Pellegrino in 1159. Five hundred years later, as the infectious wrath of the plague took hold of the city, she appeared before a lost hunter and promised to save Palermo. She did. Savvy political leaders have recently used the plague as a metaphor for the Mafia (*Cosa Nostra*). She is credited with saving Palermo from that threat, too.

Sicily's other major cities, including **Catania** and **Messina**, also have female patron saints. Sant'Agata, virgin martyr of Sicily, died following extreme torture, during which her breasts were cut off. Today, she protects against breast cancer and has a role in stopping dangerous lava flows from Mount Etna.

Opposite Palermo on the other side of the triangular island, everyone from schoolchildren to taxi drivers starts the day with a quick read of the steam coming from the massive volcano that casts a shadow over Catania. When wind breaks up the steam that usually billows from its crater, Etna – always assigned a male gender – is 'a bit down'. When the clouds of steam are defined and thick, he's 'back up'. This primitive barometer measures not only the volcano's mood, but the city's.

Smack in the middle of the Mediterranean, Sicily really is a crossroads of east and west, north and south, old and new. Almost every major military force – from the Greeks, Arabs, Romans, Spanish and French to Garibaldi's troops in the days of 'the Leopard' – has marched across the island. Pagan rituals have merged with Catholic symbols to create a spirituality unique to this island. The Arabs left behind irrigation technology and cooking ingredients that flavour today's famously delicious *cucina siciliana* in which couscous and curry make appearances. A cluster of towns near Palermo are home to an Albanian community that settled here in the 15th century. *Arbëreshe* (an archaic version of Albanian) is still spoken and taught in schools, and residents in Piana degli Albanesi observe Byzantine rites based on the Christian Orthodox Church. Unique Sicilian and Norman gene-blending has produced stunningly attractive Sicilians with dark skin, blond hair and blue eyes.

With the exception of Enna, located at the geographical centre of the island, most of Sicily's cities are on the sea. The provinces of **Agrigento, Caltanissetta, Catania, Enna, Messina, Palermo, Ragusa, Syracuse** and **Trapani** make up the most densely populated island in the Mediterranean. Inland Sicily consists of vast expanses of agricultural plains and vineyards, but few people. Palermo has always been associated with organised crime and the brutal murders of two anti-Mafia judges in the 1990s have only cemented negative stereotypes. The truth is Palermo has been cleaned up and beautified and formally crime-ridden neighbourhoods are now swarming with people looking for investment properties.

Many foreigners own homes near **Taormina, Noto** and **Syracuse**. English families settled near the town of Marsala and made famous fortified wine to ship back home. Today, the area makes excellent wine from indigenous ansonica and nero d'avola grapes.

Beach-house-hunters should seriously consider Sicily. One reason is because of its architectural wealth. Byzantine columns and Islamic arches make for added value. Another reason is price. An apartment in the centre of Palermo costs €3,000 to €4,000 per square metre although prices are rising very fast. Listings in Catania are about the same. Once burdened with the country's highest crime rate, Catania has also been restored, cleaned up and 'reborn'. It is also close to some of Sicily's cleanest beaches. **Cefalù**, near Palermo, is another excellent spot for a holiday home.

# Sardinia

This, Italy's third largest region, owes a lot to the bikini. Before French fashion house Chanel turned sun-tanning into the latest rage by showcasing darker

## Tiscali.com

A walk through the canyon of Gorroppu, near Dorgali, leads to the prehistoric village of Tiscali. Today, the name has been borrowed by new economy guru, Sardinian-born Renato Soru, who founded Tiscali, Italy's first free Internet company and one of the biggest Internet service providers in Europe. A top performer on Milan's index for high-growth companies, Tiscali is a symbol of a wired, tech-savvy Italy.

models on its Paris runways, the Tyrrhenian island was largely made up of rocks and goatherds. Many of its towns were built inland for protection against repeated Saracen raids during the Middle Ages and for proximity to pastoral plains. As a result, Sardinia's inhabitants never really took to fishing. Kilometre after kilometre of pristine white- and pink-coloured sand beaches, alternating with hidden coves and sheer cliffs soaring above sparkling emerald waters, were deemed utterly useless. However, as bathing suits got smaller, the crowds grew bigger and the island's natural resources turned to gold.

Indeed, gold is the primary colour of Sardinian style. Bleached blondes match their golden tans with gold-coloured sandals and sunglasses. Boutiques in the posh Porto Cervo resort town showcase seashells enamelled in the precious metal and even hotels have gilded bathroom fixtures. A summer holiday on the island is a fashion statement among the nation's élite. However, behind the glitz and golden glare lies a cultural crossroads severed from the mainland.

Now a symbol of Sardinia, there are the *nuraghe*, or truncated round towers built by a mysterious people who settled here in 1500–800 BC. Following them, the Phoenicians, Carthaginians, Romans, Byzantines, Saracens, Pisans and Genovese, the Aragons of Spain and the Austrians all passed through and left their marks before the island went to the House of Savoy. In Alghero, for example, the Catalonian influence on the local dialect is strong.

Sardinia's main cities are **Cagliari**, a port on its southern tip, **Nuoro**, birthplace of author Grazia Deledda, **Oristano** and **Sassari**. Sunbathers will fancy one of Sardinia's satellite islands – **Sant'Antioco, San Pietro, Asinara**, the **La Maddalena** archipelago and **Caprera**. On some, pink sand made from crushed seashells, granite and coral is so precious that guards have been hired to stop beachgoers from pocketing the grains.

However, most come to the Emerald Island for its nature. Isolation has made Sardinia the Galápagos of the Mediterranean. Hidden among the scrub are Sardinian sparrows, wild goats, Sardinian partridges and fallow deer found nowhere else. In the clear waters and on rocky outcrops, monk seals thrive. The Stagno di Molentargius wetlands are even home to pink flamingos. The diversity of the landscape is so great – from mountains, to beaches, to deserts – that Hollywood directors in the 1960s borrowed Sardinia's 'Wild West' scenery as a backdrop, making spaghetti westerns here.

*Flavours of Sardinia*

The island cuisine has been inspired first by its shepherds, then by its fishermen. *Mirto* (myrtle) is paired with meat, and the bitter berry is fermented into a tasty after-dinner drink. *Carta da musica* ('music sheets') is a thin, cracker-like bread. Sardinia produces a cheese so 'aged' that live worms wiggle inside; enzymes inside the creatures are said to improve the taste, and die-hard cheese fans wouldn't dare pull them out. *Merca* is small fish wrapped in herbs and left to 'ripen' for several days, and *spaghetti alla bottarga* is pasta served with female lobster eggs that have been pressed and dried in the sun like raisins.

Vineyards in Campidano, north of Cagliari, produce unique grape varieties such as girò, cannonau (a relative of granacha from Spain), nuragus (believed to have been brought by the Phoenicians), torbato, vernaccia di Oristano and monica. The bark from a special oak, called *sughero*, makes the world's best wine corks.

If you intend to buy property, avoid the painful thought that, not too long ago, landowners couldn't unload beachfront property no matter how low the price. Now buyers are faced with the opposite scenario – with prices as high as €2,000 per square metre in cities and up to four times that for seaside villas.

# The Smaller Islands

Good things always come in small packages. The tiny islands off Italy's coast offer a natural beauty that rivals the mainland, in addition to privacy and seclusion. Transport to and from can be patchy, however, and many islands rely on ships for everything from mail to drinking water. However, that is precisely why they make perfect holiday hideaways.

**Elba**, off the Tuscan coast, is where Napoleon spent his final days, and **Isola del Giglio**, facing Porto San Stefano, is laid-back and rustic. **Montecristo** is now a nature reserve and home to exactly two people: a man and woman guardian who are literally stranded together. The **Isole Ponziane**, with ferries from Anzio or Gaeta, are stunningly beautiful. Houses overlooking white cliffs and blue water include underground rooms to guarantee cooler temperatures. Campania includes a lucky load of islands, such as **Capri**, **Procida** and **Ischia**. Puglia, on the Adriatic side, has the three-island **Tremiti** group. Although this tiny archipelago, some 40km from the coast, hosts only about 50 full-time residents, the islands' population soars to more than 100,000 during the summer months.

The Mediterranean's biggest island, Sicily, is surrounded by plenty of smaller satellites. The most famous collection is that of the seven **Æolian Islands** – Stromboli, Panarea, Lipari, Salina, Vulcano, Filicudi and Alicudi. A perfect black cone rising from the sea, Stromboli is a very active volcano with eruptions every 15 minutes that look like fireworks against a dark sky. Legend says that Odysseus used it as a beacon. Stromboli is also home to the world's smallest port, into which exactly two fishing boats can barely squeeze. Energy is provided by solar panels and residents rely on mobile phones. When a storm hits, they cope without outside contact for days.

The island of **Ustica** is associated with an unresolved DC-9 passenger jet crash in 1980 that still feeds hundreds of conspiracy theories. The islands facing Trapani – **Favignana**, **Levanzo** and **Marettimo** – are known for their good fishing and sunbathing. **Pantelleria** is home to plantations of oversised capers and **Lampedusa** is often in the news as the first European stop for illegal immigrants from North Africa. But both are gorgeous summer holiday spots.

### Case Study: Island Life

When Janet, a former teacher at an English-language high school in Rome, purchased a property on Ponza more than a decade ago, she knew she was among the last generation of foreign home-owners on the tiny island. 'You can't touch housing here any more; prices have gone through the roof and it has now become impossible to build or restore without buckets of money and very good friends at town hall.' She might complain how Ponza has changed now, but a wink and a subtle smile give her true feelings away. 'I know, I'm darn lucky. I have a house in paradise.'

Ponza is paradise to citizens of Rome and Naples, who regularly board the boats that connect the island to the mainland and settle down in rented boats or on rocky beaches to enjoy the sun, fishing and scenery. You can swim between natural rock arches and wedge a small boat into one of the many watery *grotte* (caves) illuminated from underneath by the sun's reflection.

As Ponza grew in popularity with tourists, local officials decided that, in order to safeguard limited resources, severe restrictions would be put on planning permission. No new homes and very few renovations are allowed, adding one more hardship to locals who rely on ferry service for water, mail and food and are faced with the sky-rocketing costs associated with island life. 'Getting a washing machine repair man out here is a major ordeal,' says Janet.

'If you want to buy here, the only thing to do is find an old cave and dig and dig until you've carved out a home.' That's exactly what Janet did. Many homes on the island are in fact former shepherd's storage caverns within the island's soft stone. Home-owners convert these into residences by pushing deeper into the rock, away from the glaring sun and outdoor heat. Janet's house has views of the main port and is steps away from the Frontone beach, where ancient Romans carved bathing pools in the stone that are still enjoyed by swimmers today. 'But the part I love the most is that I have the best views of the spectacular fireworks display each year, during the San Severio patron saint celebrations.'

Property prices depend on the island, with Pantelleria, Stromboli, Panarea, Ischia and Capri costing the most. On those posh islands, summer homes can cost as much as €7,000 or more per square metre. Less posh property can be had for €2,000 a square metre. Near deserted islands, such as far-flung Filicudi and Alicudi, are very, very rustic, and prices there reflect problems such as sporadic water supplies, unpaved roads and a weekly mail service.

# Selecting a Property

04

If the time has come to turn intentions into actions, you'll need to answer the last questions that are the pillars of basic house-hunting. 'Why Italy?' and 'Why buy?' have already been discussed, and 'Where in Italy?' was the focus of our tour of the regions, but the first phase of actually buying in Italy includes searching for a suitable property and knowing what to do to prepare for the search. So now is the time to ask questions such as, 'What do I need to know before buying?' and 'When am I going to be ready to buy?' And, along the way, you'll need to plan a trip to Italy.

# Travelling to Italy

With two major international airports and some 30 smaller ones that cater to international air traffic, going by plane is the easiest, fastest and surprisingly often the cheapest way to get to Italy. But if you are bringing furniture – or anything else that doesn't fit into two pieces of luggage and a carry-on – you might consider driving to Italy as many expatriates or second-home-owners do. Rail and coach are less popular options.

One very important thing to keep in mind when planning your trip is that strikes are a basic component of Italian life. There are air traffic control walkouts that will ground hundreds of flights in a single day. Petrol station strikes could leave you stranded, and paralysing train strikes are timed down to the minute to make the rush-hour commute as horrific as possible, but there is good news: industrial action is usually announced in advance to give travellers time to make alternative plans. If you travel frequently, you should get into the habit of consulting the website of the Ministry of Transport, **http://www.infrastrutture trasporti.it/page/standard/site.php?p=scioperi**, offering a constantly updated page on national and inter-regional strikes.

## Air

Chances are your entry point will be Milan's Malpensa airport or Rome's Leonardo da Vinci airport (located in the nearby town of Fiumicino and often referred to as Fiumicino airport). These are the country's biggest and most trafficked airports catering to all foreign carriers with services to Italy. Of Italy's 137 airports, 32 offer international connections. As well as Milan and Rome, airports in medium-sized cities like Venice, Florence, Bari and Palermo cater to a limited number of international carriers.

For many years, state-owned Alitalia reigned supreme in the Italian skies and had the final word when it came to pricing. But, since the mid-1990s, when airline deregulation splintered monopolies, fuelled tariff wars and heralded the arrival of budget airlines, Alitalia's grasp on the market has loosened. Now there is a whole new generation of low-cost airlines with services to Italy from many European cities. But this new generation of budget airlines is a volatile bunch. Some change schedules or destinations at the last minute and others disappear altogether following a sudden bankruptcy only to reappear a few months later with a different name. But most, like the exceptional Ryanair, promise not only to stick around but to revolutionise air travel. The main carriers are:

• **Alitalia** (**t** 0870 544 8259; **www.alitalia.co.uk**) has numerous direct flights to Italy each day departing from the UK and Ireland: London Heathrow (eight flights per day to Milan; one to Rome); Manchester (two flights per day to Milan); Dublin (one flight per day to Milan). House-hunters might consider the 'Visit Italy' AirPass, which allows you up to five destinations in Italy for a very reduced fare and is great for hopping around the peninsula.

• **British Airways** (**t** 0870 850 9850 for fares and booking or **t** 0870 551 1155 for 24-hour flight arrival and departure information; **www.ba.com**) also has many flights per day to Italy departing from London Heathrow and Gatwick, including six or seven daily to Rome depending on the day of the week and eight to Milan (both Linate and Malpensa airports) from Heathrow, and three to Venice, one to Turin, three to Naples and Pisa from Gatwick.

• **Ryanair** (**t** 0906 270 5656; **www.ryanair.com**) services Italy from London's Stansted Airport and Luton, with more Italian destinations than any other. It connects Stansted to Turin, Ancona, Trieste, Brescia, Parma, Bologna, Genoa, Pisa, Pescara, Palermo, Lamezia, Bari, Brindisi, Alghero; both Stansted and Luton to Venice, Milan and Rome (also from Liverpool, East Midlands, Dublin and Glasgow). At the time of the writing, most one-way fares averaged about £40, but prices can go lower (or higher, depending on how last-minute your booking is). For example, Ryanair advertised one promotional fare for as little as £10 each way for its Stansted–Ciampino (Rome) route.

• **easyJet** (**t** 0905 821 0905 (65p/min); **www.easyjet.co.uk**) will take you to several Italian towns: from London (Gatwick, Stansted or Luton) to Milan, Rome, Venice, Turin, Naples, Cagliari, Olbia; from Bristol to Venice, Pisa and Rome; from Newcastle to Rome; from East Midlands to Rome and Venice; from Belfast to Rome.

• **British Midland/BMI** (**t** 0870 607 0555; **www.flybmi.com**) flies from Heathrow to Milan (Linate), Naples and Venice; from Manchester to Naples and Venice; from Leeds to Milan (Linate) and Venice; from Dublin and Belfast to Milan (Linate) and Venice; from Glasgow, Aberdeen and Edinburgh to Milan (Linate), Naples and Venice.

• **Jet2** (**t** 0871 226 1737; **www.jet2.com**). This new low-cost company connects Leeds to Milan, Rome, Pisa and Venice; Manchester to Rome and Pisa; Newcastle, Edinburgh and Belfast to Pisa. At the time of writing, one-way fares cost £19 on average.

# Road

The drive from England (or rather from the French Channel ports) is about 24 hours or so, with short stops and one overnight stay, to the Italian border. The fastest route is from Calais, heading towards Italy via Nancy, Lucerne and Lugano for a total of 1,042km (650 miles). The most scenic and hassle-free route is through the Alps, but if you drive through Switzerland you will have pay steep fees for motorway use and mandatory extra car insurance.

Make sure you bring your vehicle registration documents and driving licence. You can obtain an international driving permit, which is basically a translation of your licence, but most Italian police are familiar with UK driving licences so this is not strictly necessary. Third-party insurance is the minimum require-ment, although it is good sense to carry more. You should obtain a 'green card' (*carta verde*) from your insurer that proves you are fully covered. It is valid in most European countries. If you have an accident, you will have to fill out a European Accident Statement form. These are available from your insurer or from the Automobile Club of Italy (**www.aci.it**). If the situation is amicable, both parties can share one, fill it out together and keep a copy each (the form has multiple layers). For more information on the pains and pleasures of driving in Italy, *see* pp.70–72.

To reach Italy by car you must select one of the alpine border passes or tunnels that open on to the Italian peninsula. Expect to pay a toll as high as €35 at the tunnel entrance – round-trip discounts are available. Some passes close in winter months or during heavy snowfall and drivers should be prepared with chains or snow tyres (for more information, visit **www.travel-italy.com**). Some of the tunnels have web pages and these are listed below so that you can check weather conditions before departure. The main tunnels and other passes are the following.

• **Mont Blanc Tunnel**: Reopened in 2002, three years after a tragic fire, this tunnel is 11.67km (7 miles) long and connects France with Italy. The altitude at the Italian entrance is 1,381m (4,500ft) and is uphill at a 2.5 per cent gradient. The French part is downhill at a 4.5 per cent gradient and exits at 1,264m (4,150ft) in altitude. This is the most popular tunnel with British travellers.

• **Fréjus Tunnel** (**www.tunneldufrejus.com**): Measuring 12.96km (8 miles) long, this tunnel joins the region of Piedmont with southeastern France. Opened in 1980. Another tunnel popular with British travellers.

• **San Bernardo Tunnel** (**www.grandsaintbernard.ch**): Connecting Italy and Switzerland, the Italian entrance is 1,740m (5,700ft) in altitude and has a maximum gradient of 5 per cent. It is 5.8km (3.6 miles) long. In the tunnel, vehicles must maintain a speed of not less than 40km per hour (25mph) and not more than 80 (50mph). Open all year.

• **St Gotthard Tunnel** (**www.gottardtunnel.ch**): Also connecting Italy and Switzerland, this is the longest alpine tunnel at 16.42km (10 miles) long. There is no toll. The southern entrance is at Airolo at 1,114m (3,650ft) in altitude and the northern entrance is at Goschenen at 1,080m (3,540ft). Up to 1,800 vehicles per hour can pass through the tunnel in either direction.

• **Brenner Pass (Brennero)**: Connecting Austria and Italy at 1,370m (4,500ft) in altitude, this is the lowest alpine road pass (not a tunnel) and is open all year between Innsbruck and Vipiteno.

• **Monte Croce Carnico Pass**: Open from June to October between Tolmezzo and Lienz, this is a mountain pass rather than a tunnel. It is useful for visitors arriving from Eastern Europe.

# Rail

There are mixed views on travelling to Italy from England by train. Some find the journey, usually via Paris, to be painfully long and monotonous. Others are able to sleep soundly in their *couchettes* and awake fresh and energised at their Italian destination.

If you decide to come to Italy by rail from London, you have the following options. First, take the Eurostar to Paris Gare du Nord. Then take the *métro* to Paris Gare de Bercy to board one of Europe's great overnight express trains to Italy. There are two main lines. The *Palatino* leaves Paris every night at 7pm and arrives the next morning at Piacenza, Parma, Bologna, Firenze and Rome. The other great express is the *Stendhal*, which leaves Paris at 8.28pm bound for Milan. These departure times do change, so you should check when booking.

There are other options from Paris (Gare de Lyon) to Turin and Milan. The first, EC *Manzoni*, departs at 8.04am; the *Dumas* and *Caravaggio* at 2.24pm and 3.50pm respectively.

**Fares** vary depending on the size of your sleeping quarters (the cheapest is a compartment sleeping six, the most expensive is one for two people with a private bathroom) and the route you select.

To buy tickets online for London–Paris–Italy routes, contact **Rail Europe** (**t** 08708 371 371; **www.raileurope.co.uk**). From London to Paris, check the **Eurostar** times and fares (**t** 08705 186 186; **www.eurostar.com**). From Paris to Italy, or within Italy, go to **www.trenitalia.it** (or, from within Italy, call **t** 89 20 21). This Italian site is also in English.

# Coach

Travel by coach is not much cheaper than the train and it takes much longer. **National Express Eurolines** runs coaches from London to Italy several times a week. Contact them (**t** 0870 580 8080; **www.nationalexpress.com**) for more information.

## Sea

There are no direct ferry links to Italy from the UK unless you want to take an extremely long route but, if you are considering buying (or already own) a home on one of Italy's islands, there are various options for flying or driving to a port in Italy or France and then completing your journey by sea (*see* pp.73–5).

# Travelling around Italy

Once arrived, you'll need to know how to get around. One mode of transport that should not be underestimated is rail travel. Yes, trains do run on time thanks to Il Duce, who also established an incredibly elaborate railroad network that reaches into the most remote corners of Italy. National air carriers have slashed prices, making travel down the peninsula often cheaper than trains or cars. Ferries and hydrofoils will zip you over to Italy's paradise-like islands, although reservations should be made in advance during the summer. In addition to cars, mopeds and scooters are favourite vehicles for enjoying life on the road.

Travelling in Italy, you join the ranks of among the most mobile people on the planet. On average, Italians travel 26km (16 miles) per day, according to the national institute for transport, and spend more than an hour per day in movement (or stuck in traffic, as it may be). Surprisingly, most short trips are for pleasure – visiting friends and family or shopping – rather than work. One quarter of all short commutes are done on bicycle or foot. Overall, journeys in private cars outrank buses, trams and metros by a ratio of seven to one.

## Air

Besides Alitalia, there are three other private carriers that service the nation. These are **Meridiana** (**www.meridiana.it**), **Airone** (**www.flyairone.it**) and **Air Europe** (**www.aireurope.it**). These airlines often engage in tariff wars, especially during the busy summer months, to attract customers and earn a bigger slice of the market. Some offer fares as low as €40 one way – Milan–Naples, for example. Besides these national airlines, there are also many regional airlines servicing islands like Sardinia, the mountainous north, Florence and the rest of Tuscany, and the south. These include **Air Dolomiti** (**www.airdolomiti.it**), **Alpi Eagles** (**www.alpieagles.com**) and **Volare** (**www.volareweb.com**).

If your destination is Milan's Malpensa or Rome's Leonardo da Vinci airports you will find there are easy connections to the centres, although both airports are located far from the cities they service. From Malpensa, some 70km (44 miles) away, the Malpensa Express train departs every 30 minutes for Milan's central Cadorna station. Alternatively a bus departs half-hourly for Milan's main train station. From Rome's airport, a train connects with Stazione Termini in Rome's centre, departing every 30 minutes or so.

Both Milan and Rome have secondary airports for national and limited international flights. Milan's Linate Airport is conveniently located within the city. Rome's Ciampino Airport, mostly for military flights, is also used by some international budget airlines. Ciampino is connected by metro to the centre (although the metro station is a few stops by bus from the airport).

A chart of regional airports, with contact numbers and trip times to their cities, is available at **www.travel-italy.com**.

# Rail

Without a doubt one of the best ways to get around Italy is by train. Tracks were laid down with fervour before and after the Second World War to demonstrate that Italy was a modern nation with industrial muscle. Rail travel is very cheap compared with other European nations and it can get you almost anywhere. There are some exceptions, such as in Tuscany (*see* p.73). The Ligurian line (Genoa–Ventimiglia) is a nightmare as there is only one track in either direction, forcing all trains – from express to local – to travel at the same speed. The journey is about two hours longer than it should be, although the coastal views are worth the extra time. Trains to Sicily still must engage in a silly ritual that involves separating the cabins and putting them in a ferry to cross the Straits of Messina.

There are some private lines, but the majority of Italy's rail system is operated by Ferrovie dello Stato (FS). This government holding bequeathed on Italians one of the most revolutionary gifts of modern times: a functioning website (**www.trenitalia.it**). Before its existence, travellers had to go to the nearest station in person to get train information as phone lines were permanently busy. The site has an English version and up-to-date and accurate schedule information. It even tells you which trains allow you to board with a bicycle. However, you cannot buy tickets online unless you register.

The basic types of trains are as follows.

- **Eurostar (ES)**: Italy's fastest trains, with first- and second-class seating. A dining service is often available, for which reservations are not required. Eurostar trains leave Rome every hour for Florence, Bologna and Milan. These are new trains, with air-conditioning, clean bathrooms and legroom; you'll miss these qualities when on any other kind. A supplement, or *supplemento rapido*, included in the ticket price, is required for this service.

- **Eurocity (EC)**: An international express train that stops only at major stations in Italy and beyond its borders (for example, Rome–Paris). There is first- and second-class seating, and a supplement is payable for this high-speed service.

• **Intercity (IC)**: These are express trains with first- and second-class seating, stopping at major stations in Italy and a limited number just beyond the nation's borders. A supplement is payable on this service; reservation is only recommended. On the other hand, on the modern and more comfortable train called **Intercity Plus (ICplus)**, reservation is mandatory. There is also **Intercity Notte (ICN)** travelling by night, with sleeping carriages.

• **Espresso (EXP)**: A long-distance train that stops at major stations. No supplement is required.

• **Diretto (DIR)**: A much slower train that often only has second-class seating; a standard fare is charged with no supplement.

• **Interregionale (IR)**: No supplement required and sometimes it is really convenient in order to travel from one region to another. It is the fastest train for local transport, with few stops on its way.

• **Locale and Regionale (R)**: This train stops at every station. Not recommended for long trips unless you have a lot of reading to catch up on. A standard fare is charged with no supplement.

After buying your ticket, you must validate it in one of the small red or yellow machines near the platform. Not doing so results in a €5 fine. If your ES, EC, IC or ICN train is more than 30 minutes late on arrival at your destination, you can apply to have a portion of the ticket refunded (ask the ticket office for a bonus request, *richiesta di bonus*, fill it in, enclose your ticket and send it to the station). If you can make a seat reservation in advance, do so. On holidays and weekends some trains are so packed that you will be lucky to find sitting room in the WC.

## Road

Most travel guides warn visitors of the perils of driving in Italy, and some go as far as suggesting that first-time motorists abandon any temptation to get behind the wheel. The simple truth is that the 'defensive' approach to driving just won't cut it here. Driving in Italy should be seen as a challenge, a liberation from rules, an exercise in personal freedom and expression and a way of purging passivity from your system. The key is to change perspective and enjoy the road, not fear it. But if you can't keep pace, it's best you move into the slow lane.

That said, many of the horror stories you've heard about driving in Italy are really modern myths. Motorways, or *autostrade*, are well maintained, brightly lit and have service stations with snack bars or restaurants and petrol every 25km (15 miles) on average. The majority of *autostrade* have tollbooths at which you pay as you leave with cash, credit cards or a pre-paid 'Viacard' (available at tobacconists). Driving on smaller roads, *strada statale* (SS) or *strada nazionale* (N), through regions such as Tuscany or Sicily is one of the biggest pleasures life affords. Last, despite city traffic that will make you suicidal, driving from one city to the next is really quite fast. The network of motorways makes it feasible to

## Roadworks Ahead

In an effort to follow through on public works projects promised but never delivered, the Italian government in 2001 pledged that €34 billion would be spent over six years – with half the funds directed at the south – to build 2,900km (1,800 miles) of new roads and motorways. Italy now averages 25km (15.5 miles) of new road every three years, compared to France's 200km (124 miles) each year.

The public works minister produced a list of 18 'high priority' projects targeted for the money. These included long-awaited highways along the Adriatic and Tyrrhenian coasts, or the *autostrade del mare*, a new Messina–Palermo motorway and new highway intersections in the port cities of Genoa and Mestre – important shipping hubs. Tolls along the Salerno–Reggio Calabria motorway – Italy's most dangerous stretch of road – were considered to raise money for renovations, the construction of extra lanes and a junction connecting it to existing littoral highways. The 'high priority' list also includes a controversial new mountain pass on the congested Bologna–Firenze motorway, although the feasibility of this project is still under debate.

In July 2005 it seemed likely that work would be carried out on the A12 – Cecina to Civitavechia (on the road from Livorno and Pisa towards Roma); the A18 – Siracusa southwards, to Gela; the A20 Messina to Palermo; the A28 north of Venice (but there is no connection between the A28 and the A27 yet); the SS3 from Viterbo to the west coast; road from Asti to Cuneo (south of Torino, completion date 2010); the northern bypass of Milan; the road from Milan to Bergamo and Brescia; and the bridge to Sicily (the plan is to start building in 2005 and open for traffic in 2011).

Separately, Italy is also unlocking funding for new high-speed trains.

Spending on infrastructure has dramatically declined in the country that led motorway construction in Europe after the Second World War. In 1970, GDP spending on infrastructure was 1.4 per cent. That figure plummeted to 0.2 per cent in 1995. Public spending on infrastructure dropped from 30 to 5 per cent in that time. The crippling effects of *Tangentopoli*, the anti-corruption probe that unleashed a tidal wave of bribery convictions in the public works sector in the early 1990s, are partly to blame. In addition, Italy's budget planners tightened the belt on public spending in an effort to meet stringent requirements to join the European Monetary Union in 1998.

visit Florence or Naples from Rome in a day trip (for more information, visit **www.autostrade.it**).

Unfortunately, the Italian art of driving is not a myth. Italians are known for turning and passing without signalling, and for an acute and incurable inability to stay within the painted boundaries of the lane. (You will find it does in fact make more sense to drive on top of the white lines rather than between them because they are easier to see that way.) It has often been said that a red light is a mere suggestion to stop, not a requirement. Motorists take a quick look to the left and right before sailing through the intersection no matter what colour the light. City parking is another situation where normal road rules fail to be applied – faced with no alternative, motorists double- and triple-park, crossing their fingers that the traffic police, or *vigili urbani*, won't notice. One of the most important rules of the road, however (that is not only respected but revered), is not passing on the right. If you wonder why a blue Alfa is tailgating you and flashing its full beam centimetres from your back bumper, it's because: a) you are a snail, and b) you shouldn't expect *him* to break the law and pass on the right. Incidentally, Italian male drivers are to blame for seven out of eight of the country's road accidents, according to a study published by Rome's La Sapienza University. Anthropologist Gioia di Cristofaro Longo attributed the massive disparity to what she described as men's tendency to use cars as 'mechanical prostheses' rather than as a means of transportation.

**Speed limits**, like traffic lights, are also open to interpretation. The speed limit on motorways is 130km per hour (80mph) for vehicles over 1100cc and 110km per hour (70mph) for all others. In cities, it is 50km per hour (30mph) and 110km per hour (70mph) outside city limits. Secondary state roads are usually 90km per hour (55mph). The wearing of front seatbelts (and back seatbelts too, for children) is mandatory, although Italian drivers too commonly 'forget' them.

## Mopeds and Bikes

Enter Rome for the first time and one thing that stands out above all else is the overwhelming number of *motorini*, or scooters. They come from left and right – and even head-on in one-way traffic. If you can't beat them, join them. Crash helmet regulations mean that nowadays you won't be riding with the wind in your hair on the back of a Vespa, like Audrey Hepburn in *Roman Holiday*, but nonetheless this mode of transport is not only convenient, it's fast. In fact, in a city like Rome, plagued by eternal gridlock, mopeds are the fastest way to twist through traffic. They're also easy to park.

Another uniquely Italian mode of transport is the ape, a three-wheeled covered 'mini-truck' fitted with a scooter engine.

## Car Hire

There is nothing that makes renting a car in Italy different from anywhere else in the world, but it is worth noting that rates are often cheaper if you reserve your rental car from abroad and pay for it in advance by credit card rather than turning up at the rental agency and paying Italian rates. All the big companies service Italy, such as Hertz (**www.hertz.com**) and Avis (**www.avis.com**). As well as normal cars, Maggiore (**www.maggiore.it**) rents mini-vans – perfect for moving furniture – at low weekend rates. Europecar (**www.europecar.com**, **www.europecar.it**) offers low fares across the board.

Leasing a car rather than renting one will save you money if you need a vehicle for three weeks or more. Travellers can lease a car for anything from 17 days to six months, and cars can be picked up or dropped off in a number of countries (**www.europebycar.com**).

# Bus and Coach

Where trains cannot travel, public buses and coaches are good alternatives for regional transport. Each region has its own operator, but they all fall under the authority of **SITA**, or Società Italiana Trasporti Automobilistici (**www.sita-on-line.it**). For example, many towns in Tuscany, including Montepulciano, Pienza and Montalcino, are more easily reached by bus, and even Siena–Florence is better by coach than train, since they depart more frequently and travel via the 'Si–Fi' motorway, which is a more direct connecting line between the two cities. Tuscany is an anomaly in this respect, although Sicily is another region where buses are sometimes better than the train. In other regions, you might resort to buses during one of the many rail strikes. Each town has a SITA bus depot – usually located near the train station – and tickets are purchased in advance from a ticket booth at the bus station or from a tobacconist. When these are closed, tickets can usually be bought from the driver. Long-distance regional buses operated by SITA are painted blue.

If you are taking a bus within a city, look for an orange coach. Each city has its own operator. Public buses, trolleys and trams all operate by the same basic principle: the honour system. You buy a ticket in advance at a news-stand, tobacconist or at the public counter of the operator, situated outside a train station or at the beginning of the bus route (usually a green hut). Automatic ticket dispensers are more common, especially in bigger cities. Once on board, validate the ticket by punching it in the machine near the front door or at the middle of the vehicle. Chances are no one will come to check your ticket and, for this reason, many take the risk and ride for free. If a ticket controller makes a surprise appearance, however, there are steep fines for not having a ticket. In most cities, 75 minutes of bus travel (and sometimes metro travel too) costs around €1.

# Sea

Italy relies heavily on ferries and hydrofoils (*aliscafi*) to its numerous islands, and there is a wide range of Italian and non-Italian companies operating from port cities such as Genoa, Naples, Brindisi and Palermo. The main Italian companies are **Tirrenia** (**www.gruppotirrenia.it**), **Grimaldi** (**www.grimaldi.it**), **Moby Lines** (**www.mobylines.it**), and **Sardinia Ferries** (**www.sardiniaferries.com**). Most ferries can carry cars and larger vehicles.

## Bridge over Troubled Waters

At over 5km (3 miles), it will be the longest suspension bridge on the planet. The ancient Romans were the first to float the idea of a bridge connecting Sicily to mainland Italy over the Straits of Messina, but centuries of political bickering have failed to turn paper plans into steel and cement. Now it looks as though that may change – the government pledged to start work on Italy's biggest public works project in 2004, but it never started because politicians still disagree about its usefulness and argue on the urgency of making it before other important works. The €6 billion bridge would take at least seven years to build, meaning that the earliest it could be operative would be 2014.

Bridge blueprints propose a suspension bridge held in place by four gigantic cables. Each one will be 132cm (52in) in diameter and will connect to two 380-metre (1,246ft) towers at either end. The bridge will carry six lanes of traffic plus two emergency lanes and four rail tracks.

Connecting Sicily to mainland Europe would jump-start the island's economy and represent a blow to the Mafia, which allegedly controls the ferry services that now cross the Straits. Promoters of the project say it will bring in more tourists and create job opportunities, but environmentalists say it will disturb marine life in the Straits and threaten areas of countryside on both shores. Many also fear it will never be safe against the threat of terrorism or fully protected in this earthquake-prone land.

Some islands, like the Aeolians, rely exclusively on ferries for mail, supplies and fresh water. When seas are rough and the boat service is suspended, islanders have to go for days in isolation. Even the gigantic island of Sicily relies exclusively on trucks loaded onto boats for the transportation of many of its supplies, as a long-debated project to connect it to the mainland by bridge has not yet materialised. A few years ago, Sicilians – even in big cities like Palermo and Catania – went without fresh milk, pharmaceutical supplies and petrol when a truck drivers' strike (sparked by the high tolls truckers are forced to pay to cross the Straits of Messina) virtually paralysed the island's economy.

There are too many small ferry operators to list in this book, but for a general overview of services, go to **www.snav.it** or the websites of the companies listed above. The main routes to the islands are as follows.

• From Liguria, the ports of Savona and Genoa serve Corsica and Sardinia (13 hours to Olbia, 20 hours to Cagliari). Genoa also has boats to Naples and Palermo (24 hours).

• Tuscany's Livorno has services to the large Mediterranean islands as well as to smaller ones such as Capraia (2 hours). They also run to Lipari (22 hours) and Palermo (18 hours).

• Further south in Tuscany, near Piombimo, you can catch a ferry to Elba (1 hour), or from Orbetello to the island of Giglio (1½ hours).

- Lazio's Civitavecchia, the region's biggest port, services three points on Sardinia at Olbia (7 hours), Arbatax (9 hours) and Cagliari (13 hours).
- The port of Anzio has high-speed boats to the Pontine islands (1½ hours). Gaeta, further south, has a slower boat that gets you there in the same amount of time.
- Naples and Salerno serve Ischia and Capri (a little more than 1 hour each). Naples also has an overnight boat to Stromboli and the other Aeolian islands (9 hours), making them easy to reach from Rome. Naples serves Messina (10½ hours) and Palermo (10 hours) too.
- From the Gargano Peninsula on the Adriatic there are ferries to the Tremiti islands (1½ hours).
- On Sicily, Messina runs a ferry to the Aeolian islands (1½ hours); Palermo connects with Cagliari (13 hours).

# Climate and Geography

## Geography

The peninsula extends from the southernmost part of the European continent to the southeast into the Mediterranean Sea. Some 1,200km (800 miles) in length, it divides the Adriatic Sea to the east from the Tyrrhenian Sea to the west. The Gulf of Taranto is at the arch of the boot-shaped country, while to the west, across the Tyrrhenian Sea, lie Corsica and Sardinia. To the south, across the narrow Straits of Messina is the triangular island of Sicily. The 'toe' of Italy seems poised to give it a good kick.

Parts of the peninsula and Sicily are volcanic, with extinct volcanoes on its western flank forming mountain peaks. Three active volcanoes exist in the country today: Vesuvius south of Naples, Mount Etna in Sicily, and Stromboli. Earthquakes are common on the eastern side of the country from Umbria downwards, and in Calabria and Basilicata.

Italy is divided into three distinct geographical regions that have each helped shape its history. The first is the *pianura*, or the great plains of the Po river, located where Italy is widest (250km/155 miles across). Italy's largest river, the Po drains a massive area of land and there have always been marshlands at its mouth. Geographically it is often included as part of central Europe. In fact, the ancient Romans referred to this region as Gallia Cisalpine (or 'this side of the Alps') and initially did not consider it part of Italy.

The peninsula narrows to about 150km (90 miles) in width. The Apennines form a backbone running its entire length and divide Italy into two more geographic regions. There is a narrow strip of land on the Adriatic side where mountains descend sharply to meet the sea, and a broad plain on the west that gently slopes up to the mountains and that was the cradle of Italy's ancient civilisations. Latium (Lazio) is where the city of Rome was founded on the banks of the Tiber. To its north lay Etruria, land of the Etruscans, now Tuscany.

Unlike Greece, which enjoys a coastline rich with bays and inlets, Italy has few natural harbours on either its western or eastern flank. However, Naples, Brindisi and Ancona were important seaside ports to the ancients. Rome was intentionally located some 20km (12 miles) inland where the Tiber river was too shallow for navigation. This allowed adequate warning should attackers come by sea. From the navigable portions of the river, the Romans had excellent access to both the sea and trade routes. With such shrewd city planning, it is no wonder that it became the seat of a world empire.

# Climate

Italy is blessed in this department. The moderating influence of the sea, and protection from northern winds by the alpine barrier, form a temperate climate. But Italy's weather does change considerably according to how far you are from

## The Weather Forecast

The world may envy Italy's climate now, but the peninsula could face a catastrophic future. According to a study by New York's Columbia University on the effects of global warming on the environment, Venice will be underwater by the year 2060, while Sicily will be an arid desert and Rome will be surrounded by marshland within the next 100 years.

The most damaging outcomes of global warming are rising temperatures – calculated to increase by 3°C by 2100 – and rising sea levels. That translates into a 67cm (26in) rise in sea water, enough to flood, and therefore permanently lose, a huge 4,500 sq km (1,737 sq miles) – or 8 per cent of the Italian peninsula.

The study predicts that, within 30 years, the Adriatic coast between the city of Monfalcone, near the Slovenian boarder, and Cattólica, north of Ancona, will be flooded. The regions of Tuscany and Puglia, between Taranto and Brindisi, will forfeit 5–11m (16–33ft) of beach. Higher sea levels will flood the Tiber delta, pouring water into the Pontina area. Formerly swampland, Pontina was painstakingly drained and turned into fertile farming fields under land development programmes in the 1930s. The inland valley of Volturno, in the Campania region, will also become marshland.

The study says that the north of Italy will be subject to warmer winters and humid summers. This will cause rivers to swell and make flooding a recurring problem. In the south, annual precipitation will be halved, turning 27 per cent of the territory into barren wasteland thanks to rampant deforestation. The beaches of Sicily, Sardinia, Basilicata and Puglia are already drying up and salt content in the land is quickly reaching toxic levels, posing a risk to wildlife and making agriculture impossible.

the sea or mountains. Winters are cold in the Alps, of course, but also cold and foggy in the Po river plain and the central Apennines and snowfall is common. Those same months are mild to warm on the Ligurian Coast, the Amalfi Coast and on the islands. Summers are hot and dry in those areas, but coastal regions are cooled by sea breezes. Inland cities like Milan and Rome are humid and hot in summer and, despite its proximity to the sea, Venice is very humid in summer yet bone-chillingly cold in winter.

The summer heat in Rome is somewhat cooled by the celebrated *ponentino* wind that brushes over its seven hills, but another wind, the *scirocco* from Africa, heats up the whole country in August. Not only does it bring high temperatures – well above 30°C (90°F) – but the *scirocco* also carries sand from the Sahara that leaves a dirty film on cars and patios. Arid climates in the south, Sicily and Sardinia during the summer make those areas very prone to forest fires – tragically, most ignited by arsonists.

Much of the nation experiences thunderstorms at the end of August, marking the beginning of autumn. More rain comes in October, November, March and April, and Venice is often flooded during those months. During *acqua alta*, tourists and locals stomp about the Lagoon City in rubber boots. However, between the extremes of winter and summer, spring and autumn are glorious times when temperatures settle at perfect levels.

For a regional temperature and rainfall chart, *see* **References**.

## When to Go

By and large the climate is so mild that you can house-hunt any time of year, but there are a few 'blackout' dates during which you should not come to Italy if you intend to get down to business, make appointments with estate agents, find a *notaio* or sign contracts. These are during the month of August, and during the Christmas and Easter breaks. Italians take their *feste*, or holidays, very seriously and vacate cities for the country, beach or mountains. Milan and to a lesser extent Rome become ghost towns as owners of cinemas, family-run shops and even pharmacies padlock their doors and disappear. Forget trying to find anyone in the property world to answer your questions. You will also have a difficult time tracking down home-owners, so it becomes impossible to visit properties. The most you can do is 'window-shop', or admire properties from the comfort of your car.

The Christmas and Easter holidays are easier to work around because they are generally shorter. Doing business in Italy becomes difficult by 20 December and isn't a possibility again until after the *Befana* holiday (6 January, or Epiphany). Easter slows things down for about a week, and the Monday after Easter Sunday, known as *Pasquetta* ('little Easter'), is a national holiday. Making a business call on that day is a *faux pas*. However, the biggest golden rule in Italy is 'avoid August'. The whole month should simply be removed from your business calendar. A problem with this is that the dates of 'August' are not as clear as you would think – sometimes it starts in mid-July and lasts until mid-September. Although you might succeed in getting things done during the tail-end periods, be prepared for less and less to happen the closer you are to 15 August, or *ferragosto*. On that day, businesses are closed tighter than a bank vault.

# Choosing a Location

It cannot be stressed often enough that pinpointing a desired location is the most important step in house-hunting. Deciding where to buy a house is not just a matter of settling on which Italian region you like best. It entails deep thought and on-the-ground research of other significant factors such as the property's proximity to shops, schools for your children, businesses, doctors, transport and a friendly community. You might stumble across your dream home on a hilltop near Tuscany's Monte Amiata, but when you realise that the nearest foreign newspaper shop is in Siena, some 50km (30 miles) away, that image of the castle in the sky might lose some of its lustre. There are city-dwelling foreigners who buy country homes based purely on the aesthetic impact of the property drenched in golden sunshine but, once the sun sets, they realise that what they thought was 'quaint isolation' during the day becomes a *Friday the 13th* terror at night. They lie in bed with eyes wide open listening to the deafening silence of nature: screeching owls, human-like wails of felines in heat and the pitter-patter of rats scurrying on the roof tiles. After just one night, they're ready to sell up and move back to the city.

There is a slew of practical issues to consider. The first is shopping. Country homes are usually only serviced by a small collection of food shops located in the nearest hamlet. They sell the basics like bread, sugar, cold meats, canned goods and cleaning detergents. Some of these *alimentari* shops are rather depressing and exhibit a 'minimalist' décor reminiscent of Bulgaria during the Cold War. Only larger cities are flanked by supermarkets – or, better yet, hyper-markets – that sell everything from British chocolate to mountain bikes. If you cannot live without the plentiful resources of a full-blown retail centre, you're best off closer to a city or town.

If you are prepared to brave country life, make sure you have a large vehicle. Your shopping expeditions will be as momentous as when Noah filled his ark. Besides food shopping, you'll have to think about things like building equipment such as plywood and bricks, plumbing parts and gardening materials. And, you'll need to keep an eye on services available nearby. For example, if your water heater has a tendency to break down, getting a customer service representative to travel kilometres over dirt roads might be more trying than braving ice-cold showers.

Choosing a location also means checking out the nearest hospital and accessible doctors. This is especially important if you are older, or have young

# Profiles
# of the Regions

# The North

Painters and poets have flocked to
Lombardy's lake region and the lagoon
city of Venice for centuries in search of
artistic inspiration. They find it, too, in
the spectacular Alps that descend
dramatically to the fertile plains of the
Po River valley. Italy's north marches
forward at a faster, more determined
pace than the rest of the nation. Yet
there are also timeless regions of forest
and farmland to be enjoyed. From smart
city lofts to country estates, ski lodges to
seaside apartments, European workers
and second-homeowners alike have a
wealth of choice.

1 Dozza, Emilia-Romagna
2 Wooden house, Dolomites
3 Carnival, Ivrea, Piemonte
4 House, Dolomites
5 Wooden house, Dolomites
6 Window, Val di Fassa, Dolomites
7 Near Castel del Rio

8 Near Castel del Rio
9 Castel landscape
10 Castle, Imola, Emilia-Romagna
11 Rooftops, Modena, Emilia-Romagna
12 Frescoed house, Dozza
13 Canal, Venice, Veneto

11

12

13

1 5000 ITL

POSTE ITALIANE

14 Portofino, Liguria
15 Port, Rapallo, Liguria
16 Shells, Portovenere, Liguria
17 Port, Rapallo, Liguria

# The Centre

This part of the peninsula holds both the honour and the responsibility of being the cradle of western civilization. If one were to select a single image to represent the country as a whole, it would undoubtedly come from here: Italy's heart and soul. While the dream homes of 'Chiantishire' are now the prerogative of celebrities, other regions, like the Marches, still hide affordable abandoned castles and even whole villages waiting to be restored to life.

*1 Landscape, Tuscany*
*2 Farmhouse, Tuscany*

3 Cypress trees, Tuscany
4 Farmhouse, Tuscany
5 View to the sea, Sperlonga, Lazio
6 Bagno Vignoni, Tuscany
7 Rooftops, Florence, Tuscany
8 Duomo, Florence, Tuscany
9 Lucca, Tuscany

10 *Piazza Navona, Rome*
11 *Fiat, Rome*
12 *Doorway, Rome*
13 *Trevi fountain, Rome*
14 *Street detail, Rome*
15 *Scooter, Florence*
16 *Vicolo della Pace, Rome*

14    15

16

# The South

The rest of the world is drawn here and to Italy's islands by the vibrant natural beauty, unspoilt seashores, cuisine based on spices and seafood, and sheer charismatic appeal. For foreigners who take the time to understand them, Naples, Bari and Palermo easily become favourite cities, while house-hunters are starting to snap up quaint fishermen's cottages and mysterious domed *trulli* houses as unique holiday homes. But what really distinguishes the south is its people. They are seductive, superstitious, savvy, stylish and sunny all in one.

1 Port at Ponza, Pontine Islands
2 Stromboli, Sicily
3 Trulli, Puglia
4 Painted tiles, Campania
5 Fish market, Mondello, Sicily
6 Lemons and peppers

7 Cathedral, in Palermo, Sicily
8 Near Stromboli, Sicily
9 Amalfi, Campania
10 Ravello, Amalfi coast, Campania
11 Trulli cones, Puglia
12 Villa Rùfolo, Ravello, Campania
13 Campania

14 *Sicily*
15 *Harbour, Mondello, Sicily*
16 *Main cathedral, Cefalù, Sicily*

children, but even small medical concerns – like the availability of your brand of contact lens solution – should be factored in. You'll need to know if there are schools in your area for your children. If you want them to have an English-language education, this will further limit your choices. Thought should be given as to whether you want to live near a gym, swimming pool or golf club. Again, most of these things are easier to find the closer you get to an urban centre. This might make it seem that country areas in Italy are completely desolate. Be forewarned: many are. If you want to live in a city, you might want to limit your choices to within the ancient city walls or ring road that circles it. Most small towns have Roman or medieval walls that still play an important part in urban planning. Bigger cities have a ring road, or *tangenziale*. In Rome, it is called the GRA, or *Grande Raccordo Anulare*.

Transport is another major concern. If you often travel for work, you can still live in isolated bliss surrounded by olive groves; just make sure that you find a farmhouse near an airport. People in the southern parts of Umbria can drive to Orte easily, where there are good train and bus connections to Rome and its Leonardo da Vinci international airport an hour away. But if you live any further north, say near Perugia, or Arezzo in Tuscany, your transport options become limited. From these areas, you must change trains numerous times and plan around an erratic schedule that offers only a few connections per day to Florence and Rome. Once you get to Florence's Amerigo Vespucci airport, you'll probably have to connect through Rome or Milan for international travel. If you live near Volterra, or further south in the Maremma area of either Lazio or Tuscany, near Grosseto, you will need a car to get to train stations, bus depots or airports. Locations in the north – such as Lombardy, Piemonte and the Veneto – are better connected because you can take advantage of a larger infrastructure network. The south and Sicily, except for areas near a medium-sized airport like Palermo, Brindisi and Naples, are also difficult in terms of access. Properties here are usually purchased by people looking for a summer home or an investment property. They are less convenient for people in perpetual motion, unless they have a copious travel budget.

Foreign home-owners are faced with an additional concern that does not apply to Italians. This is finding a location near to – or away from – other expatriates. There are two kinds of foreigner in Italy. The first group is intent on successful full immersion into Italian culture. These are Britons who would prefer to live as far away as possible from other Britons. They speak Italian fluently, read Italian newspapers and have many Italian friends. They fall into the 'lone-ranger' category. One extreme example of their way of life is observed on the island of Stromboli. On the far side of the volcano, away from the main port, is the tiny town of Ginostra, with something like 14 full-time inhabitants of which exactly half are foreigners. These people use solar panels for energy, mobile phones for communication and candles for midnight reading. They are not hermits *per se*, but they are interested in preserving the most authentic and rustic qualities of life on their island. The other seven inhabitants are island natives. Their priority is to bring in more tourism, enlarge the tiny boat docking area and plug into state utilities and modern comforts. The seven foreign 'conservationists' and the seven local 'modernists' have been at odds for years, and their battle has become known as the 'war of Ginostra'. It's a dirty war. If you visit Ginostra today you will see homes marred by offensive graffiti and neighbours harassing neighbours by pinning cartoon caricatures to their front door.

The second expatriate group is made up of 'cultural colonialists'. They are much larger in number and their concern is to make Italy feel a little bit like home. They watch the BBC on satellite to keep up with the news, they send their children to English schools and surround themselves exclusively with people who can understand their affection for two countries (these are almost always other expatriates). Within this group are extremes: those who never make the effort to learn Italian and those who find a happy medium between the 'lone ranger' and the 'cultural colonialist' castes. People who live in Italy for extended periods tend to find this harmony eventually. They conclude that it makes as little sense to box themselves into an Italian-only lifestyle as it does to sever all ties with home.

## Where the Expatriate Communities Are

If you are interested in locating other foreigners, you should know about the following sightings. In the north there are clusters of Britons on the perimeter of the lakes, in towns like Pallanza on Lake Maggiore or Cernobbio on Lake Como. Financial capital Milan is home to a thriving foreign population tied into the city's banking, publishing and fashion industries. Turin also has appeal, although the wine country in its foothills, around Asti and Alba, is quickly becoming one of the hottest rural areas for foreign house-hunters. The entire Ligurian Coast – from picturesque Bordighera to posh Portofino – is a long ribbon of expatriate homeowners. The Veneto shines with its main jewel, Venice, and smaller gems such as Bassano del Grappa (set against stunning countryside) and Verona. University town Bologna is popular with English and foreign students, as is Florence, but it is Florence's region, Tuscany, that takes the cake in terms of foreign presence. From Sting to Tony Blair to Sarah, Duchess of York, it's almost easier to list those who don't holiday or have a home in Tuscany. The British presence there is so strong that it has long become cliché.

Elbowing expatriates and soaring property prices have forced some to migrate east to Umbria, but a farmhouse near Todi (one of the most popular expatriate stomping grounds) is just as expensive as one in Chiantishire. Todi has special allure among writers, film-makers, artists and intellectuals, and a vibrant community has developed. Some foreigners are marching towards the Marches, although their numbers amount to little more than a trickle. This is a region to keep an eye on. The 'wild west' of Italy, Maremma, draws foreigners

## Case Study: From Beasts to Beauty

One afternoon, Joan Curci was more than a bit perplexed when a helicopter swooped down from the sky and landed in her back garden. A couple disembarked and approached, saying they had heard that she was selling her house near Porto Ercole. 'What could I say?' she recalls. 'I told them they had been incorrectly informed.' But Curci should prepare herself for more guerrilla tactics from eager house-hunters. A former barn that she bought and transformed into a summer estate is situated in the Argentario, now one of Tuscany's chicest, most expensive and sought-after resort areas.

Her relationship with Porto Ercole, once an inauspicious fishing village, goes back 20 years to when she bought a ruined peasant house that had been void of human inhabitants for more than 30 years. 'The floor was dirt and the structure of the house was such that animals slept on the ground floor and their body heat gave warmth to the upper levels,' she says. It took years to transform a beastly property into a beauty (including installing non-animal heating). But the road has not always been an easy one. She has seen her share of profiteers and Machiavellian schemes. At one point she got a notice from the government informing her that she qualified for a 25 per cent discount on property tax due in 1968 – years before she had even set eyes on the place. 'My lawyer advised me to pay it,' she explains, 'and I did, because I didn't want to miss out on the discount.'

who love riding horses and sitting in thermal baths. Prices are still affordable and the natural beauty of the area is immense, so this is another area to watch. The Argentario, or the coastal area of Tuscany near Ansedonia and Porto Ercole, was 'discovered' decades ago. Easily reached from Rome and boasting pristine beaches, it's difficult to find affordable properties here, but it is easy to run into other foreigners. Magnetic and seductive, Rome itself is home to thousands of Britons who come for both business and pleasure – mostly pleasure. Expatriates in Rome tend to become 'lifers'; in other words, they never do make that return flight home.

The bottom third of the peninsula sees foreigners grouped south of Naples, in the heavenly stretch of land that curves sensually from Sorrento to Salerno. This is the famed Amalfi Coast, and houses are as hard to come by as parking spaces in this sliver of land between sea and mountains. On the Adriatic side, foreigners are buying seaside homes on the Gargano peninsula and in the whitewashed hamlets of Ostuni and Alberobello.

Sardinia has wealthy foreigners comfortably rooted in its most beautiful bays and seaside towns. Sicily, an exciting new frontier for foreigners, is already home to expatriate communities in Taormina, Erice and Milo. Italian singers and film stars have already picked up prime specimens of real estate there. Last, the charm of islands such as Lampedusa, Pantelleria and Lipari has rubbed off on foreigners.

# Italian Homes

If one were to peel away like the petals of a flower all the remarkable qualities of Italy – food, wine, art, history, quality of life, friendly people – one of the deepest and most tenacious ones would be architecture. By buying a house in Italy, you own a tiny fraction of the country's enormous artistic heritage. For home-owners, this is the most satisfying and exceptional reward of the entire experience. Often, what you think is only a treasure on the outside reveals hidden bonuses within. More than 2,000 years of thriving civilisation on this tiny finger of land dipping into the Mediterranean has resulted in multiple layers of history, building styles and personal touches – some made by the family that lived in your home 500 years ago.

Italy will tickle your fancy. Whether you are partial to neoclassical stairways, Romanesque stonework, cherrywood-panelled libraries, Baroque interiors, stained-glass windows, rustic ironwork, Venetian blinds, chiselled entrance-ways, medieval passageways, underground wine-cellars, beamed ceilings, Moorish courtyards, vine-covered verandas, frescoed walls, alpine cabins, Roman pillars, marble floors, country kitchens, or rooftop terraces – they're all here.

There are many fantastic stories that have made the annals of estate agent lore. A couple who bought an apartment in the historic centre of Orvieto, adjacent to a church, discovered a 15th-century fresco under inches of paint and stucco applied in the centuries since. The artwork, they determined, once adorned the priests' living quarters of the church but had been covered for so long that no one knew of its existence. Another home-owner, near Salerno, pulled up the modern machine-made floor tiles to find a priceless treasure: 400-year-old hand-painted glazed tiles with floral designs. This person had suddenly acquired a 60 sq m (654 sq ft) room blanketed with the precious tiles. Just one similar tile fetches €80 in a nearby antiques store. Another home-owner tore down a wall and found a human skeleton stuffed in a tiny pocket between bricks.

Some areas are known for their unique architectural interpretations. In fact, drive two hours in any direction and you're likely to stumble across dozens of different building styles. In Liguria, south of Genoa, most houses are adorned with *trompe l'œil*. From far away, these painted houses look very elaborate and wealthy (intentional, of course), but move closer and you'll see that what you thought were travertine bricks and marble frames were in fact deceptively applied with a paintbrush. Some houses have *trompe l'œil* vines, flowers and terraces, and one even has a painted cat looking out on to the road from a painted windowsill. You could swear it was alive. The windows themselves are fitted with complicated shutters that open not only out but up, allowing cool air in and keeping sunbeams out.

It is common to find homes built in and around Etruscan tombs in the central regions. This productive ancient indigenous population left behind so many remnants that it is almost impossible to buy a house without their traces. Today, Etruscan tombs are converted into wine-cellars and basements. One home-owner even enlarged his to house an indoor swimming pool. In Tuscany, farmhouses were built in the form of a large cube with a smaller cube on top. Walls are thick and windows small to seal in warm or cool air, according to season. The top cube is the *fienile*, or hay storage area. By putting it on the roof, animals' food was protected from humidity and predators. Other *casali*, or country homes, are made out of stone or brick, depending on where they are, and, in most, flooring was never added because animals lived on the ground floor. Two- and four-legged beings shared a single roof in the name of convenience and safety. In Italy's northeastern corner, in the area known as Carnia, there were so many roaming bandits that all homes were built in clusters around a central courtyard like little fortresses. When danger approached, the door was shut, and multiple families plus their livestock were safe within.

In Milan, many apartments are in so-called *casa di ringhiera*. This is a traditional style in which homes overlooking a central courtyard are connected by long, thin metal balconies. Both Naples and Milan, two very different cities,

## Living with History

Wedged between the Colosseum and the Forum is one of Rome's most picturesque neighbourhoods. In ancient times it was known as the Suburra, or great slum, home to prostitutes, gypsies and thieves, and it was the place where Julius Caesar sent his troops to unwind after battle. More than 2,000 years later, police still occasionally raid the illegal brothels tucked away there. Now called Rione Monti, Rome's oldest working-class quarter is regarded by many as the most authentic and tourist-free district in the city.

In the square-mile neighbourhood, you're likely to see snippets of Italian living from a bygone era. Residents of top-floor apartments, reluctant to climb three or four flights in the heat, let down wicker baskets from their windows by ropes and yell down to nearby shopkeepers to fill them. Once a month, a man circles the streets with a tiny motorised cart to sharpen dull cutlery and fix broken umbrellas.

Despite its location at the city's centre, Monti is a safe island of tranquillity. You can wander through the *vicoletti*, or alleys, and examine architectural details without the traffic and noise present in much of Rome. Buildings on the tiny via degli Ibernesi on Monti's southwestern edge represent a cross-section of architectural history. For centuries, residents have added floors to existing structures. You might see a medieval *palazzo* built on ancient Roman foundations, with a third floor from the Renaissance and a 1950s concrete roof terrace. One woman owns a house near the Forum that has columns from a Roman temple in the basement. In fact, Monti is built on top of scores of unexcavated Roman-era monuments, and smugglers and bandits are said to have created a network of secret passages through this netherworld.

are famous for their spectacularly elaborate *cortili*. These courtyards were built to preserve a sense of posterity, not of protection. The idea was that a family's wealth should only be shown to a select few: those invited into the courtyard. Pedestrians passing these seemingly modest buildings outside had no idea of the beauty locked within. The Romans, on the other hand, put much of their wealth on the outside of their buildings to make their fortunes obvious to all. Outside the capital is a neighbourhood known as EUR. Built by Mussolini, it showcases some of the finest examples of fascist architecture. Strong, neoclassical and often made using white travertine stone, this style is profoundly attractive – although it might be an acquired taste.

In the far north, alpine homes were built on stilts to buffer the cold from the frozen ground. These homes are known as *mas* or *maso*, which comes from an ancient Celtic word for 'home'. Many have roofs of heavy black slate cut individually from quarries and untouched by time. In the far south, country estates are called *masseria*, after the same Celtic root. Surrounded by hectares of olive groves, many were fitted with an olive press inside the courtyard. If you buy a home here today, you will often find the ancient machinery still intact. With so much space on the outside, southern estates were built with football field-sized sitting rooms and gigantic kitchens.

In the most isolated territories, architecture was completely improvised. Puglia is famous for its cone-shaped *trulli*, mysterious in both form and function. On the island of Pantelleria, you will find *dammusi*, or cube houses with domed roofs. This architectural style has been traced back to the Arab period. And the island of Ponza is famous for its homes cut into the soft stone of its hillsides. The further you walk into a room, the deeper you are penetrating the rock.

## Property Types

What follows is a general breakdown of the properties on the market today.

• **Estates**: Normally located in the country, but within 50km (30 miles) of a major city, these are summer palaces built by nobles who could afford their own personal holiday paradise. There are grounds, parks and gardens surrounding a home that can include 15 or more rooms. You can find them in the north as well as the south. Many were built during the late Renaissance and Baroque periods.

• **Villas**: Smaller country homes built by aristocrats. These are different from *casali*, or farmhouses, which only housed peasants. Don't confuse these with *villette*, 'small villas' (also called *villini*), which are usually modern two-storey homes built in suburban areas.

• *Casali*: A rustic country house is what most foreigners dream of owning. Once shared by both man and beast, today they are lovingly restored and sold for many times their initial value. You can find thousands of them in Tuscany, Lazio and Umbria. Most were built in the 16th–18th centuries.

• **Farmland**: If your priority is more outdoor space, rather than room indoors, you could purchase some hectares of olive or chestnut grove. Large parcels of land usually include a small stone house or barn that might be transformed into a residence.

• **Vineyards**: Each of Italy's 20 regions makes wine. If you buy a vineyard in a DOC or DOCG area, expect to pay a very high price. (DOC stands for Denomination of Controlled Origin, while DOCG is not only controlled but also guaranteed. DOC and DOCG wines are reputable label indicators, ensuring by law that the wines are of the geographic zone, correct varieties and quality.) However, there are also vineyards available off the oenologist's map that are just as attractive.

• **Castles and monasteries**: These can often be found for sale in any region but, more often than not, they go on the market after being abandoned for years, sometimes centuries, so expect to pay as much as, if not more than, the purchase price in restoration costs. Some foreign corporations buy them to convert into hotels or conference centres.

• **Ghost towns**: Mass emigration in the south left entire towns empty, and these often go on the market as well. You'd be surprised how low the asking price can be, but don't be deceived, restoration costs are astronomical. Although most of them are located in poor and isolated parts of the south, with little infrastructure or transportation, a lucky few buyers have purchased abandoned towns in more popular central regions. Again, they are usually turned into hotels or subdivided into small residences by investors with very deep pockets.

• **Apartments in a rural setting**: These include apartments in small urban centres either in the country or on the coast. You can find old ones with beamed ceilings and terracotta floors, or modern ones in resort villages. The plus of investing in one of these is that you avoid costly maintenance fees associated with swaths of land.

• **Apartments in an urban setting**: These include residences in cities ranging from Palermo to Milan. If you work, or are looking for an investment property to rent, this is a promising option.

• **Modern homes**: Some people are not turned on by the prospect of having to repair outdated plumbing and crumbling walls. They want new and modern properties, and Italy is chock full of these as well. For example, two residential neighbourhoods outside Rome – Olgiata and Casal Palocco – are gated communities with three-storey houses, tennis courts, swimming pools and two-car garages.

• **Modern apartments**: Immediately outside city centres or in resort areas are apartments that were erected in the 1950s, 1960s and 1970s. Fewer were built after those decades.

• **Commercial properties**: Shops, boutiques, restaurants, artisan outlets, hotels, bed-and-breakfasts, office space, artists' studios, laboratories and all other types of commercial property are available throughout the nation. Make sure your commercial property is licensed for the type of activity you hope to pursue. Applying for a new business licence is a long and tedious process, which falls within many restrictions set by the state. For example, if one neighbourhood has reached its limit of snack bars, you won't be permitted to open a new one. It is easier and cheaper to buy out someone else's snack bar licence. For more on setting up or buying a business, *see* pp.205–207.

## Guide Prices

Data on prices per square metre can be obtained from the Bologna-based Nomisma real estate research unit, the nation's most respected independent authority on such matters. For more information, go to **www.nomisma.it** (the site is in English too) .

A good rule when estimating prices is to factor in the annual estimated increase. By using the following calculation, you should be able to foresee prices in 2006, 2007 and beyond.

- **New or completely restored properties rise 7.68 per cent per year.**
- **Partially restored old or used homes rise by 7.48 per cent per year.**
- **Properties for renovation rise by 8.66 per cent per year.**

These indicators were provided by Gabetti, Italy's largest estate agency, with 500 offices nationwide and headquarters in both Rome and Milan. According to them, 'fixer-upper properties' are rising faster in value because they are in greater demand. If you go to their website you will find more price indicators (**www.gabetti.it** with English-language translations) and information on their annual publication, the *Guide for Foreign and National Investors*. Whereas Nomisma tracks official national price estimates, Gabetti has more experience in the field and their property index tends to reflect higher prices. Another very useful resource when determining the price you should expect to pay can be found on the website of the Federazione Italiana Agenti Immobiliari Professionali (**www.fiaip.it**). It has an excellent database of property prices not only by region but by city, including the smallest towns. The only problem is that data is always one year old.

To get a better understanding of what property is worth in Italy, consider the following examples of listings published in 2005.

### €20,000

- **Building plot of 1ha in the south, or other remote area.**
- **Unrestored cottage with no land in Sicily or Puglia.**
- **Small dairy store in Pegli (Genoa).**
- **Unrestored traditional stone house overlooking little Lake Corbara, near Orvieto.**

**€30,000**

- One-bedroom studio apartment near Avellino.
- Unrestored farmhouse in Molise.
- Small apartment in the Abruzzo mountains.

**€40,000**

- Studio apartment, Naples' outskirts.
- Little *trullo* just outside Alberobello.

**€50,000**

- Recently renovated two-bedroom property in Friuli.
- Studio apartment on the outskirts of Padua or Verona.
- Commercial property in the immediate outskirts of Lucca.

**€60,000**

- Chalet with garden and forest in Fornovo (Parma).
- Three-bedroom cottage near Salerno.
- Internet Point venue in Asti.

**€80,000**

- Studio apartment in Agrigento.
- Small house needing restoration in Liguria or Emilia-Romagna.
- Large apartment near the ski slopes in Gignese, Piedmont.
- Building plot of 1 ha near Orvieto.
- Small wine bar in central Perugia.

**€100,000**

- Chalet in Valle d'Aosta.
- Cottage with garden in Campania.
- Penthouse apartment in medieval Candelo, Biella.
- Farmland with planning permission in Umbria.
- One-bedroom apartment just outside Parma.

**€120,000**

- Unrestored farmhouse near Volterra or in Umbria.
- One-bedroom apartment in the centre of Ascoli Piceno.
- Three hectares of land and three ruined buildings near Isernia.
- Two-bedroom apartment in Livorno.

€140,000
- Three-room apartment near Como.
- Studio apartment with terrace and sea view, Amalfi.
- Small rural building in Tuscany's Garfagnana.

€160,000
- Two-bedroom apartment in Vigevano, Lombardy.
- Large parcel of land, set in green pine forests, in Pollino National Park.
- Farmhouse with garden in the Marches.

€180,000
- Small two-bedroom villa in San Teodoro, Sardinia.
- A group of *trulli* in need of renovation, Puglia.
- Modern apartment on Viareggio coast.

€200,000
- Two-bedroom apartment in Gallipoli, Lecce.
- Modern apartment with roof garden in Treviso.
- Six-bedroom house on three floors in Frassinoro, Modena.
- Commercial property in central Brescia.

€250,000
- Large farmhouse and barn needing complete restoration in Umbria.
- One-bedroom apartment in the centre of Lerici, La Spezia.
- Studio apartment in Florence near Santo Spirito.
- Two-bedroom apartment in Spoleto, Perugia.

€300,000
- Studio apartment near the Navigli, Milan.
- Seven-bedroom *masseria* in inland Puglia with olive groves.
- Stone farmhouse and barn in the Emilia Apennines.
- Renovated farmhouse with courtyard garden in Monferrato, Piedmont.

€350,000
- Two-bedroom apartment in the centre of Bologna.
- Bed & breakfast in Maratea, Basilicata.

€400,000
- Bar-*tavola calda* in Rome near Porta Pia.
- Three-bedroom apartment in the centre of Mantua.

**€500,000**
- Commercial property in the centre of Verona.
- Modern villa on two floors, with private beach, on Lake Maggiore.
- Four-bedroom villa with sea views in Roseto degli Abruzzi.

**€600,000**
- Two-bedroom apartment with terrace, medieval part of Cervo, Imperia.
- Panoramic Attic, 3 bedrooms, in Pompei and Ercolano, Naples.
- Three-bedroom villa with terrace on the Sicilian island of Favignana.

**€700,000**
- Two-bedroom apartment near Piazza del Campo in Siena.
- Large stone farmhouse on two floors in the Chianti.
- Two-bedroom villa on two floors, with a large garden, near Chiusi.
- Large apartment in the centre of the historic town of Matera.

**€800,000**
- Newly built villa on three floors, in the hills between Tuscany and Umbria.
- Three-bedroom apartment in Trastevere, Rome.
- Bar-restaurant in the centre of Turin.

**€900,000**
- Attic in central Rome.
- *Agriturismo* in Lavagna, Genoa.
- Studio apartment in Venice, facing Grand Canal.
- Little villa in Posillipo overlooking the Bay of Naples.

**€1,000,000 and upwards**
- Historic apartment in Venice.
- Large apartment with view over Torre di Pisa.
- Modern villa close to the sea in Costa Smeralda, Sardinia.
- Completely renovated two-floor 17th-century villa, outside Ferrara.
- *Agriturismo* with restaurant in San Benedetto del Tronto.
- Luxury country house with swimming pool near Lago di Garda.

**€2,000,000 and upwards**
- DOC or DOCG vineyard with working cellar in Tuscany.
- Whole tourist village with all comforts in the Lazio hills.
- Small (2 ha) island on the Venice lagoon.
- Lakefront estate on Lake Maggiore.

# Research and Information Sources

House-hunting these days usually starts in front of the computer with a thorough search of properties listed on the Internet. Enter a few keywords and your search engine is likely to throw thousands of web links back at you. Some of the most popular ones include **www.tuscandream.com**, **www.tuscany-on-thames.com**, **www.real-estate-european-union.com**, **www.escapeartist.com**, **www.italian-realestate.com** and **www.goitaly.com**. The website **www.casa.it** has an excellent database. If you go to **www.vladi-private-islands.de** you can even find listings of small islands for sale off the Italian coast or in the Venice area. There are simply too many to list in this book but a careful search will produce mouthwatering photographs of properties that go on and off the market each week. For more than 30 other property websites, *see* **References**.

Alternatively you can start your research with more traditional media. In the UK, *World of Property* and *International Homes* are two publications with ample listings in Italy. *Italy* magazine is also building up its property listings. You might find more, however, by looking at some Italian publications. The most beautiful are *Case & Casali* and *Ville & Casali* (**www. villeecasali.com**) – they can be bought at Italian news-stands and at some London newsagents and include tempting photography and text in both English and Italian. Classified advertisement publications, such as *Porta Portese* in Rome and *Seconda Mano* (**www.secondamano.it**) in Milan, Bergamo, Bologna, Genoa, Monza, Lecco, Como, Parma, Piacenza, and Turin, all have thick property sections, and virtually all Italian daily newspapers include a property insert at least once a week. For example there is *La Pulce* in Florence, *Più Case* in Milan and the lake region and *Panorama Casa* in Tuscany. Just ask your vendor for the *immobiliare*, or property, section. Some local English-language magazines, like *Wanted in Rome*, also have listings (**www.wantedinrome.com**). In Milan, *Easy Milano* (**www.easymilano.it**) has English-language listings. There are also free leaflets and journals published by the estate agencies, including the latest offers. You can find them on the racks just outside the shops' door.

## Property Exhibitions

France and Spain are especially well represented at property shows in the United Kingdom, while Italy is to a lesser extent. Although you will find entire trade shows focused on one or other of the former two, properties in Italy are usually grouped together with those of other European countries. However, there are many such exhibitions and you should be able to find one with enough to interest you. At these events you can meet estate agents with listings in Italy, as well as solicitors for consultations and financial advisers who can explain face-to-face the intricacies of foreign-property mortgages. There may also be a series of short seminars covering those topics. Most importantly,

**Trulli** *Exclusive*

There's one site you're not likely to find on your own but that is worth a peek. Started by Milan-based architect Ado Franchini, **www.sitidoltremare.it** (in Italian and English) features Italy's unique and mysterious houses – the *trulli* – only found in one tiny corner of Puglia (*see* p.52) as well as *masserie* or larger palaces dating from the 16th century.

these exhibitions give you a chance to look through thousands of photographs and particulars, giving you a good idea of what is available where, and for how much. Exhibitions usually take place over two days, at the weekend, at the end of each month.

There are two main exhibition series: Homes Overseas and World of Property. For information on when and where the next trade show will take place, log on to **www.tsnn.co.uk** or **www.internationalpropertyshow.com**.

# Estate Agents

Without wronging many of the fine professionals who operate in this field, it must be said that estate agents are the subject of frequent complaints among foreign home-buyers. Unfortunately, they have been tagged with every insult imaginable – from unprofessional, disorganised or greedy to dishonest – but it must also be said that, while laments were common in the past, today's world of real estate has evolved and matured beyond recognition. The Internet represents the biggest system of checks and balances. Competition is fierce, good properties few and far between and, most importantly, buyers can preview properties from their own home without moving an inch. They can form impressions – whether positive or negative – with just a few clicks of the mouse. The Internet makes the estate agent's job both easier and, at times, more difficult. Easier because the Internet connects sellers to agents, and agents to buyers; more difficult because the estate agent can no longer rely on tempting adjectives in an advertisement to attract customers. They have learned that a picture really is worth a thousand words – especially when it can be compressed and downloaded within seconds to buyers abroad. In short, the Internet means they can't afford to misrepresent the truth.

Remember that you are paying a part (usually half) of the commission for your estate agent's services. If services rendered are not up to par, go to another one. If the agent seems uninterested or lethargic, find another. Be honest and clear with your agent about your likes and dislikes, worries and concerns. The more information you feed the agent, the better he or she will be equipped to help you. And treat the estate agent with respect. Courteous and appropriate behaviour is especially appreciated in Italy, where many professional relationships include a touch of what can only be described as friendship. If you make an appointment, keep it. If you need to cancel for any reason, make sure you do so in advance (especially if you booked a weekend appointment). Ultimately, a good rapport with your agent can led to better understanding and a shorter journey to finding your dream home.

There are two main groups of *agenti immobiliari* (estate agents) and *agenzie immobiliari* (estate agencies). Sometimes they are also called *mediatori*. The first are Italian and the second foreign, and there are pros and cons to both. Some buyers swear by Italian estate agents, especially the ones headquartered very close to the property in question, because they have a deeper understanding of the practical issues – such as zoning regulations, possible problems and the neighbourhood. Many estate agents are also close friends or relatives of the people surrounding your target property (or even of its owner), which guarantees an insider's approach. And, since one unfortunate myth about foreign buyers is that they are all rich, having an Italian agent to represent you might remove some of the seller's temptation to overcharge. On the other hand, a foreign estate agent – and many are British – can speak your language and therefore better understand your needs. For example, a foreign estate agent has probably dealt more extensively with buyers who went on to restore their properties. He or she might be more useful to you if you intend to do the same. The downside to a foreign agent is that they tend to charge slightly higher fees. In addition, it is probably easier to negotiate a fee downwards with an Italian estate agent. Choosing between the two groups might ultimately be decided by your fluency in Italian, as good communication between agent and buyer is paramount.

Italy's most respected agencies are Gabetti (**www.gabetti.it**), Grimaldi (**www.grimaldi.net**, be careful not to connect to Grimaldi ferry lines) and Tecnocasa (**www.tecnocasa.it**). You will find their branch offices spread throughout the peninsula. Besides these 'big three' that operate on a national level, other agencies – both Italian and foreign – usually pinpoint a specific geographical area and work within its boundaries. In fact, the vast majority of estate agents are local. That means you will probably have to deal with many agents at once if you are not sure of the exact location you want. There is a list of more than 50 websites, covering both Italian and foreign estate agents, in **References**, 'Resources and Reference', pp.266–8.

Many buyers, particularly those with a good command of Italian, opt to buy property directly from the seller, thus avoiding the agent's fee. There is nothing wrong with this – in fact, many buyers prefer not dealing with a middle man. Unagented properties are common in Italy, although foreigners often miss them because they instinctively head towards agencies.

With no exceptions, all estate agents in Italy must have the correct qualifications. The industry is regulated by the state to guarantee that individuals and agencies are licensed and carry insurance. Your agent should be registered with the local *camera di commercio*, or chamber of commerce, or hold a certificate with the closest *comune*, or municipality. They should also be a member of either the Federazione Italiana Mediatori Agenti d'Affari (Italian Federation of Mediators and Agents) or the Federazione Italiana Agenti Immobiliari Professionali (Italian Federation of Professional Real Estate Agents), founded in 1976 and with 3,000 members nationwide. Their websites are **www.fimaa.it** (this is only in Italian but you can find the names of listed agents under *elenco iscritti*) and **www.fiaip.it** (which also has a database of property prices).

An agent's fee is usually 3 per cent, but sometimes it can swell to 8 per cent depending on the property. Very often the fee is divided between buyer and seller. For example, each might pay 3 per cent. Rather than a percentage of the sale price, some agents prefer to charge a flat fee. For example, you might be asked to pay a fee of €2,000 on a property that you bought for €50,000, or you could pay as much as €8,000 in agent's fees on a sale of €300,000. If you are offered this sort of arrangement, be very clear what you are being charged – sometimes it can amount to a lot of money. Unfortunately, whichever method of charging you opt for, the cheaper the property, the higher the agent's fee as a percentage of the final price. Do not confuse the agent's fee with the additional fees and taxes that you will be required to pay on purchase.

## Case Study: Estate Agent Alert

Peter Kennealy spent months looking for the perfect apartment in Florence and estimates he visited 50 places. 'I guess you could say I'm fussy.' That's why he immediately wrote a cheque for five million lire (about €2,500) to reserve a top-floor apartment with a roof terrace and views of the Renaissance skyline in the San Frediano area. He handed the cheque to the estate agent and left to make his next appointment at another apartment. 'I figured that, even if the second apartment was better than the first, the money would have been well spent,' he says.

'The main problem is estate agents,' says the 44-year-old who works at the European University and has lived in Italy for 20 years. 'Every aspect of their behaviour is completely duplicitous.' In Kennealy's experience, dealing with them means learning a whole new language and paying attention to the subtleties of individual words themselves. 'An apartment that is described as *illuminoso* is really a dark pit. You've got to look for *illuminosissimo*. An apartment that is *tranquillo* is not as quiet as one that is *tranquillissimo*,' he explains. Superlatives aside, he generally recommends avoiding anything that is advertised as a 'fixer-upper' (*da ritoccare*) or to restore (*da restaurare*). And, as Kennealy explains, if he hadn't reserved his apartment with hard cash he would have had no guarantee that the agent would not have shown it to other clients.

Although he bought his home just six years ago, Kennealy thinks the situation has already improved, thanks to the Internet and the fact that more pictures are included with property listings so that buyers can form impressions before making appointments.

Many agents will ask that you sign a document before they show properties, in which you promise to pay the fee if you buy. This is to ensure that you do not go behind the agent's back and make a deal directly with the seller. To further avoid this temptation, the seller is not usually introduced on the first visit to a property. You are expected to pay the agent's fee after the preliminary sales agreement has been signed, not when the final act occurs – an arrangement that many foreign buyers dislike and which comes as a surprise to them.

# Viewing Trips

When you make an appointment to visit a property, bring a notepad, a digital camera and a map. Also take copies of the checklist in the **Appendix** of this book (*see* pp.271–6). If you see more than four homes in one day, it is likely that details concerning the first house will become indistinguishable from those of the last. To keep them straight in your mind, take notes and pictures of rooms you might like to restore, bathroom fixtures you might like to move, gardens you'd like to plan or anything else that strikes you about the property. These will come in handy when you come back for a second visit. If you are making appointments with agents from abroad via the Internet, note the reference or tracking numbers of properties that you wish to see, and check the property's availability

## Case Study: Clause Wars

'He was a smartly dressed *notaio* with a Roman accent and deep tan, in a rust-beige suit elegantly crumpled in all the right places,' recalls James Walston, a Rome resident of 28 years, writer, and seasoned Italian property buyer, 'but somewhere along the line I began to suspect that his elegance was inversely proportional to his competence.'

In the mid-1980s James bought an apartment on Via dei Serpenti in the Rione Monti neighbourhood of the Eternal City. He met the notary charged with the sale of the property, who read the contract aloud. 'It said the buyer will accept all liabilities on the property, to which I replied, "I'd be quite happy if I knew what those were." I was told the clause was "just a formality" and not to worry about it, but when I insisted that it be taken out I was sharply told, "it can't be removed".'

James Walston's resolve would not be swayed and he decided to wage his battle not unlike gunslingers who duel out their differences on a dusty street in a Wild Western town. 'We spent more than an hour locked in an airless office fighting over that single clause. It was ridiculous because all I wanted to know was what the liabilities were.' The Cambridge native was the victor, despite the *notaio*'s best efforts to keep the contract intact. After a long battle of wills, the clause was struck from the contract, and this happy home-owner never did find out what the fight was all about.

often. Turnover rates are high and you wouldn't want to travel all the way to Italy to find that the home you came to see has already been sold.

After you've seen a batch of possibilities, find a good restaurant, relax with a glass of wine and your notepad scribbled with impressions and discuss, discuss, discuss.

# What Questions to Ask

As well as the questions we asked earlier in the book, as you get closer to selecting your property there are many other questions that you should ask yourself or others.

• **What is your budget, and can your finances support it?** As a rule of thumb, most second-home-buyers purchase properties that cost 1.5 to 2.5 times their annual income.

• **Do you need to secure a loan?** You could qualify for a loan in Italy – although interest rates are high – or take out equity on your home in the UK. Make sure your bank will mortgage your home for a property abroad.

• **Do you plan to remodel or renovate?** Make sure that has been factored into your budget.

• **Should you spend money on a home inspection?** Yes, yes, yes. Make an appointment with a surveyor to check plumbing, roofs, floors and humidity as soon as possible (*see* pp.109–12).

• **Are there outstanding mortgages or loans on the property?** Mortgages from two, three or even four owners ago can suddenly become your responsibility.

• **Are there outstanding property taxes?** The same applies to these, too.

• **Are there outstanding utilities connected to the property?** You can unwittingly inherit water, gas and electricity bills from old owners even if those utilities are not in your name.

• **Is there an outstanding refuse (rubbish) tax on the property?** The refuse tax is a tenacious one that always has a way of catching up with you. In fact, it is almost considered a form of property tax. Make sure it's been paid off (*see* p.157 and p.192).

• **Does the property have the relevant building licences?** If a window has been enlarged, or an extra room added, make sure it has been recorded on the property deed. Fines connected to unauthorised modifications become your responsibility.

• **What is the water situation?** Some country properties have shared wells. Check that all relevant neighbours have given their consent for water use.

• **Is the property being sold by an individual or group (such as a family)?** Check for consent of sale by all family-registered owners.

- **Have you checked the zoning?** If you plan to turn a barn into a residence, make sure it is zoned for such a change.

- **Is there a tenant in the property?** When you buy a property with a sitting tenant, you usually have the option of drawing up a new lease for them or terminating the lease altogether. The second option allows you to replace the old tenant with a new one of your own choosing or not have one at all. However, you must do this as soon as you buy the property, otherwise the old lease is automatically continued under the agreements drawn up by the previous owner. Give the tenant notice as soon as the property becomes yours – they then have a few months to move out.

- **Have you been asked not to declare the full amount paid for the property?** Unfortunately this form of tax evasion (which is called sottodichiarazione) on the part of the vendor is so common in Italy that most sellers don't even blink an eye. The notaio handling the transaction is likely to simply 'leave the room' when the moment comes to declare, indicating subtle complicity. In most cases, about half the transaction is declared. Some daring sellers push to declare as little as 40 or even 35 per cent of the actual price paid. Remember, the declared property sale figure should agree with the official value in the Land Registry. Although this book does not condone illegal behaviour, failing to warn that this is a very common occurrence in Italy would be a disservice to readers. *See* p.127.

- **What taxes and fees do you face?** Total fees for buying a property are usually between 10 and 20 per cent of the purchase price. Registration tax should be 10 per cent of the declared price for urban property and up to 17 per cent for a property with land (*see* pp.141–4).

- **Are you dealing with a licensed estate agent?** Make sure you are.

- **Are you dealing with a local *notaio*?** It is always best to hire the services of one who is familiar with the land, the surroundings and the possible problems connected with the property. *See* p.126.

# Temporary Accommodation

It doesn't make sense to book hotels while you house-hunt, unless you plan to stay in any given area for four days or less. Hotels are very expensive (on average €100 and upwards per person) and prices rise the closer you are to public transport and the city centre. Hotels really only cater to tourists and overnight business trips – and you fall into neither category. There are many other options for you. The best is a *pensione* or *residence*. These are flats in either the city or country that you can rent weekly or monthly. In the long term, their rates are quite affordable compared to *alberghi* (hotels), which charge daily rates. If you are in the countryside, you might also try to reserve a room at an *agriturismo*. This is a cross between a hotel and a residence, in that you can choose to stay just a few days and then move on or you can stay for weeks. Most are situated in old farmhouses and are surrounded by opportunities for hiking, horseriding or wine-tasting. The *agriturismo* is what Italians opt for when they go to the country for extended holidays. In general, prices also include meals (usually mouthwatering country cooking). Half board is *mezza-pensione* and means you only get breakfast, which could be nothing more than leftover bread, jam and coffee. Full room and board is *pensione completa*. Places only offer this when they can truly claim cooking talent. To find out about these options you should consult either a guidebook to Italy or the Internet. Look for *residence ed appartamenti ammobiliati*. The website **www.italianhousing.com** has many options.

You could also stay in a rented apartment while you house-hunt (leasing information is provided below), stay with friends or house-sit for people on holiday (some Internet chat rooms have bulletin boards where this option is listed). Or you could drive to Italy with a mobile home – there are various sites in rural areas where you can set up base camp while you scout for property.

# Renting before Buying

The cautious often prefer to live in an area before committing their hard-earned cash. If you feel that moving abroad could be too much culture shock to absorb at once, you might consider finding a house or flat to let in the area you are most interested in, to test it out and start the slow process of establishing some roots.

Like buying a house, your alternatives for finding an apartment include hiring an agent, scanning the Internet and searching through local publications (like *Wanted in Rome* if you are in the Eternal City) or one of the property sections of a local newspaper. The best way, though, is word of mouth.

On rental properties, estate agents usually ask for one month's rent as a fee for their services. Alternatively, they ask for 10 or 20 per cent of the first year's rent. If you are renting for less than a year, make sure to negotiate a percentage, as paying one month's rent will not be cost-effective.

Under new laws, the standard lease in Italy is for four years and is renewable. Contracts lasting three months, six months, one year or any length of time you desire can be negotiated with the owner or the agent. A wise move is to include a 'diplomatic clause' in the contract. This lets you terminate the agreement if you must leave Italy sooner than you foresee. Many tenants are asked to produce proof of income such as a bank statement or pay slips showing monthly income to prove that they are solvent.

You will be required to pay one or two months' rent up-front as a safety deposit, and some owners ask for three. If the property is found to be in good condition on your departure, the deposit is refunded.

In addition to the monthly rent, you will be expected to pay the *spese*, or utilities, and other expenses. These include water, gas for heating, phone service, electricity, cleaning and maintenance of the building (*spese del condominio*), elevator expenses and the porter's fee (*portinaio*). The last is usually paid quarterly and is calculated by the administrator of the building based on the size of your apartment and the floor it is on (for the elevator fee). Don't be surprised if you get caught with a refuse (rubbish) tax as well. All utilities are paid by the tenant according to consumption.

Make sure you check all appliances well (especially the refrigerator and washing machine) before renting. The high calcium content in Italian water makes dishwashers and washing machines clog easily and you don't want to be burdened with the cost and inconvenience of repair if the damage was done by a previous tenant. Also make sure the *caldaia*, or water heater, functions well. Check all appliances with the owner before signing the lease agreement.

As a rule of thumb, major repairs such as wiring, plumbing and blinds are the owner's responsibility. Minor repairs due to wear and tear are your responsibility.

It's a good idea to make a detailed list of all the furniture, cutlery, kitchen and bathroom items before you sign the contract. Itemise everything and make a note of its condition. If an inventory is given to you, you should check it and draw attention to any disparities.

Semi-furnished apartments usually include major appliances, like a cooker and refrigerator, but little or no furniture. Unfurnished apartments are usually bare, with tubing for water and gas protruding from the walls for you to connect your own appliances.

The *portinaio*, or custodian, usually lives on the ground floor of an apartment building and sits in a little booth at the entrance. He or she does light repairs and cleaning, collects mail, signs for packages that don't fit in the letterbox (important if you're not often home) and guards the building against strangers during working hours. You should tip the *portinaio* at Christmas and when extra services are rendered.

Rent is paid monthly (or sometimes quarterly) by direct bank transfer (*bonifico bancario*), by cheque or cash. Most contracts call for six months' advance notice in writing prior to the termination of the lease agreement. It is called the *disdetta* and should be sent registered-return-receipt mail (*lettera raccomandata con ricevuta di ritorno*). Three months' notice is required on leases of one year. If you help the landlord find an another tenant to replace you, you can usually leave or agree on your departure date with the owner without waiting six months.

# Buying to Let

Buying property for income-generation is quickly becoming a popular option with foreigners. As a foreigner yourself, you are well equipped to understand

and meet their needs. You can advertise from home, send out brochures, and pass news of your rental property on to friends and co-workers to secure short-term tenants. When the apartment is not occupied, you can take a break there yourself. It's a business that virtually runs itself.

The best news is that, among those who have purchased property for income-generation, there is an overabundance of success stories. People with income properties in tourist cities like Florence and Venice, and popular country areas like Tuscany, report that they are always flooded with prospective clients. They make a killing during holiday seasons and also do well in the off-seasons.

There are a few basic guidelines for letting your property (for more detailed information, *see* **Letting Your Property**, pp.233–46). The first is that the shorter the stay, the more you must charge per night to cover cleaning expenses such as sheets and towels. For example, you might let a two-bedroom apartment in Rome for €200 for a weekend, €500 for a week, and €1,500 for the month. Prices like that make good sense for you, and for your tenant (who is still paying less than at most hotels). Contact a cleaning agency who can take care of preparing the home between tenants and calculate how much they will cost you per week or month. Then, factor those expenses to determine a fair rent (based on the location and size of your property).

You should also calculate for how long you need to let your property in order to earn back your initial capital investment. Add the cost of the property, plus renovation expenses, to determine when you are likely to see a profit. Many people who have taken out a mortgage to buy a second home in Italy let their property as a way of meeting mortgage payments. If this is handled correctly, you can generate sufficient income to pay off a ten-year mortgage by the end of a decade.

One of the most important points to remember, if you intend to let, is that it is much, much better to lease to non-resident foreigners than it is to let to Italian citizens, because non-residents are not protected under Italy's rigid housing laws. If a resident (who is officially registered with the *anagrafe* using your property's address) fails to pay rent, you will face a long and tedious process to evict them. This point should not be underestimated. No matter how much you trust your tenants, disagreements do occur, and you need to be sure you can get your property back if you so choose. Despite warnings from everyone who is familiar with Italy's housing scene, this situation is much more common than you would think – especially among naïve foreign owners. If your tenant is a resident of Italy, remember, too, that the eviction of unemployed people, preg-nant women, mothers with children or people on pensions is almost impossible. It would involve a long court process in which a judge can opt to terminate your lease agreement, but the procedure is so lengthy and costly that it might well be impossible. Only if you can prove one of the following three things is the eviction process easier: that you intend to sell the property; that you need it for your offspring; or that the property is your primary residence. If you can demonstrate one of those things in a court of law, you'll have a better chance of getting the property back – but only after several years have passed. Even if your tenant fails to pay rent, you won't have an easy time. The worst situation occurs when the tenant does not pay rent and can prove he or she is unemployable. In that case the state steps in and pays rent for them (based on their own interpretation of rental prices). If that happens, you might as well kiss your property goodbye. Some home-owners resort to extreme tactics in order to free their property of the tenant – snipping the satellite cable or cutting off utilities and heating – but these rarely work and will eventually get you in trouble with the law.

Be especially careful if you buy property with a sitting tenant. In many cases, when you sign the deed to your new property, you have the option of terminating the existing lease agreement. Take that option and plan on looking for a tenant yourself later. Once that opportunity passes, you're not likely to get another one. (*See* p.96.)

# Building from Scratch or Renovation

Prepare an abundant reserve of 'elbow grease' if you plan on building or restoring your property. If you are not fond of do-it-yourself labour (*fai da te*), or if you are not incredibly rich, you are better off buying a modern or restored home. There is no shortage of derelict property in Italy available in all stages of decay – from 'a pile of rocks' up to 'a pile of rocks that could resemble a habitable structure with the help of a healthy imagination'. A shift away from farming in the past centuries has forced entire families to move to the cities or abroad. Now they return to sell what's left of their ancestors' homes to buyers who have the energy and inclination to restore them to their long-lost beauty. House restoration in Italy has become the focus of a sociological trend, spurred by the recent literary successes of *Under the Tuscan Sun* (about an American woman who restores a farmhouse near Cortona) and the ensuing barrage of copycat books. If you want to be part of that movement, here's what you need to know.

First, building a new home costs about €800 per square metre for finished work (unfinished work, which is just walls and plumbing but not decorative details like carpeting or tiling, is about half that). Restoring an old home also costs €800 per square metre for finished work. However, in most cases, renovation costs more in the long term because demolition costs must also be factored in. Don't think you are getting a bargain by buying a 'pile of rocks'.

The only way to bring down renovation costs is to do most of the work yourself, hence the need for 'elbow grease'. You are helped by the fact that labour is cheaper in Italy than in England and, better yet, prices fall the further south you go, but you will face steep costs if you need to install electric lines, water, a septic tank, air-conditioning, broadband wiring for Internet services, a well or a swimming pool or have to connect up to utilities that are far away. Remember that an old *casale*, or peasant's farmhouse, rarely has these amenities. Although do-it-yourself materials are readily available in Italy, they are more expensive than in the UK. In addition, there is 20 per cent IVA (VAT) tax on such goods. Many foreigners drive over with carloads of supplies, such as paint, that cost less at home. There are also things that are not as common in Italian construction that you might consider importing – for example, tubes of silicone sealant for sealing windows are hard to find. Otherwise, Italy is full of *fai-da-te* stores and other businesses that specialise in fireplaces, above-ground swimming pools, porcelain for bathrooms, lighting fixtures and everything else you'd find in a DIY warehouse. You can also find junk yards or salvage dealers who sell antique bathtubs, masonry and ironwork.

Once you have an idea of what you'd like to do, you can hire the services of either an *architetto* (architect) or a *geometra* (a convenient hybrid between an architect and a surveyor that exists only in Italy). They can advise you on work to be done, and lend a hand in the tedious permit process that will follow once you have drawn up plans. They can also recommend the rest of the crew that you will rely on, such as a *costruttore* (builder), *muratore* (builder or mason), *decoratore* (interior decorator), *elettricista* (electrician), *fabbro* (locksmith or blacksmith), *falegname* (carpenter), *giardiniere* (gardener), *idraulico* (plumber), *imbianchino* (painter) or an *ingegnere* (engineer). And, last, a well-stocked *ferramenta*, or hardware shop.

There are two things that you should know about Italian labour. The first is that it is highly specialised and extremely good. Many builders consider themselves *artigiani*, or artisans, and take great pride in being perfectionists and carrying out the trade that was probably passed on to them by their fathers. Only in Italy can you find painters specialised in the *trompe l'œil* techniques used in Liguria or who are capable of carving limestone the way their forefathers did during the Baroque period. The second thing is that much labour is done *al nero*, or 'under the table'. If you don't ask for a fiscal receipt for labour rendered, the unwritten rule is that you get a 'discount' equal to the 20 per cent VAT. If you need a receipt for tax deductions or for any other reason, make sure to specify that you require a *ricevuta fiscale*, or a fiscal tax receipt. One important reason for getting a receipt is that it represents a guarantee on the work should something should go wrong or break. By law, the IVA tax should always be included in estimates. It is illegal for your builder to add on 20 per cent extra after the work is done and when you ask for a fiscal receipt. Your builder should have factored in the IVA from the start, as it would be ridiculous for him or her to assume you didn't want to pay the tax (although many do).

You can also find builders by consulting the *Albo dei Artigiani* or artisans' work order at your local town hall, or by asking your neighbours. Asking your estate agent might not be the best idea as they are known to take commission. Approach more than one builder to compare estimates (*preventivi*) and shop

## Learning the Hard Way

In a brazen move by the state, bulldozers moved into the Valley of the Temples in Agrigento, Sicily, a few years ago to demolish a collection of illegally built (*abusivo*) homes, despite protestors' efforts to stop them. Six of the 'skeletons' – as the half-built homes are called – were levelled as their owners watched. They represent a fraction of the 654 illegally built homes targeted by bull-dozers in Poggio Muscello and the other neighbourhoods that surround the celebrated archaeological site. The high-profile demolitions were meant to underline the regional government's commitment to combat illegal construc-tion, a widespread problem in Sicily. Among the wreckage was one home reputed to belong to a Mafia boss.

The 1,200ha (3,000-acre) Valley of the Temples became a protected cultural site more than 30 years ago. and construction inside its periphery was outlawed. Despite the ban, illegal buildings continued to sprout up – many are second or holiday homes for the wealthy. According to the environmental lobby Legambiente, some 6,000 illegal homes, representing €400 million in real estate, are built each year in Sicily.

Five temples in the area include the eight-pillar Temple of Hercules, the oldest, and the larger Temple of Concord. Known as the 'Golden Temples' for the warm light cast on them by the setting sun, they are the remains of a wealthy Greek settlement of 580 BC. 'Why don't they destroy the temples since they are the real illegal constructions in this area?' asked one angry protestor.

around for the lowest prices. You will either be charged by the hour or by the square metre, and there are pros and cons to both – by the hour could work out longer and more costly, but with better results; by the metre could be done too fast, but cheaper. You will usually be asked to pay a deposit of 10–25 per cent before the work starts, and follow this up with monthly payments. Never give too much money up-front, and check the price of materials to make sure you are not being overcharged. Establish a completion date with your builder so that the work doesn't carry on for eternity. As anywhere else, there are stories of builders taking deposit money and then disappearing, or builders who get halfway through the project and then disappear, leaving you roofless or water-less. Some foreigners prefer to bring foreign workers with them, but this is usually more costly and means you will miss out on Italy's artisan tradition. It's best to polish up on your Italian, find someone to translate or become very proficient in mime and go with local labour. If you will not be present to super-vise work, hire a *direttore dei lavori* (usually an architect or a *geometra*) who will take 10 per cent of the total restoration cost to be your eyes and ears. Total absenteeism by owners while their property is being worked on is a recipe for disaster.

Another important thing to keep in mind is that renovation or modernisation costs are almost never recouped when you eventually sell the property. For this reason alone, many experts would discourage buyers from seeking dilapidated properties if they intend to put them back on the market. The only reason to ignore this advice is if the restoration is a labour of love for you. Be forewarned that a house advertised as a 'fixer-upper' probably really is a pile of rocks. A house that is 'partially' restored might just have running water. Read property ads with a very critical eye and always assume that the actual state of the property is one, if not more, levels removed. If you are told that a property needs repairs to the roof, this should be a warning signal. Replacing an old tiled roof can cost up to €80,000 and requires specialist builders who know how to install terracotta roofing without breaking the tiles. Check that the ceiling beams and wooden supports are not eaten by termites or weakened by time. Make sure the walls and foundations of the home are in good condition. If they are not, you will probably have to tear them down and rebuild from scratch. Check for cracks in the chimney – seismic shifts in the land can tip or sway the stonework and that can drastically reduce the property's value. Another thing to look for is signs of dampness, such as bubbling paint on walls or discoloured patches. Water is pulled up from the ground through the walls of stone houses by capillary action. Once damp starts, there's very little you can do to stop it. Have your *geometra* check the wiring (many electrical systems were put in place before new building codes were established and are downright dangerous today), heating, plumbing, bathroom and kitchen.

Check your water source. If you are running off a well, check its depth and reliability; digging a new well can cost as much as the property itself. Some aquifers are seasonal and others dry up for good. Wells built in sandy soil have a tendency to clog every few years, leaving you without water until you clean the system. If you plan to irrigate crops, grapevines or a large garden, you might consider getting a secondary source of water. These concerns are also valid if you want to install a pool. (Be aware that you will have a hard time getting a permit for one in an area with water shortages, and having a pool can put your property in a higher tax bracket.)

If you are in an earthquake-prone area, you might need to reinforce the walls under the Unità Minima d'Intervento (minimal intervention unit) standard, and that can cost 25 per cent of the value of the house. Installing a new septic tank is also an expense worth factoring in. Make sure yours is not old or leaking. New models can manage other waste on top of sanitary needs (*see* also pp.190–92).

The next step is to get a building permit or planning permission (*concessione edilizia*) from your local *comune*, town hall or municipality. In general, all exterior changes require a permit. These include adding more rooms to the property (or anything else that would increase the square metres officially registered with the land registry or *catasto*), enlarging windows or doors and adding balconies. Some properties are protected by the *belli arti*, or the culture ministry, and no changes to their external appearance are allowed. In other areas, changes must be carried out with local materials and in traditional style.

Tuscany is notorious for its rigid approach to renovations – all buildings must have a Tuscan-style roof and the exterior colours must match pre-determined shades and hues. In all other cases you can apply for a permit for renovations, but you are by no means guaranteed to receive it. Smart buyers put a clause in the initial contract (*compromesso*) saying that the purchase is contingent on obtaining permission. Some sellers claim already to have obtained permission. If this is the case with your prospective purchase, check the validity of the permit and make sure it is good for at least another year, or for as long as you intend to wait before starting construction. Getting a permit can take six months or longer and costs anywhere from €500 to €2,000 for bigger renovations.

More than any other country, Italy has gained a sorry reputation for being incredibly inefficient and bureaucratic when it comes to granting planning permits. Many home-owners resort to bribery (which usually works) or simply put in illegal changes and wait for either a fine or a state-sanctioned *condono*, or pardon. There are entire areas marred by illegally constructed, or *abusivo* ('abusive'), buildings. When coffers run dry, a *condono* is a quick way for the state to raise cash. You pay a steep fine and your illegal changes are suddenly forgiven. These 'pardons' usually happen every few years.

The website **www.proprietaricasa.org** has a list of the latest laws concerning planning and building permits. Unfortunately, the site is only partially translated into English but you will find more building and renovation-related links at **www.italiansites.com**.

If you intend to build a house from scratch, you will have to hire the services of an architect and go through the same planning permit procedures with your *comune*. Building costs about €800 per square metre or more, depending on your needs. Make sure your land is zoned to include a residence.

# Making the Purchase

**John Howell**
**Solicitor and international Lawyer, John Howell & Co.**

Buying a property in Italy is as safe as buying a property in England. A book such as this – which must explain the potential pitfalls if it is to serve any useful purpose – can make it seem a frightening or dangerous experience. But if you go about the purchase in the right way it is not dangerous and should not be frightening. The same or similar dangers arise when buying a house in England. If you are in any doubt, look briefly at a textbook on English conveyancing and all the horrible things that have happened to people in England. You don't worry about those dangers because you are familiar with them and, more importantly, because you are shielded against contact with most of them by your solicitor. The same should be true when buying in Italy. Read this book to understand the background and why some of the problems exist. Ask your lawyer to advise you about any issues that worry you, and leave him or her to avoid the landmines!

## Law

This book is intended primarily for people from England and Wales. For this reason I have drawn comparisons with English law. Scots law is somewhat different. Where the points apply also to Scots law I have tried, depending on the context, to refer to either UK or British law. The law is intended to be up to date as at 1 July 2005.

## Disclaimer

Although we have done our best to cover most topics of interest to the buyer of a property in Italy, a guide of this kind cannot take into account every individual's personal circumstances, and the size of the book means that the advice cannot be comprehensive. This book is intended as a starting point that will enable people who are thinking of buying property to understand some of the issues involved and ask the necessary questions of their professional advisers. **IT IS NO SUBSTITUTE FOR PROFESSIONAL ADVICE**. Neither the authors nor the publishers can accept any liability for any action taken or not taken as a result of this book.

# Finding a Property in Italy

At the moment we are in a property 'boom'. It is, in most popular areas, a seller's market. Property – and, in particular, attractive, well-located and well-priced property – sells very quickly. A few years ago it was fairly simple to go to Italy, look around, see a few properties and then come back to England to ponder which to buy. Today someone doing this could well find that the house they wanted to make an offer on had sold to someone else in the few days after they saw it.

As a result of this, people who are serious about buying property in Italy should do some research and make some preparations before they go on a visit to look at property. When they go on a visit they should do so with the intention that, if they see something they really like, they will make an offer and commit themselves (at least in principle) to the purchase while they are still in the area.

# What Preparation Should You Make?

## Understand the System

The system of buying and selling property in Italy is, not surprisingly, different from the system of buying property in England or Scotland. On balance, neither better nor worse – just different. It has many superficial similarities, which can lull you into a false sense of familiarity and overconfidence. *The most important thing to remember is that buying a home in Italy is just as safe as buying a home in Cardiff – providing that you take the right professional advice and precautions when doing so.* If you do not take such advice there are many expensive traps for the unwary.

## See a Lawyer

It will save you a lot of time and trouble if you see your lawyer *before* you find a property. There are a number of preliminary issues that can best be discussed in the relative calm before you find the house of your dreams rather than once you are under pressure to sign some document to commit yourself to the purchase. These issues will include:

- **who should own the property, bearing in mind the Italian and British tax consequences of ownership.**
- **whether or not to consider mortgage finance and if so in which country.**
- **what to do about buying the euros needed to pay for the property.**
- **how to structure your purchase to minimise taxes and cost.**
- **if you are going to be living in Italy, sorting out the tax and investment issues that will need to be dealt with *before your move* if you are to get the best out of both systems.**

Only UK lawyers who specialise in dealing with Italy will be able to help you fully. Your normal English solicitor will know little or nothing of the issues of Italian law, and a Italian lawyer is likely to know little or nothing about the British tax system or the issues of English or Scots law that will affect the way the transaction should be arranged.

The lawyer may also be able to recommend estate agents, architects, banks, surveyors, mortgage lenders and other contacts in the area you are looking.

A physical meeting is still the best way to start an important relationship. It has a number of advantages. It allows you to show and be shown documents and to wander off more easily into related topics. Most importantly, it is usually easier to make certain that you have each understood the other in a face-to-face meeting than it is by letter. But, these days, 'seeing' your lawyer does not need to involve an actual meeting. If it is more convenient to you, it could be done by telephone conference call, by videoconference or over the Internet.

## Decide on Ownership

Who should be the owner of your new home? This is the most important decision you will have to make when buying a property. Because of the combination of the Italian and British tax systems, getting the ownership wrong can be a very expensive mistake indeed. It can lead to totally unnecessary tax during your lifetime and on your death. Even on a modest property, this unnecessary tax can amount to tens of thousands of pounds. This subject is dealt with more fully later.

## Get an Offer of Mortgage/Finance

These days, with very low interest rates, more and more people borrow at least part of the money needed to buy their home in Italy. Even if they don't need to do so, for many it makes good business or investment sense.

If you want to borrow money to finance your purchase it is better to get clearance before you start looking at property. Your lawyer should be able to get a preliminary mortgage offer within about 72 hours.

# Estate Agents

The role of Italian estate agents (*agenzie immobiliari*) is similar to the role of the British estate agent. Their job is to find buyers for properties entrusted to them by a seller, but there the similarity ends.

In the UK a person can be a plumber today and, without any qualifications or experience, set up an estate agency tomorrow. They cannot do this in Italy. In Italy in order to practise as an estate agent you must be professionally qualified and hold a licence to practise. You must also have indemnity insurance. All this is partly an example of the generally greater paperwork and red tape prevalent in Italy and partly a useful consumer protection measure.

There are certain agents operating in Italy without a licence. That is, they are operating illegally. Many are foreigners servicing the foreign buyer: British selling to British, Germans to Germans, etc. Some of these 'illegals' are excellent, skilled people who offer a service at least as good as many of the legal agents.

Despite this, you are better dealing with a 'proper' agent or his genuine employee as you will then be covered by the legislation and the codes of conduct to which the agents must adhere.

For more on estate agents and viewing properties, *see* pp.91–6.

# Property Inspection

Whatever property you are thinking of buying, you should think about having it inspected *before* you commit yourself to the purchase. It costs just as much and causes just as much disruption to repair property in Italy as in the UK, so you don't want any surprises. In fact – foolishly – very few buyers of property in Italy do this.

A new property will be covered by a short guarantee running from the date of handover and covering minor but not trivial defects in a new property. The property will also benefit from a guarantee in respect of major structural defects that will last for 10 years. As a subsequent purchaser you assume the benefit of these guarantees. After 10 years you are on your own. For property more than 10 years old (and, arguably, for younger property too) you should consider a survey.

If you are buying a rural property that is being split off from a larger property you must use a surveyor to establish your boundaries.

Most surveys can be carried out in seven to ten days.

## Who Can Provide a Survey?

### Do-it-yourself

There are several things that you can do yourself. These will help you decide when to instruct a surveyor to do a proper survey and help direct him or her to any specific points of interest, *see* the 'Checklist' in **Appendix 1**.

### Estate Agent's Valuation and 'Survey'

It may be possible to arrange for another local estate agent to give the property a quick 'once-over' to comment on the price asked and any obvious problem areas. This is far short of a survey. It is likely to cost about £200.

### Mortgage Lender's Survey

This is no substitute for a proper survey. Many lenders do not ask for one and, where they do, it is normally fairly peremptory, limited to a check on whether it is imminently about to fall over or not and if it is worth the money the bank is lending you.

## Italian Builder

If you are going to do a virtual demolition and rebuild, then it might make more sense to get a builder to do a report on the property. A reputable and experienced builder will also be able to comment on whether or not the price is reasonable for the property in its existing state. Make sure you ask for a written quotation for any building work proposed. As in any country, it is as well to get several quotes, though this can be tricky. There is a lot of work for builders at the moment.

## Italian Surveyor

The person doing a fuller survey is usually the *geometra*. Your lawyer can put you in touch with the right people. In most rural areas there will be limited choice but if you prefer you can select 'blind' from a list of local members supplied by the surveyors' professional body. The cost of a structural survey (*perizia strutturale*) is typically £500–1,500.

You will find that the report is different from the sort of report you would get from an English surveyor. Many people find it a little 'thin', with too much focus on issues that are not their primary concern. It will, hardly surprisingly, usually be in Italian. You will need to have it translated unless you speak very good Italian and have access to a technical dictionary. Translation costs amount to about £100 per thousand words, depending on where you are located and the complexity of the document. Incidentally, always use an English person to translate documents from Italian into English. An alternative to translation of the full report would be to ask your lawyer to summarise the report in a letter to you and to have translated any areas of particular concern.

A few Italian surveyors, mainly in the popular areas, have geared themselves to the non-Italian market and will produce a report rather more like a British survey. They will probably also prepare it in bilingual form or at least supply a translation of the original Italian document.

## UK-qualified Surveyor Based in Italy

A number of UK surveyors – usually those with a love of Italy – have seen a gap in the market and have registered and set themselves up in Italy to provide UK-style structural surveys. As in this country, they usually offer the brief 'Homebuyers' Report' or the fuller 'Full Structural Survey'. This is not as simple as it would first appear. To do the job well they must learn about Italian building techniques and regulations, which are different from those in Britain. Without this knowledge the report will be of limited value. Prices are generally slightly more expensive than for an Italian report, but it will be in English and so avoid the need for translation costs. Your UK lawyer should be able to recommend a surveyor able to do a survey in your area. Alternatively, look for advertisers in the main Italian property magazines.

Check they have indemnity insurance covering the provision of reports in Italy. Check also on the person's qualifications and experience in providing reports on Italian property and get an estimate. The estimate will only be an estimate because they will not know for sure the scope of the task until they visit the property and because travelling time means that visits just to give estimates are not usually feasible.

## UK-based Surveyor

Some UK surveyors provide reports from a base in the UK. These can be very good but travelling time often makes them impractical – especially in remote areas – and expensive. Make the same checks as for a UK surveyor based in Italy.

# Contracts 'Subject to Survey'

This is unusual in Italy. Legally there is nothing to stop an Italian preliminary contract containing a 'get-out clause' (*condizione risolutiva*) stating that the sale is conditional on a satisfactory survey being obtained. It is unlikely to meet with the approval of the seller or his agent unless the transaction is unusual. In an ordinary case the seller is likely to tell you to carry out your survey and then sign a contract.

# General Points about Surveys

Whichever report you opt for, its quality will depend in part on your input. Agree clearly and in writing the things you expect to be covered in the report. If you do not speak Italian (and the surveyor doesn't speak good English), you may have to ask someone to write on your behalf. Your UK lawyer would probably be the best bet. Some of the matters you may wish to think about are set out below. Some of these will involve you in additional cost. Ask what will be covered as part of the standard fee and get an estimate for the extras.

Here is a list of things you may ask your surveyor to check:

- **Electrical condition and continuity.**
- **The drains, including assessing them to the point where they join the mains sewers or a septic tank.**
- **The septic tank itself.**
- **For rot.**
- **Adequacy of foundations.**
- **Earthquake resistance if in an earthquake zone.**
- **Cement condition, in property constructed out of cement.**
- **Underfloor areas, where access cannot easily be obtained.**

- Heating and air-conditioning.
- Pool and all pool-related equipment and heating.
- For wood-boring insects.
- For evidence of asbestos.
- For evidence of radon gas – if it is in an affected area.

# Raising Finance to Buy a Property

In these days of low interest rates many more people are taking out a mortgage in order to buy property abroad.

If the property is viewed simply as an investment, a mortgage allows you to increase your benefit from the capital growth of the property by 'leveraging' the investment. If you buy a house for £200,000 and it increases in value by £50,000, that is a 25 per cent return on your investment. If you had only put in £50,000 of your own money and borrowed the other £150,000, then the increase in value represents a return of 100 per cent on your investment. If the rate of increase in the value of the property is more than the mortgage rate, you have won. In recent years property in the most popular areas has gone up in value by much more than the mortgage rate. The key questions are whether or not that will continue and, if so, for how long.

If you decide to take out a mortgage you can, in most cases, either mortgage (or extend the mortgage on) your existing UK property or take out a mortgage on your new Italian property. There are advantages and disadvantages in both cases. Many people buying property in Italy will look closely at fixed-rate mortgages so they know their commitment over, say, the next 5, 10 or 15 years. Again there are advantages and disadvantages to these.

## Mortgaging your UK Property

At the moment there is fierce competition to lend money and there are some excellent deals to be done, whether you choose to borrow at a variable rate, at a fixed rate or with one of the hybrid schemes now on offer. Read the Sunday papers or the specialist mortgage press to see what is available, or consult a mortgage broker. Perhaps most useful are mortgage brokers who can discuss the possibilities in both the UK and Italy.

It is outside the scope of this book to go into detail about the procedures for obtaining a UK mortgage.

### Advantages

- **The loan will probably be very cheap to set up.** You will probably already have a mortgage. If you stay with the same lender there will be no legal fees or land registry fees for an additional loan. There may not even be an arrangement fee. If you go to a new lender, many special deals mean that the lender will pay all fees involved.

• **The loan repayments will be in sterling.** If the funds to repay the mortgage are coming from your sterling earnings then the amount you have to pay will not be affected by fluctuations in exchange rates between the pound and the euro. At the time of writing (July 2005) most experts are predicting that the pound will probably fall further in value against the euro. If sterling falls in value then your debt as a percentage of the value of the property decreases. Your property will be worth more in sterling terms but your mortgage will remain the same.

• **You will be familiar with dealing with British mortgages, and all correspondence and documentation will be in English.**

• **You can take out an endowment or PEP mortgage or pension mortgage or interest-only mortgage, none of which is generally available in Italy.** Normally only repayment mortgages are available in Italy, though interest only morgages are beginning to appear.

• **You will probably need no extra life insurance cover.** This can add considerably to the cost of the mortgage, especially if you are getting older.

## Disadvantages

• **You will pay UK interest rates which, at the time of writing (April 2005), are higher than Italian rates.** Note, however, that Italian rates, over the last few years, have generally been higher than UK rates. British rates are about 5.5 per cent variable. Italian rates vary from about 3.8 per cent variable. Make sure you compare the overall cost of the two mortgages. Crude rates (which, in any case, may not be comparable as they are calculated differently in the two countries) don't tell the whole tale. What is the total monthly cost of each mortgage, including life insurance and all extras? What is the total amount required to repay the loan, including all fees and charges?

• **If sterling increases in value against the euro, a mortgage in euros would become cheaper to pay off.** Your loan of €60,000 (now worth about £41,500 at €1 = £0.69p) would only cost about £33,000 if the euro rose to about £0.55.

• **If you are going to let the property, it will be difficult or impossible to get Italian tax relief on the mortgage interest.**

• **Many people don't like the idea of mortgaging their main home – a debt which they may only just have cleared after 25 years of paying a mortgage!**

• **Some academics argue that, in economic terms, debts incurred to buy assets should be secured against the asset bought, and assets in one country should be funded by borrowings in that country.**

All in all, a UK mortgage is generally the better option for people who need to borrow relatively small sums and who will be repaying it out of UK income.

# Italian Mortgages

An Italian mortgage is one taken out on your Italian property. This will either be from an Italian bank or from a UK bank that is registered and does business in Italy. You cannot take out a mortgage on your Italian property from your local branch of a UK building society or high street bank.

The basic concept of a mortgage to buy property is the same in Italy as it is in England or Scotland. It is a loan secured against the land or buildings. Just as in the UK, if you don't keep up the payments the bank will repossess your property.

## The Main Differences Between an English and an Italian Mortgage

• It can be expensive to take out an Italian mortgage. Set-up fees, administrative costs, legal fees and taxes can easily amount to 3–4 per cent of the amount borrowed.

• An Italian mortgage (*mutuo ipotecario*) is almost always created on a repayment basis. That is to say, the loan and the interest on it are both gradually repaid by equal instalments over the period of the mortgage. Endowment, PEP and pension mortgages are not known in Italy, though interest-only mortgages are beginning to appear.

• There are often restrictions on or penalties for early payment of the loan.

• The formalities involved in making the application, signing the contract subject to a mortgage and completing the transaction are more complex and stricter than in the UK.

• Most Italian mortgages are usually granted for 15 years, not 25 as in England. In fact the period can be anything from five to (in a few cases) 25 years. Normally the mortgage must have been repaid by your 70th (sometimes 65th) birthday.

• The maximum loan is generally 80 per cent of the value of the property and 60 per cent is more common, especially for non-residents. As a planning guide, you should think of borrowing no more than 60 per cent of the price you are paying.

• Fixed-rate loans (*tasso fisso*) – with the rate fixed for the whole duration of the loan – are more common than in England. They are very competitively priced.

• The way of calculating the amount the bank will lend you is different from in the UK. As you would expect, there are detailed differences from bank to bank, but most banks are not allowed to lend you more than an amount the monthly payments on which come to 30–33 per cent of your net disposable income. *See* 'How Much Can You Borrow', opposite.

- There will usually be a minimum loan (say £20,000) and some banks will not lend at all on property that is less than a certain value. Some will not lend in rural areas.

- The way of dealing with stage payments on new property and property where money is needed for restoration is different from in England. *See* sections below.

- The paperwork on completion of the mortgage is different. There is often no separate mortgage deed. Instead the existence of the mortgage is mentioned in your purchase deed. It is prepared by and signed in front of a notary public (*notaio*).

## How Much Can You Borrow?

Different banks have slightly different rules and slightly different ways of interpreting the rules. Generally they will lend you an amount that will give rise to monthly payments of up to about 30–35 per cent of your net available monthly income.

The starting point is your net monthly salary after deduction of tax and National Insurance but before deduction of voluntary payments such as to savings schemes. The following income is also taken into account:

- **Two salaries if there are two applicants.**

- **Any investment income or a pension.**

- **Your pension and investment income if you are over 65 (but your earnings will not be taken into account).**

The following income *may* also also taken into account:

- **If you are buying a property with a track record of letting income.**

If your circumstances are at all unusual, seek advice as approaching a different bank may produce a different result.

| e.g. | Mr Smith – net salary | £3,000 |
| --- | --- | --- |
| | Mrs Smith – net salary | £2,000 |
| | Investment income | £1,000 |
| | **Total income taken into account** | **£6,000** |

The maximum loan repayments permitted will be 30 per cent of this sum, less your fixed commitments.

i.e.    Maximum permitted loan repayment £6,000 x 30% = £1,800

Regular monthly commitments would include mortgage payments on your main and other properties, any rent paid, HP commitments and maintenance (family financial provision) payments. Repayments on credit cards don't count. If there are two applicants, both their commitments are taken into account.

e.g.    Mr and Mrs Smith – mortgage on main home          £750
        Mr and Mrs Smith – mortgage on second home in UK  £400
        Mrs Smith – HP on car                             £200
        **Total pre-existing outgoings**                  **£1,350**

Maximum loan repayment permitted = £1,800–£1,350 = £450 per month. This would, at today's rates, equate to a mortgage of about £60,000 over 15 years.

If you are buying a property for investment (rental), the bank may treat this as commercial lending and apply different criteria.

The table below gives an idea of how much you would have to pay if you take out a mortgage.

## Monthly Mortgage Repayments per £1,000 (UK or Italy)

| Period of Repayment | 2% | 3% | 4% | 5% | 6% | 7% | 8% |
|---|---|---|---|---|---|---|---|
| 5 years | £17.50 | £17.92 | £18.36 | £18.79 | £19.24 | £19.69 | £20.14 |
| 10 years | £9.19 | £9.63 | £10.09 | £10.56 | £11.05 | £11.54 | £12.05 |
| 15 years | £6.42 | £6.89 | £7.37 | £7.88 | £8.40 | £8.94 | £9.49 |
| 20 years | £5.05 | £5.53 | £6.04 | £6.57 | £7.13 | £7.71 | £8.31 |
| 25 years | £4.23 | £4.73 | £5.26 | £5.82 | £6.41 | £7.03 | £7.67 |

Rates vary depending on formula used by the bank

# Applying for an Italian Mortgage

Once again, the information needed will vary from bank to bank. It will also depend on whether you are employed or self-employed.

Applications can receive preliminary approval (subject to survey of the property, confirmation of good title and confirmation of the information supplied by you) within a few days.

Allow four weeks from the date of your application to receiving a written mortgage offer as getting the information to them sometimes takes a while. It can take longer than four weeks. Once you receive the offer you will generally have 30 days from receipt in which to accept it, after which time it will lapse. You should have the mortgage explained in detail by your lawyer.

# Payments for New Property

In Italy, when buying a new property one normally makes payments as the development progresses and takes title at the end. This can pose problems for banks, as you do not own anything you can mortgage until you make the final payment and take title. In most cases the mortgage will therefore only be granted to cover the final payment. As this is often 60 or 70 per cent of the total cost of the property, this is seldom a problem. In some cases if the earlier payments are more substantial the banks will offer a credit facility to make the earlier payments. Once the property has been delivered to you (and thus the full loan has been taken), the normal monthly payments will begin.

## Property Needing Restoration

Not all banks will finance property that needs restoration. If you have enough money to buy a property but need a mortgage to renovate it, you must apply for the mortgage before buying, as it can otherwise be difficult to find a lender.

## The Cost of Taking out a Mortgage

This will normally involve charges amounting to about 3–4 per cent of the sum borrowed. These charges are in addition to the normal expenses incurred when buying a property, which normally amount to about 12 per cent of the price of the property.

You will probably be required to take out **life insurance** for the amount of the loan, though you may be allowed to use a suitable existing policy. You may be required to have a medical. You will be required to **insure the property** and produce proof of insurance – but you would probably have done this anyway.

The offer may be subject to **early redemption penalties**. Early payment penalties are of particular concern in the case of a fixed-rate mortgage.

## The Exchange Rate Risk

If the funds to repay the mortgage are coming from your sterling earnings then the amount you have to pay will be affected by fluctuations in exchange rates between sterling and the euro. Do not underestimate these variations. In the period since the launch of the euro it has varied from €1 = £0.53 to €1 = £0.73. This can make a tremendous difference to your monthly mortgage repayments. A monthly mortgage repayment of €725 (about £500 at today's value) would on some occasions during the last three years have meant paying £384 and on other occasions £529. Equally, if sterling falls in value, then your debt as a percentage of the value of the property increases in sterling terms. Your property will be worth more in sterling terms but your mortgage will also have increased in value. This is probably not of too much concern to most people. If sterling rises in value against the euro, then the situation is reversed.

This is less of a worry if you have income in euros, for example from letting the property.

## Mortgaging Your Italian Property: Summary

### Advantages

• **You will pay Italian interest rates which, at the time of writing (July 2005), are lower than UK rates.** British rates are about 5.5 per cent variable. Italian rates vary from about 3.8 per cent variable. Make sure you compare the overall cost of the two mortgages. Crude rates (which, in any case, may not be comparable as they are calculated differently in the two countries) don't tell the whole tale.

What is the total monthly cost of each mortgage, including life insurance and all extras? What is the total amount required to repay the loan, including all fees and charges?

• **If you are going to let the property, you may be able to get Italian tax relief on the mortgage interest, depending on how you structure the legal ownership of the property you purchase.**

• **The loan repayments will usually be in euros.** If the funds to repay the mortgage are coming from rental income paid to you in euros, this will give you something to spend them on!

• **Many people don't like the idea of mortgaging their main home – a debt which they may only just have cleared after 25 years of paying a mortgage!**

• **Some academics argue that, in economic terms, debts incurred to buy assets should be secured against the asset bought, and assets in one country should be funded by borrowings in that country.**

## Disadvantages

• **The loan will probably be expensive to set up.** Arrangement fees, inspection fees, notaries' fees and land registry fees can come to about 3–4 per cent of the amount borrowed.

• **You will incur further fees to pay to clear the record of the mortgage off your title once it has been paid off.** This will usually only be a problem if you want to sell the property during the two years following paying off the mortgage.

• **The loan repayments will usually be in euros.** If the funds to repay the mortgage are coming from your sterling earnings, then the amount you have to pay will be affected by fluctuations in exchange rates between sterling and the euro. At the time of writing (July 2005), most experts are predicting that the pound will fall further in value against the euro. Equally, if sterling falls in value then your debt as a percentage of the value of the property increases in sterling terms. Your property will be worth more in sterling terms but your mortgage will also have increased in value.

• **You will be unfamiliar with dealing with Italian mortgages, and all correspondence and documentation will usually be in Italian.**

• **Normally only repayment mortgages are available – i.e. mortgages where you pay off the capital and interest over the period of the mortgage.**

• **You will probably need extra life insurance cover.** This can add considerably to the cost of the mortgage, especially if you are getting older.

Generally speaking, Italian euro mortgages will suit people letting their property regularly or who intend to live in Italy.

## Saving Money on Your Euro Repayments

Your mortgage will usually be paid directly from your Italian bank account. Unless you have lots of rental or other euro income going into that account, you will need to send money from the UK in order to meet the payments.

Every time you send a payment to Italy you will face two costs. The first is the price of the euros. This, of course, depends on the exchange rate used to convert your sterling. The second cost is the charge that will be made by your UK and Italian banks to transfer the funds – which can be substantial. Some Italian banks make no charge for transferring funds to pay off mortgages. These deals are worth looking out for if the other terms are competitive.

There are steps that you can take to control both of these charges.

As far as the **exchange rate**, is concerned you should be receiving the so-called '**commercial rate**', not the tourist rate published in the papers. The good news is that it is a much better rate. The bad news is that rates vary from second to second and so it is difficult to get alternative quotes. By the time you phone the second company, the first has changed! In any case, you will probably want to set up a standing order for payment and not shop around every month.

There are various organisations that can convert your sterling into euros. Your bank is unlikely to give you the best exchange rate. **Specialist currency dealers** will normally better the bank's rate, perhaps significantly. If you decide to deal with a currency dealer you must deal with one that is reputable. They will be handling your money and, if they go bust with it in their possession, you could lose it. Ask your lawyer for a recommendation.

As far as the **bank charges** are concerned, differing banks make differing charges. This applies both to your UK bank and to your Italian bank. Discuss their charges with them. In the case of your UK bank there is usually room for some kind of deal to be done.

Another possibility for saving money arises if you '**forward buy**' the euros that you are going to need for the year. It is possible to agree with a currency dealer that you will buy all of your euros for the next 12 months at a price that is, essentially, today's price. You normally pay 10 per cent down and the balance on delivery. If the euro rises in value you will gain, perhaps substantially. If the euro falls in value – *that's life!* The main attraction of forward buying is not so much the possibility for gaining on the exchange rate but the certainty that the deal gives you. Only enter into these agreements with a reputable and, if possible, bonded broker.

Bearing in mind the cost of conversion and transmission of currency, it is better to make **fewer rather than more payments**. You will therefore have to work out carefully whether, taking into account loss of interest on the funds transferred but bank charges saved, you are best sending money monthly, quarterly or every six months.

## Foreign Currency Mortgages

It is possible to mortgage your home in Italy and borrow not in euros but in sterling – or US dollars or Swiss francs or Japanese yen.

There may be some attractions to borrowing in sterling if you are repaying out of sterling income. The rates of interest will be sterling rates, not euro rates. This will currently mean paying more. Usually the rates are not as competitive as you could obtain if you were remortgaging your property in the UK, as the market is less cut-throat. You will have all the same administrative and legal costs as you would if you borrowed in euros – about 5 per cent of the amount borrowed.

This option is mainly of interest to people who either do not have sufficient equity in their UK home or, for whatever reason, do not wish to mortgage the property in which they live.

# Who Should Own the Property?

There are many ways of structuring the purchase of a home in Italy. Each has significant advantages and disadvantages. The choice of the right structure will save you possibly many thousands of pounds in tax and expenses during your lifetime and on your death. Because, in Italy, you do not have the total freedom that you have in the UK to deal with your assets as you please, on your death the wrong choice of owner can also result in the wrong people being entitled to inherit from you when you die. This is a particular problem for people in second marriages and unmarried couples.

## The Options

### Sole Ownership

In some cases it could be sensible to put the property in the name of one person only. If your husband runs a high-risk business or, if he is 90 and you are 22, this could make sense. It is seldom a good idea from the point of view of tax or inheritance planning.

### Joint Ownership

If two people are buying together, they will normally buy in both their names. Your half is yours and your fellow owner's is his or hers. On your death your half will be disposed of in accordance with Italian law. A person who owns in this way, even if they own by virtue of inheritance, can usually insist on the sale of the property. So if your stepchildren inherit from your husband they could insist on the sale of your home.

If you decide to buy together then, in certain cases, it can make sense to split the ownership other than 50/50. If, for example, you have three children and your wife has two, then to secure each of those children an equal share on your death you might think about buying 60 per cent in your name and 40 per cent in your wife's name.

It is very important to seek clear advice from your lawyer about the form of ownership that will suit you best, with regard to the consequences both in Italy and in the UK.

## Adding Your Children to the Title

If you give your children the money to buy part of the property and so put them on the title now, you may save quite a lot of inheritance tax. On your death you will only own (say) one-fifth of the property rather than one-half. Only that part will be taxable, and it may be such a small value as to result in a tax-free inheritance. This only works sensibly if your children are over 18. Of course, there are drawbacks. For example, if the gift is not properly structured it could become subject to gift tax in Italy immediately. If the children fall out with you they might insist on the sale of the property and on receiving their share. If they divorce, their spouse may be able to claim part of the property. If you die within seven years then the gift of the money in the UK (which allows them to buy the property) will be taxed in whole or in part as part of your UK estate; seek advice from your lawyer. If they die before you, then you may end up inheriting the property back from them and having to pay inheritance tax for the privilege of doing so.

## Putting the Property in the Name of Your Children Only

If you put the property only in the name of your children (possibly reserving for yourself a life interest – *see* below) then the property is theirs. On your death there will be little or no inheritance tax and there will be no need for them to incur the legal expenses involved in dealing with an inheritance.

This sounds attractive. Remember, however, that you have lost control. It is no longer your property.

A **life interest** is the right to use the property for a lifetime. So, on your death, your rights would be extinguished *but* your second wife or partner, who still has a life interest, would still be able to use the property. Only on their death would the property pass in full to the people to whom you gave it years earlier. This device can not only protect your right to use the property but also save large amounts of inheritance tax, particularly if you are young, the property is valuable and you survive for many years. As ever, there are also drawbacks, not least being the fact that after the gift you no longer own the property. If you wish to sell you need the agreement of the 'owners', who will be entitled to their share of the proceeds of sale and who would have to agree to buy you a new house. If you wish to do this you must structure the gift carefully, otherwise it could be taxable at once in Italy.

## Limited Company

For some people, owning a property via a limited company can be a very attractive option. You own the shares in a company, not a house in Italy. There are various types of company.

### Italian Commercial Company

Ownership via a company can, in certain circumstances, reduce your tax bill. Ownership in the form of a company also gives rise to certain expenses: accountancy, filing tax returns, etc.

Buying through an Italian company gives rise to a host of potential problems as well as benefits. The plan needs to be studied closely by your advisers so that you can decide whether or not it makes sense in the short, medium and long term.

### UK Company

It is rare for a purchase through a UK company to make sense for a holiday home or single investment property. This is despite the fact that the ability to pay for the property with the company's money without drawing it out of the company and paying UK tax on the dividend is attractive. Once again, you need expert advice from someone familiar with the law of both countries.

### Offshore (Tax Haven) Company

This has the added disincentive that, in Spain, France and Portugal, the governments have passed laws to combat such ownership. For example, in Spain and France you will have to pay a special tax of 3 per cent of the value of the property every year. This is to compensate the government for all the inheritance and transfer taxes that they will not receive when the owners of these companies sell them or die. This tax treatment has more or less killed off ownership via such companies, yet they still have a limited role to play.

These rules do not yet exist in Italy but anyone thinking of buying in this way should, in the light of harmonisation of taxes in Europe, bear them in mind.

If the person who controls the offshore company is tax resident in the UK, he may be treated as a director or shadow director of the company. He may thus be liable to UK income tax on the 'benefit in kind' he gets if the company allows him to use the property in Italy. If the property would let for £1,000 per week then this can amount to a lot of benefit – for most people, taxed at 40 per cent.

This does not mean that this type of ownership is never a good idea. A 93-year-old buying a £10,000,000 property, or someone who wishes to be discreet about the ownership of the property, might think the cost is a small price to pay for the avoidance of inheritance tax or privacy respectively.

## Your Self Invested Personal Pension (SIPP)

For a time in 2005, this looked like a 'new' option. It has been possible to buy commercial property via a SIPP for several years – but there was a prediction that the rules would be changed to give people the right to own residential property via a pension fund, starting in April 2006. However, at the last minute the UK chancellor changed his mind, and so this attractive option is sadly not available at present. See John Howell & Co's website – **www.lawoverseas.com** – for an up-to-date statement of the situation.

## Investment Clubs

Some people cannot afford to invest enough in an Italian property to buy the property they would like to own. Others prefer to own a portfolio of properties in several countries, joining with others for this purpose. This can spread your risk by diversification in a way that might not be possible on your own. Some will prefer to share one splendid property rather than own an average property outright. For all of these people the investment club is a serious possibility. You can group together with up to 19 friends, relatives, workmates or strangers and buy between you. The structure is tax transparent, always in the UK and usually in Italy too – which means that you simply pay tax on your share of the income and gains when they occur.

An investment club requires a constitution in order to function. See your specialist UK lawyer.

## The Use of Trusts

As a vehicle for owning a property, trusts are of little direct use. Italian law does not fully recognise trusts and so the trustees who are named on the title as the owners of the property would be treated as 'private individual' owners, having to pay all of the income, wealth and inheritance taxes applicable in their case. In a few cases this could still give some benefit, but there are probably better ways of getting the same result.

This does not mean that trusts have no place for the owner of property in Italy. A trust could still, for example, own the property via a limited company if this fitted the 'owner's' overall tax and inheritance planning objectives.

Again, careful specialist advice is essential.

# Which is Right for You?

The choice is of fundamental importance. If you get it wrong you will pay massively more tax than you need to, both during your lifetime and on your death. The tax consequences arise not only in Italy but also in your own country.

For each buyer of a home in Italy, one of the options set out above will suit perfectly. Another might just about make sense. The rest would be an expensive waste of money. The trouble is, it is not obvious which is the right choice. You need, in every case, to take specialist advice from a UK lawyer familiar with international property transactions. If your case is simple, so will be the advice. If it is complex, the time and money spent will be repaid many times over.

# The Process of Buying a Property

## The Law

As you would expect, this is complicated. A basic textbook on Italian property law might extend to 500 pages. There are certain basic principles, however, that it is helpful to understand.

1. The main legal provisions relating to property law are found in the civil code. The analysis of rights reflects the essentially agrarian society of late 18th-century Italy and pays limited attention to some of the issues that today would seem more pressing. That has only partly been remedied by the later additions to the code.

2. The civil code declares that foreigners are to be treated in the same way as Italian people as far as the law is concerned.

3. Italian law divides property into two classes – moveable property and immovable property. The whole basis of ownership and transfer of ownership depends on which classification property belongs to. The distinction is similar to the English concept of real and personal property *but it is not exactly the same*. Immovable property includes land and buildings, but not the shares in a company that owns land and buildings.

4. The sale of immovable property – basically land and buildings – located in Italy must always be governed by Italian law.

5. The form of ownership of land is almost always absolute ownership. This is similar to what we would call freehold ownership. There are other lesser property rights, including 'surface rights' (*diritto di superficie*), which allows someone to build on land and own the buildings *but not the land they stand on*. On the expiry of the surface right, the owner of the land becomes the owner of the building.

6. It is possible to own the buildings – or even parts of a building – on a piece of land separately from the land itself. This is of particular relevance in the case of flats, which are owned 'freehold'.

7. Where two or more people own a piece of land or other property together they will generally own it in undivided shares (*comunione*). That is to say the piece of land is not physically divided between them. Each owner may, in theory, mortgage or sell his share without the consent of the others – though

the others might have certain rights of pre-emption (the right to buy the property in preference to any outsider). On the death of one of the owners the property will pass by inheritance in accordance with his will or the rules of Italian law, if those apply.

8. Where a building or piece of land is physically divided between a number of people, a condominium (*condominio*) is created. The land is divided into privately owned parts – such as an individual flat – and communally owned areas. The management of the communally held areas is up to the owners of the privately held area, but can be delegated to someone else. If there are more than four owners they must appoint an administrator. If there are more than ten co-owners there must be a set of rules governing their conduct.

9. In the case of a sale of land, certain people may have a right of pre-emption. These include a tenant farmer cultivating the land or, if there is no such farmer, tenant farmers on adjoining land.

10. Transfer of ownership of immovable property is usually by simple agreement. This will usually be in writing as only a written contract can be registered. That agreement binds both the parties to it but is not effective as far as the rest of the world is concerned, who are entitled to rely on the content of the land register (*pubblici registri immobiliari*). Ownership can also be acquired by possession, usually for 20 years.

11. Other rights – short of ownership – can exist over land. These include rights of way, tenancies, life interests, mortgages and option contracts. Most require some sort of formality in order that they are valid against third parties but are always binding as between the people who made the agreements.

12. There are two land registers. Each area maintains a tax register (*catasto*). In this, all the land in the district is divided into plots and assessed for tax purposes. The second register is the deed and mortgage register (*ufficio dei pubblici registri immobiliari* or *conservatorie dei pubblici registri immobiliari*). Not all land is registered here. Land is registered in the name of the individual owner. The entries (size, boundaries, etc.) do not necessarily correspond in the two registers.

## General Procedure

The general procedure when buying a property in Italy seems, at first glance, similar to the purchase of a property in England: sign a contract; do some checks; sign a deed of title. This is deceptive. The procedure is very different and even the use of the familiar English vocabulary to describe the very different steps in Italy can produce an undesirable sense of familiarity with the procedure. This can lead to assumptions that things that have not been discussed will be the same as they would in England. This is a wrong and dangerous assumption. Work on the basis that the system is totally different.

# Choosing a Lawyer

## The Notary Public (*Notaio*)

The notary is a special type of lawyer. He or she is in part a public official but is also in business, making his or her living from the fees charged for his services. Notaries also exist in England but they are seldom used in day-to-day transactions. Under Italian law, only a legalised private deed of sale (*scrittura privata autenticata*) or a public deed approved and witnessed by a notary (*atto pubblico*) can be registered at the land registry.

Although it is possible to transfer legal ownership of property such as a house or apartment by a private agreement not falling into these categories, and although that agreement will be fully binding on the people who made it, it will not be binding on third parties. Third parties – including people who want to make a claim against the property and banks wanting to lend money on the strength of the property – are entitled to rely on the details of ownership recorded at the land registry. So if you are not registered as the owner of the property, you are at risk.

The notary also carries out certain checks on properties sold and has some duties as tax enforcer and validator of documents to be presented for registration. For example, he will normally check that the property has been declared for tax purposes, that it complies with or is exempt from planning rules, that it is free of mortgages and other charges, etc.

His basic fee is fixed by law (*see* pp.141–2). If the notary undertakes extra work or the documentation is unduly long, this will increase.

The notary is, in theory, appointed by the buyer but in many cases – particularly with new property – the seller will stipulate the notary to be used. This is a practical time- and cost-saving measure. The notary has already drafted the documents gathering together all the bits of land bought by the seller and then split off the various individual plots to be sold. It makes sense for him or her to deal with all the resultant sales. Otherwise all of the powers of attorney, etc., would need to be produced before lots of different notaries, potentially all over the country.

The notary is strictly neutral. He or she is more a referee than someone fighting on your behalf. He or she is, in the usual case, someone who checks the papers to make sure that they comply with the strict rules as to content and so will be accepted by the land registry for registration. Many Italian notaries, particularly in rural areas, do not speak English – or, at least, do not speak it well enough to give advice on complex issues. Very few will know anything about English law and so will be unable to tell you about the tax and other consequences in the UK of your plans to buy a house in Italy. In any case, the buyer will seldom meet the notary before the signing ceremony and so there is little scope for seeking detailed advice. It is, anyway, rare for notaries to offer any comprehensive advice or explanation, least of all in writing, to the buyer.

For the English buyer the notary is no substitute for also using the services of a specialist UK lawyer familiar with Italian law and international property transactions. This is the clear advice of every guidebook, the Italian and British governments and the Federation of Overseas Property Developers, Agents and Consultants (FOPDAC).

## Italian Lawyers (*Avvocati*)

Most Italian people buying a home in Italy will not use the services of a lawyer (in addition to the *notaio*) unless there is something unusual or contentious about the transaction.

## English Lawyers (Solicitors)

For English people the services of the notary are unlikely to give them all the information or help they need to buy a home in Italy. They will often require advice about inheritance issues, the UK tax implications of their purchase, how to save taxes, surveys, mortgages, currency exchange, etc., which is outside the scope of the service of the notary. They should retain the services of a specialist UK lawyer familiar with dealing with these issues. The buyer's usual solicitor is unlikely to be able to help, as there is only a handful of English law firms with the necessary expertise.

# The Price

This can be freely agreed between the parties. Depending on the economic climate, there may be ample or very little room for negotiating a reduction in the asking price. At the moment (2005) the scope is limited for popularly priced properties in the main cities and tourist areas, which are in short supply. There is, however, probably rather more property available than the estate agent suggests. Italians *haggle* when it comes to the price of property – or almost anything else, for that matter.

## How Much Should Be Declared in the Deed of Sale?

For many years there was a tradition in Italy (and other Latin countries) of under-declaring the price actually paid for a property when signing the deed of sale (*rogito*). This was because the taxes and notaries' fees due were calculated on the basis of the price declared. A lower price means less property transfer taxes for the buyer and less capital gains tax for the seller. The days of major under-declarations have now largely gone. In rural areas you can still sometimes come under pressure to under-declare to a significant extent, but it is now rare. In many areas the seller will still suggest some more modest form of under-declaration.

Under-declaration is illegal and foolish. There are severe penalties. Nonetheless you may find that you have little choice but to under-declare. The seller will often refuse to sell unless you do. Fortunately, there is a semi-legitimate 'grey area' for manoeuvre over declared price, rather like doing 40mph in a 30 limit. It is wrong but you will not get into serious trouble. Seek advice from your lawyer.

## Where Must the Money Be Paid?

The price, together with the taxes and fees payable, is usually paid by the buyer to the seller in front of the notary. This is the best and safest way. You can, in fact, agree to pay in whatever way and wherever you please. So, for example, in the case of a British seller and a British buyer the payment could be made in sterling by bank transfer. This can produce some complications, particularly in a rural area where the notary has no experience of such transactions.

Try to avoid arrangements, usually as part of an under-declaration, where part of the money is handed over in cash in brown-paper parcels. Apart from being illegal, it is dangerous at a practical level. Buyers have lost the bundle – or been robbed – on the way to the notary's office. Sometimes there is a suspicion that the seller, who knew where you were going to be and when, could be involved.

# General Enquiries and Special Enquiries

Certain enquiries are made routinely in the course of the purchase of a property. These include, in appropriate cases, a check on the planning situation of the property. This enquiry will reveal the position of the property itself but it will not, at least directly, tell you about its neighbours and it will not reveal general plans for the area.

If you want to know whether the authorities are going to put a prison in the village or run a new road through your back garden (both, presumably, bad things) or build a motorway access point or railway station 3km away (both, presumably, good things), you will need to ask. There are various organisations you can approach but, just as in England, there is no single point of contact for such enquiries. If you are concerned about what might happen in the area then you will need to discuss the position with your lawyers at an early stage. There may be a considerable amount of work (and therefore cost) involved in making full enquiries, the results of which can never be guaranteed.

Normal enquiries also include a check that the seller is the registered owner of the property and that it is sold (if this has been agreed) free of mortgages or other charges.

If the person who sells to you goes bust within two years of the sale, his creditors may be able to take possession of the property. There is some protection for the person who bought in good faith but It can still be sensible to make some enquiries about the seller or to obtain a guarantee.

In order to advise you what special enquiries might be appropriate, your lawyer will need to be told your proposals for the property. Do you intend to let it out? If so, is that on a commercial basis? Do you intend to use it for business purposes? Do you want to extend or modify the exterior of the property? Do you intend to make interior structural alterations?

Agree in advance the additional enquiries you would like to make and get an estimate of the cost of those enquiries.

# The Community of Owners (*Condominio*)

This is a device familiar in continental Europe but less usual in the UK; it approximates most to the fairly new condition of 'commonhold' in blocks of flats. The basic idea is that, when a number of people own land or buildings in such a way that they have exclusive use of part of the property but shared use of the rest, then a *condominio* is created. Houses on their own plots with no shared facilities will not be members of a *condominio*.

In a *condominio* the buyer of a house or an apartment owns his own house or apartment outright – as the English would say, 'freehold' – and shares the use of the remaining areas as part of a community of owners. It is not only the shared pool that is jointly owned but (in an apartment) the lift shafts, corridors, roof, foundations, entrance areas, parking zones, etc.

The members of the *condominio* are each responsible for their own home. They collectively agree the works needed on the common areas and a budget for those works. They then become responsible for paying their share of those common expenses, as stipulated in their title.

The community is managed by an elected committee and appoints a president and secretary – both of whom are residents in the community. Day-to-day management is usually delegated to an administrator, who need not be a resident in the community. There is often also a resident caretaker.

The charges of the *condominio* are divided in the proportions stipulated in the deed creating the *condominio*. You will pay the same *condominio* fees whether you use the place all year round or only for two weeks' holiday. Of course your other bills (water, electricity, etc.) will vary with usage.

The *condominio* should provide not only for routine work but, through its fees, set aside money for periodic major repairs. If it does not – or if the amount set aside is inadequate – the general meeting can authorise a supplemental levy to raise the sums needed.

The rules set by the *condominio* are intended to improve the quality of life of residents. They could, for example, deal with concerns about noise (no radios by the pool), prohibit the use of the pool after 10pm, ban the hanging of washing on balconies, etc. More importantly, they could ban pets or any commercial activity in the building. These *regolamenti di condominio* are important documents. Every buyer of a property in a *condominio* should insist on a copy of the rules. If you do not speak Italian you should have them translated or at least summarised in English.

Be careful when buying a property in a *condominio*. Disputes are common and the legal framework governing the *condominio* is somewhat lacking compared with other Latin countries.

## 'Vacant Possession'

In Italy there is a tendency to sell the property stripped bare. If you want the sale to include light fittings, fireplaces, etc., you must say so.

## The Surveyor (*Geometra*)

Especially when buying in rural areas you will almost certainly need the services of a *geometra*. This will not be to carry out a structural survey (on which subject, *see* pp.109–12), but to establish the planning status of the property and its boundaries. He or she may also be needed to help subdivide a larger plot of land of which you are buying a part.

His or her fees will typically vary from about £600 to £1,200 depending on the complexity of what he needs to do.

Often the *geometra* will be linked to the selling agent or know the owner. In a small rural community there will be few surveyors and few agents, so this is not surprising. You then have the choice between using the local *geometra* – with the possibility that he might not be entirely independent – or appointing someone from further afield. This has two drawbacks: travelling time adds to the cost of the work, and he will not have the intimate local contacts on which life in Italy depends. Generally it is better to use the local person unless there are strong contraindications.

Sometimes the *geometra*'s work will be done before signing the initial contract *compromesso* (*see* below), sometimes afterwards.

## Initial Contracts

In Italy most sales start with a **preliminary contract**. The type of contract will depend on whether you are buying a finished or an unfinished property. The signing of any of these documents has far-reaching legal consequences, which are sometimes different from the consequences of signing a similar document in the UK. Whichever type of contract you are asked to sign, always seek legal advice before doing so.

Generally the preliminary contract is prepared by the estate agent – who is professionally qualified in Italy – or by the developer. Estate agent's contracts are often based on a pre-printed document in a standard format.

Some contracts coming from estate agents are legally muddled and not properly thought through. They can blur or mix different types of contractual obligation, often referring to mutually exclusive concepts in the same document – for example, referring to it as a contract of sale and an option contract.

Sometimes the contracts are extremely one-sided, giving the seller all the rights and taking away all the rights of the buyer.

It is very important that these contracts are not just accepted as final. In many cases they will need to be modified, in some cases extensively.

## If You Are Buying a Finished Property

You will be invited to sign one or more of three different documents. Each has different features. Each has different legal consequences. Each is appropriate in certain circumstances and inappropriate in others.

### Offer to Buy

This is, technically, not a contract at all. It is a formal written offer from the potential buyer to the potential seller. It will state that you wish to buy the stated property for a stated price and that you will complete the transaction within a stated period. The offer will normally be accompanied by the payment of a **deposit** to the estate agent or seller. The deposit is not fixed but will usually range from 2–5 per cent of the price offered. In return for this deposit the property should be taken off the market.

The offer must be in writing.

This document can bind you. Unless you stipulate that it is not binding, it is not a mere enquiry as to whether or not the seller might be interested in selling. If he says that he accepts the offer then you (and he) become legally bound to proceed with the transaction.

Generally we do not like written offers. We prefer the idea of making a verbal enquiry as to whether or not the seller would accept a certain price and, once he says yes, for a binding bilateral contract of sale (*compromesso*) to be signed. Often, however, the local practice is to make formal offers. It is then a case of 'when in Rome, do as the Romans'. Just make sure that the offer is very clear and that it specifies that it is not binding. If it is a binding offer, make sure that it stipulates any key conditions to which it is subject, such as 'This offer is only binding if I am offered a mortgage from X for at least €50,000 at an interest rate no higher than X per cent' or 'This offer is subject to a satisfactory survey'.

### Reservation/Option Contract

This is relatively rare but can be useful.

It is a written document in which the seller agrees to take a stated property off the market for a fixed period and sell it at a stated price to a stated person at any time within a stated period.

The seller will usually require that any person taking up his offer pays him a **deposit**. Once he has received this deposit, the seller must reserve the property for you until the end of the period specified in the contract.

This is similar to an English option contract. If you want to go ahead and buy the property you can but you are not obliged to do so. If you do not go ahead, you lose your deposit.

The contract could contain special '**get-out clauses**' stipulating the circumstances in which the buyer will be entitled to the refund of his deposit if he decides not to go ahead. The drafting of these clauses is of vital importance. See your lawyer.

If you do want to go ahead you can exercise the option at any point up to the end of the agreed period. If the seller refuses to go ahead, the buyer is entitled to claim compensation.

## Full Preliminary Contract (*Compromesso*)

The *compromesso* is, in most parts of Italy, the most common type of document. It is also known as the *contratto preliminare di vendita*.

It is an agreement that commits both parties. The seller must sell a stated property at a stated price to a stated person on the terms set out in the contract. The buyer must buy.

Other types of preliminary contract – binding only either the buyer (*promesso d'acquisto*) or the seller (*promesso di vendita*), are sometimes seen and have different legal consequences from the *compromesso*. Because they are relatively rare, they are not considered further in this book.

The *compromesso* is the most far-reaching of the three documents covered in this section and so it is particularly important that you are satisfied that it contains all the terms necessary to protect your position. Take legal advice. Remember that, under Italian law, by signing and completing this contract you become, in some senses, the owner of the property, though you will need to sign a deed of sale (*rogito*) and register your ownership to be safe as far as third parties are concerned.

The contract will contain a variety of 'routine' clauses.

- **The names of the seller and buyer should both be stated fully.**

- **The property should be described fully, both in an everyday sense and by reference to its land registry details.**

- **If the property is part of a condominium, the common parts (pool, etc.) should be described.**

- **A date for the signing of the deed of sale (*rogito*) will be fixed or the contract will permit either party to require the signing of the *rogito* at any point by giving notice to the other.**

- **A statement will be made as to when possession will take place – normally, on the date of signing the title.**

- The price is fixed.

- A receipt for any deposit is given.

- The property should be sold with vacant possession.

- The property should be sold free of any charges, debts or burdens and all bills should be paid up to date before signing the *rogito*.

- It will provide for who is to pay the costs of the purchase.

- It may confirm the details of any agent involved and who is to pay his commission.

- It will set out what is to happen if one or both of the parties breaks the contract.

- It will establish the law to cover the contract and the address of the parties for legal purposes.

It will probably also contain some '**conditional clauses**' (*clausoli resolutivi*). These are clauses that say, in effect, if X is not true or does not happen then the deal is off and you get your deposit money back. Examples might be as follows.

- The seller has good title. (You might not have been able to get confirmation of this before signing the *compromesso*, especially if you were under pressure to sign quickly or lose the property.)

- The seller has planning permission.

- You will be successful in an application for planning permission – for example, to build a pool.

- There are no pre-emption rights or they will not be exercised.

- The property is to be surveyed (or inspected for mortgage purposes) and the sale is conditional on a satisfactory outcome to that inspection.

- The seller is required to fix various things or complete some work on the property.

- You are applying for a mortgage and the sale is conditional on that mortgage being offered.

- The sale is conditional on the sale of your exising property within a certain time.

These all need careful drafting if there are not to be any 'loopholes'.

If the buyer or seller drops out of the contract or otherwise breaks it, various arrangements may be made.

A **deposit** is paid at the time of signing the contract. Normally a special type of deposit is payable by the buyer. If he fails to complete he will lose the deposit. If the seller fails to satisfy the conditions imposed on him, and to complete, he will have to return double the deposit paid. Alternatively the contract may provide for a deposit to be paid as a simple part of the price of the property. The contract can provide for all or part of this deposit – and any other sums paid up to the relevant moment – to be lost if the buyer does not proceed. It is important to understand the difference.

The amount of this deposit varies from place to place and seller to seller. It is sometimes the 'standard' 10 per cent we are used to in the UK but often it is 20, 30 or even 33 per cent. The larger deposit is a mixed blessing. Obviously it puts more strain on your cashflow and puts you at greater exposure if anything goes wrong and you have to recover it from the seller. Getting money back is never as simple as paying it over, however strong your legal position. On the other hand, if you have paid 30 per cent, this acts as a very real barrier to the seller's pulling out of the transaction – or entering into a transaction where there are conditions he is not going to be able to meet. This is because if he can't go ahead he will usually be required to give you back double that amount – 60 per cent of the price of the property.

If, as is often the case, you are to pay all or a part of the **estate agent's fees** on top of the price of the property, you will often be expected to pay these at the time when the *compromesso* is signed. This will typically be 3 per cent of the price of the property.

If the parties fail to comply with their obligations there is the ultimate remedy of seeking a court order. As in any country, this is very much a last resort, as it is costly, time-consuming and (as in any country) there is no guarantee of the outcome of a court case. If a court order is made in your favour, this order can be registered at the land registry.

## If You Are Buying an Unfinished Property

### Reservation Contract

Often in these cases there is a preliminary contract. This is the reservation contract (*see* above). This allows you to reserve a plot when you see it and allows you time to sign one of the other types of contract when you have made the necessary enquiries.

### Full Contract

There are three likely types of contract in this case.

- **Contract for immediate sale of the land.**

You sign a contract agreeing to sign the title deed in respect of the land – and anything the seller has so far built on it – now. This involves paying for the land and work so far undertaken in full at this stage. At the same time you enter into a contract to build your house on the land. This will normally be an *appalto*. The contract contains detailed provisions as to what will happen, for example, if any changes are needed to the works agreed or costs rise and as to arrangements for inspection and handover of the property.

As the building continues, it automatically becomes the property of the buyer. The buyer, of course, has the obligation to pay the agreed price, usually by instalments dependent on the progress of the building work.

This has the great advantage of securing the money you pay to the builder. If the builder goes bust, you own the land and everything built on it. It only really works for property built on its own plot rather than, say, apartments. It can be tax- and cost-inefficient.

- **Contract 'on plan'.**

You agree to buy a property once it has been built and agree to make payments in stages as the construction progresses. Sometimes the payments are dependent on the progress of the building works. On other occasions they are due on set dates. The latter are now the more common option, though less attractive to the buyer.

Once the property has been built, you will sign the deed of sale and pay the balance of the price. It is only then that you become the owner of the property and register your title. Until then, if the builder goes bust you are simply one of many creditors.

The contract can provide for an independent guarantee to secure completion of the construction in the event, for example, that the seller went bust. Remember that big companies and honourable men go bust. Rolls-Royce. Barings Bank. Enron. Refco.

Where possible it is much better to have separate contracts for the purchase of the land and subsequent building work.

- **Contract to buy once the property has been built.**

You agree to buy a plot of land and building. You agree to pay once it has been built. Simple! You take title and pay the money at the same time. This is really the same as buying a resale property. This type of contract is little used.

## Other Documentation

Has the property got planning permission/a building licence?

You should be given a full specification for the property, a copy of the community rules and constitution if the property shares common facilities, and a copy of any agreements you have entered into regarding ongoing management or letting of the property. All are important documents. Pay particular attention to the specification. It is not unknown for the show flat to have marble floors and high-quality wooden kitchens but for the specification to show concrete tiles and MDF.

# Checklist – Signing a Contract

**Property in the Course of Construction**       **Existing Property**

Are you clear about what you are buying?

Are there any 'extras' included in the sale?

Have you taken legal advice about who should be the owner of the property?

Have you taken legal advice about inheritance issues?

Are you clear about the boundaries?

| Property in the Course of Construction | Existing Property |
|---|---|
| Are you clear about access to the property? | |
| Have you seen the seller's title? | |
| | Are you sure you can modify/add to the property as you want? |
| | Are you sure you can use the property for what you want? |
| | Is the property connected to water, electricity, gas, etc? |
| | Have you had a survey done? |
| Have you made all necessary checks OR arranged for them to be made? | |
| Have you included 'get-out' clauses for important checks not yet made? | |
| Is your mortgage finance arranged? | |
| Is the seller clearly described? | |
| If the seller is not signing in person, have you seen a power of attorney/mandate to authorise the sale? | |
| Are you fully described? | |
| Is the property fully disclosed with regard to land registry details? | |
| Is the price correct? | |
| Can the price increase and are the extra expenses described fully? | |
| Are the stage payments fully described? | Does contract say when possession will be given? |
| Are arrangments for stage payments satisfactory? | Is there a receipt for the deposit paid? |
| Is the date for completion of the work agreed? | In what capacity is the deposit paid? |
| Does the property have planning permission? | Does the property have a habitation licence/permission/licence to build? |
| Is the date for signing the *rogito* agreed upon? | |
| Does the contract provide for the sale to be free of charges and debts? | |
| Does the contract provide for vacant possession? | |
| Who is the notary? | |
| Is the estate agent's commission dealt with? | |
| What happens if there is a breach of contract? | |
| Are there any financial guarantees of satisfactory completion? | |
| Are all the necessary special 'get-out' clauses included? | |

# Steps between Signing the Contract and Signing the Deed of Sale (*Rogito*)

## Searches

If you were pressured into signing a preliminary contract (*compromesso*) without doing searches or seeing proof of title, do it now. The sooner you find a problem, the sooner you can fix it or take protective action.

## Registration of the *Compromesso*?

It is possible to register the written preliminary contract at the Land Registry, so protecting your rights against third parties. This can sometimes be a good idea, particularly if there is going to be a long period from the signing of the *compromesso* and the signing of the *rogito*. It does, however, increase the costs of the purchase.

## Power of Attorney

Very often it will not be convenient for you to have to go to Italy to sign the *rogito* in person. Sometimes there may be other things that, in the normal course of events, would require your personal intervention but where it would be inconvenient for you to have to deal with them yourself.

Just as often you will not know whether or not you will be available to sign in person. Completion dates on Italian property are notoriously fluid and so you could plan to be there but suffer a last-minute delay to the signing that makes it impossible.

The solution to this problem is the power of attorney. This document authorises the person appointed (the attorney) to do whatever the document authorises on behalf of the person granting the power (the grantor). Note that being appointed under a power of attorney is nothing to do with being a lawyer; anyone can be appointed – though you need to choose the person with care, as you are giving them extensive power to do things on your behalf.

The most sensible type of power to use will be the Italian style of power that is appropriate to the situation. The power will be signed in front of a notary either in the UK or Italy. If it is signed in front of a UK notary it has to be ratified by the Foreign and Commonwealth Office for use overseas. This sounds very grand but is actually quick and simple.

The type of Italian power of attorney that you will need depends on what you want to use it for. Your specialist English lawyer can discuss your requirements with you and prepare the necessary document. Alternatively you can deal directly with the Italian notary who will ultimately need the power.

In theory an English-style power should be sufficient, but in practice the cost and delay associated with getting it recognised can be unacceptable.

Even if you intend to go to Italy to sign, it is sensible to think about granting a power just in case. It is not something that can be done at the last moment. From the decision to getting the document to Italy will take at least seven and more likely ten days. If you are able to go, the power will not be used.

Even if you have granted a power of attorney, if you get the opportunity to go to Italy at the time of the signing, it is worth doing so. It is quite interesting but, more importantly, you will be able to check the house to make sure that everything is in order before the *rogito* is signed.

## Tax Identification Number

You will need to obtain your *codice fiscale* (*see* pp.28–9) before you sign the deed of sale. This is a simple process (usually) that will be initiated by your lawyer or the estate agent.

## Getting the Money to Italy

There are several ways of getting the money to Italy.

### Electronic Transfer

The most practical is to have it sent electronically by SWIFT transfer from a UK bank directly to the recipient's bank in Italy. This costs about £10–35 depending on your bank. It is safer to allow two or three days for the money to arrive in a small local bank, despite everyone's protestations that it will be there the same day.

Europe has introduced unique account numbers for all bank accounts. These incorporate a code for the identity of the bank and branch involved as well as the account number of the individual customer. These are known as IBAN numbers. They should be quoted, if possible, on all international currency transfers.

You can send the money from your own bank, via your lawyers or via a specialist currency dealer.

For the sums you are likely to be sending you should receive an exchange rate much better than the 'tourist rate' you see in the press. There is no such thing as a fixed exchange rate in these transactions. The bank's official inter-bank rate changes by the second and the job of the bank's currency dealers is to make a profit by selling to you at the lowest rate they can get away with. Thus, if you do a lot of business with a bank and they know you are on the ball, you are likely to be offered a better rate than a one-off customer. For this reason it is often better to send it via your specialist UK lawyers, who will be dealing with large numbers of such transactions. This also has the advantage that their bank, which deals with international payments all the time, is less likely to make a mistake causing delay to the payment than your bank, for which such a payment might be a rarity.

You or your lawyers might use a specialist currency dealer to make the transfer of funds instead of a main UK bank. Such dealers often give a better exchange rate than an ordinary bank. Sometimes the difference can be significant, especially compared to your local branch of a high street bank. Although these dealers use major banks actually to transfer the funds, you need to make sure that the dealer you are using is reputable. Your money is paid to them, not to the major bank, so could be at risk if the dealer is not bonded or otherwise protected.

However you make the payment, ensure that you understand whether you or the recipient are going to pick up the receiving bank's charges. If you need a clear amount in Italy you will have to make allowances for these, either by sending a bit extra or by asking your UK bank to pay all the charges. Make sure you have got the details of the recipient bank, its customer's name, the account codes and the recipient's reference precisely right. Any error and the payment is likely to come back to you undeliverable – and may involve you in bearing the cost of it being converted back into sterling.

The bank in Italy will make a charge – which can be substantial – for receiving your money into your account.

### Banker's Drafts

You can arrange for your UK bank to issue you with a banker's draft (bank certified cheque), which you can take to Italy and pay into your bank account. Make sure that the bank knows that the draft is to be used overseas and so issues you with an international draft.

Generally this is not a good way to transfer the money. It can take a considerable time – sometimes weeks – for the funds deposited to be made available for your use. The recipient bank's charges can be surprisingly high. The exchange rate offered against a sterling draft may be uncompetitive as you are a captive customer.

### Cash

This is not recommended. You will need to declare the money on departure from the UK and on arrival in Italy. Even then, if you declare £200,000 or so, they will think you are a terrorist or drug dealer. That suspicion can have far-reaching consequences in terms of listings in police files and even surveillance. To add insult to injury, the exchange rate you will be offered for cash (whether you take sterling and convert there or buy the euros here) is usually very uncompetitive and the notary may well refuse to accept the money in his account. Don't do it.

### Exchange Control and Other Restrictions on Moving Money

For EU nationals there is no longer any exchange control when taking money to or from Italy. There are some statistical records kept showing the flow of funds and the purposes of the transfers.

When you sell your property in Italy, you will be able to bring the money back to the UK if you wish to do so.

## Final Checks about the Property

All of the points outstanding must be resolved to your satisfaction, as must any other points of importance to you.

## Fixing the Completion Date

The date stated in the contract for signing the *rogito* could, most charitably, be described as flexible or aspirational. Often it will move, if only by a day or so. For this reason it is not sensible to book your travel to Italy until you are almost sure that matters will proceed on a certain day.

## Checklist – Steps Before Completion

**Property in the Course of Construction**      **Existing Property**

Prepare power of attorney

Check what documents must be produced on signing the *rogito*

Confirm all outstanding issues have been complied with

Confirm all other important enquiries are clear

Confirm arrangements (date, time, place) for completion with your lender if you have a mortgage

Confirm arrangements (date, time, place) for completion with notary

Send necessary funds to Italy

Receive rules of community

Insurance cover arranged?

Sign off work or list defects          Proof of payment of community fees

Proof of payment of other bills

# Signing the Deed of Sale (*Rogito*)

To be registered at the land registry – and so protect your ownership of your property from claims by third parties – your purchase must be either by way of a legalised private document (*scrittura privata autenticata*) or public title deed (*atto pubblico*). The deed of sale signed is called the *rogito*. The vast majority of overseas buyers buy by way of an *atto pubblico* signed in front of a notary (*notaio*). This must be signed in front of an Italian notary either by the parties in person or someone holding power of attorney for them. Generally it is at the moment of signing that the title to the property is transferred into your name.

At the same time as the *rogito* is signed, the balance of the price is paid to the seller, usually by way of an Italian banker's draft handed over in front of the notary. If you are taking out an Italian mortgage it is also at this time that the paperwork in relation to the mortgage will be completed, again by the notary. Also at this time, the various taxes and stamp duties and the notary's fees are paid.

The *rogito* will contain a variety of 'standard' clauses, largely replicating those in the contract. It will contain a statement of the price and a statement that the notary has advised you of your fiscal obligations arising out of the sale.

## Formalities

Certain procedures are followed at the signing of the *rogito*.

The parties are identified by their passports or identity cards. This will normally be done, initially, by the notary's clerk and then also by the notary.

The notary's clerk may also go through the content of the *rogito* with the parties. This tends to be very superficial and often the person concerned will have limited or no English.

The parties will then be ushered into the presence of the notary. In addition to the buyer and seller it would be possible for the group to comprise also the notary's clerk, your lawyer, a translator, a representative of your mortgage lender, the estate agent and any sub-agent appointed by the estate agent. Most of these people are there to receive money. Needless to say, if they all turn up it can get a little loud and confusing!

If you do not speak Italian, an **interpreter** should be present when you sign the *rogito*. The attitude of notaries when it comes to assessing when an interpreter is necessary varies enormously. The Italian version of the deed should be followed by the translation in English. No written translation is provided as a matter of course. If an interpreter is required, you will generally have to pay for it.

## After the *Rogito* Has Been Signed

The **taxes** must be paid.

Once the taxes are paid, your title and any mortgage should be presented for registration at the **land registry**. This should be done as quickly as possible. He who registers first gets priority. After several months the land registry will issue a **certificate** to the effect that the title has been registered.

# The Cost of Buying a Property

There are fees and taxes payable by a buyer when acquiring a property in Italy. They are sometimes known as completion expenses or completion or closing costs. They are impossible to predict with total accuracy at the outset of a transaction. This is because there are several variable factors that will not become clear until later. We can, however, give a general guide.

These costs are calculated on the basis of the price that you declared as the price paid for the property in the *rogito*. The size of these expenses, coupled with the Italian dislike for paying tax, has led to the habit of 'accidentally' under-declaring the price in the *rogito*. These days are now largely over and we can only suggest that the full price of the property is declared. *See* 'How Much Should Be Declared in the Deed of Sale', pp.127–8.

## Notary's Fees

These are fixed by law, so are not negotiable. They will depend on the type of property being bought and its price.

Typical notary's fees would be:

| Price up to (€) | Charge (€) |
| --- | --- |
| €5,000 | €1,000 |
| €20,000 | €1,300 |
| €50,000 | €1,750 |
| €250,000 | €2,600 |
| €500,000 | €3,150 |
| €1,000,000 | €3,800 |
| €2,500,000 | €4,500 |

As a general guide, if you wish to avoid the detailed calculation, allow 1 per cent. These charges may be higher in complicated and unusual transactions. If you have asked the notary to do additional work over and above the transfer of title to the property, or for advice, there will be additional charges.

# Taxes

### VAT (*Imposta sul Valore Aggiunto – IVA*)

This applies only to properties bought from a company or business. It is 10 per cent of the declared purchase price of the property unless the property is classified as a 'luxury dwelling', in which case the rate is (in certain circumstances) 20 per cent. The meaning of luxury dwelling is defined. This VAT is sometimes, but not always, included in the price of the property quoted to you. Check to see whether it is in your case.

## Stamp Duty

This is charged instead of VAT on properties bought from private individuals. The rate is usually 7 per cent. Some historic properties bear a reduced rate of 3 per cent. When the purchase is subject to VAT, there is a fixed charge of €168.

## Real Estate Taxes (*Imposte Ipotecaria e Catastale*)

If bought from an individual they are 3 per cent of the value of the property. If bought from a company they amount to approximately €336.

## Local Tax

This is based on the official tax value of the property (*valore catastale*) – not at all the same as the market value. It varies from 0.4 to 0.8 per cent of that value depending on the type of property bought, and depending on the local council.

## Mortgage Costs (If Applicable)

If you are taking out a mortgage there will be additional costs. *See* 'Raising Finance to Buy a Property', pp.112–20. These typically amount to 3–4 per cent of the amount borrowed.

## Estate Agent's Charges (If Payable by the Buyer)

If an estate agent has sold the property, his fees are often split between the buyer and seller. If this is so in your case, then you are likely to pay 3 per cent of the true price paid. This can be varied by agreement.

These fees will be subject to IVA.

## Miscellaneous Other Charges

Architect's fees, surveyor's fees, UK legal fees (typically 1 per cent), first connection to water, electricity, etc. Most of these will be subject to Italian IVA at varying rates, but your UK lawyer's fees will be outside the scope of UK VAT.

## Overall Costs of Acquisition

In the case of a house bought without a mortgage this is likely to amount to about 12–15 per cent of the declared price of the property.

# Property Insurance

Most foreign owners of property in Italy take out a multi-risk household policy. Many Italians do without insurance completely. The choice is yours.

A multi-risk policy covers the fabric of the building, its contents and any civil responsibility landing on the owner of the property other than in certain specified circumstances such as liability incurred in connection with the use of a car. Alternatively, insurance is available for the building (*edificio*) or contents (*contenuto*) separately.

Premiums are comparatively cheap in rural areas, more expensive in Rome and the main tourist areas. There are four important points to bear in mind when choosing a suitable policy.

• **Make sure that the level of cover is adequate.** Just as in the UK, if you under-insure the building and the worst happens, the company will not pay you out for the full extent of your loss. The amount for which you should be covered as far as civil liability is concerned should be a minimum of one million euros and preferably higher. Because the risk of a claim under this category is small, the premiums for this part of the insurance are low and so high levels of cover can be provided at low cost. The amount of cover you should have for the building itself should be the full cost of reconstruction of the building. If you own an apartment then the cost of the building insurance for the whole block of apartments should be included in your service charge. You will then only need contents and public liability insurance. Once this insurance value has been established, it should be increased each year in line with the official index of inflation of building costs. As far as contents are concerned, you should make a detailed estimate of the value of your furnishings and possessions likely to be in the property at any time. Remember to allow for items such as cameras that you may take with you on holiday. Pay particular attention to the details of this policy and study the small print about what you have to specify when taking out the insurance and any limitations on claims that can be made against it. Notice in particular whether there is a requirement to stipulate items of high value. If you have any items of high value it is worth having them photographed and, possibly, valued. The insurance company might specify security measures that must be in place in your home. If you don't use them, you may find that you are not covered.

• **If you are using the property as holiday accommodation (or spend long periods away from home), you must specify a policy which is a holiday policy.** If you don't, you are likely to find that one of the conditions of the policy is that cover will lapse if the property is empty for 30 or 60 days. Premiums will be higher for holiday homes because the risk is higher.

• **If you intend to let your property, you must notify the insurance company and comply with any requirements of the insurance company with regard to the lettings.** Otherwise your cover could be void. Your premiums will be higher.

• **If you need to make a claim, make it quickly.** There are usually time limits for doing so. If the claim involves a theft or break-in you will usually have to report the matter to the police. This should normally be done immediately after discovery of the incident and in any case within 24 hours. The claim should be notified to the insurance company without delay. Check the maximum period allowed in your policy, which could be as little as 48 hours. As with all-important documents in Italy, the claim should be notified by recorded delivery post. Make the claim by registered post.

There are some UK-based insurance companies who offer cover for properties in Italy. The main advantages in dealing with a UK company are that the documentation is likely to be in English and that if you have to make a claim it will be processed in English. There are some Italian companies that also have the facility for dealing with claims in English. This should not be under-estimated as an advantage. Unless your Italian is fluent, you would otherwise have to employ somebody to deal with the claim on your behalf or translate what you have said into Italian – something that is never entirely satisfactory.

# Key Points

## Property Under Construction

- Make sure you understand exactly what you are buying. How big is the property? What will it look like? How will it be finished? What appliances are included? What facilities will it enjoy?

- Think about who should own the property so as to minimise tax and inheritance problems.

- Make sure the contract has all the necessary clauses required to protect your position.

- Try to obtain a bank guarantee if you are buying 'off plan'. You now, generally, have the right to this.

- Be clear about the timetable for making payments.

- Think about whether or not you should forward-buy currency.

- When you take delivery of the property, consider carefully if it is worth incurring the expense of an independent survey to confirm that all is in order with the construction and to help draft any 'snagging list'.

## Resale Properties

- Make sure you understand exactly what you are buying. Are the boundaries clear? What furniture or fittings are included?

- Think about whether to have the property surveyed or not, especially if it is nearly ten years old and your statutory guarantee will soon be expiring.

- Think about who should own the property so as to minimise tax and inheritance problems.

- Make sure the contract has all the necessary clauses required to protect your position.

- Think about whether or not you should forward-buy currency.

- When you take delivery of the property, make sure that everything agreed is present.

## Special Points: Old Properties

By 'old property' is meant a property built more than, say, 50 years ago.

- Are you having a survey? Not to do so can be an expensive mistake.

- Are you clear about any restoration costs to be incurred? Do you have estimates for those charges?

- Are there any planning problems associated with any alterations or improvements you want to make to the property?

• When you take delivery of the property, make sure that everything agreed is present.

## Special Points: Rural Properties

• Such properties have often acquired a number of rights and obligations over the years. Are you clear about any obligations you might be taking on?

• Are you clear about your boundaries?

• You are probably buying for peace and quiet and the rural idyll. Are you sure that nothing is happening in the vicinity of your property that will be detrimental?

• If you have any plans to change the property or use it for other purposes, will this be permitted?

• If you intend to build on the site, be very clear about minimum permitted plot sizes – which can vary up to 25,000 sq m – and other planning limitations.

## Special Points: City Properties

City properties will usually be apartments, concerning which *see* below.

• Unless you are used to living in a city – and, in particular, a continental city – don't underestimate the noise that will be generated nearby. If you are in a busy area (and you are likely to be) this will go on until late at night. How good is the sound insulation?

• Are your neighbouring properties occupied by full-time residents, are they weekday only *pieds à terre* or are they holiday homes? Think about security issues.

• If you intend to use a car, where will you park?

## Special Points: Apartments and Houses Sharing Facilities

• Have you thought about a survey of the property? Will it include the common parts? This can be expensive.

• Make sure you understand the rules of the community – *see* below.

• Have you thought about a survey of the property? Will it include the common parts?

• Make sure you understand the rules of the community.

• Make sure you understand the charges that will be raised by the community.

• Make contact with its administrator. Ask about issues affecting the community. Are there any major works approved but not yet carried out? Make sure that the contract is clear about who is responsible for paying for these.

• Make contact with other owners. Are they happy with the community and the way it is run? Remember that no one is ever fully happy!

• Understand how the community is run. Once you are an owner, try to attend the general meetings of the community.

## Other Things to Do When You Buy a Property

• Insure the property and its contents. Make a full photographic record of the property. This is useful in the event of an insurance claim and for your scrap book.

• Make arrangements for your bank to pay your ICI (local property tax), water and electricity bills, etc.

• Make a will in the Italian form covering your assets in Italy. This will usually mean making small changes in your existing UK will as well.

• Appoint a fiscal representative. This is your point of contact with the Italian tax office. He will also usually complete and file your annual tax return. Your lawyer may provide this service or should be able to suggest a suitable person.

# Financial Implications

**John Howell**
**Solicitor and international Lawyer, John Howell & Co.**

# Taxation

## Introduction

All tax systems are complicated. The Italian system is no exception. The Italians would say that it is nearly as complex as ours! Fortunately, most people will only have limited contact with the more intricate parts of the system. For many owners of holiday homes in Italy their contact with the system will be minimal.

In fact, many Italian residents also have minimal contact with the tax system. Evasion is rife, but it is dangerous. It is probably also exaggerated. It has become a joke and, in reality, while it is widespread it is probably not quite as common or extravagant as is reported.

It is helpful to have some sort of understanding about the way in which the system works and the taxes that you might face. Be warned: getting even a basic understanding will make your head hurt. You also need to be particularly careful about words and concepts that seem familiar to you but which have a fundamentally different meaning in Italy. Of course, just to confuse you, the rules change every year.

In fact, it is getting a little simpler. In 2003, the Italian parliament empowered the government to implement a broad reform of the Italian tax system (Law No. 80 of April 7, 2003, the 'Law of Reform'). The reform covers companies and individuals and aims at simplifying the tax legislation and creating a favourable tax environment for domestic and foreign investment. As far as taxation of corporation is concerned, the reform has been implemented and entered into force on January 1, 2004. As far as taxation of individuals is concerned, the principles provided by the Law of Reform entered into force on January 1, 2005. At completion, the reformed tax system will be structured around five types of taxes (personal income tax, corporate income tax, VAT, tax on services and excise duties) and all taxes will be governed by one single tax code.

Just remember, simpler doesn't mean simple! There are several points in this book where I have said that the contents are only a general introduction to the subject. There is nowhere where this is more true than in this section. Books (and lengthy ones at that) have been written on the subject of Italian taxation. This general introduction does little more than scratch the surface of an immensely complex subject. It is intended to enable you to have a sensible discussion with your professional advisers and, perhaps, help you work out the questions that you need to be asking them. It is *not* intended as a substitute for proper professional advice.

Your situation when you have a foot in two countries – and, in particular, when you are moving permanently from one country to another – involves the consideration of the tax systems in both countries with a view to minimising your tax obligations in both. It is not just a question of paying the lowest amount of tax in, say, Italy. The best choice in Italy could be very damaging to your position in the UK. Similarly, the most tax-efficient way of dealing with your affairs in the UK could be problematic in Italy. The task of the international adviser and his or her client is to find a path of compromise that allows you to enjoy the major advantages available in both countries without incurring any of the worst drawbacks. In other words, there is an issue of compromise. There is no perfect solution to most tax questions. That is not to say that there are not a great many bad solutions into which you can all too easily stumble.

What should guide you when making a decision as to which course to pursue? Each individual will have a different set of priorities. Some are keen to screw the last ha'penny of advantage out of their situation. Others recognise that they will have to pay some tax but simply wish to moderate their tax bill. For many, the main concern is a simple structure that they understand and can continue to manage without further assistance in the years ahead. Just as different clients have different requirements, so different advisers have differing views as to the function of the adviser when dealing with a client's tax affairs. One of your first tasks when speaking to your financial adviser should be to discuss your basic philosophy concerning the payment of tax and management of your affairs, to make sure that you are both operating with the same objective in mind and that you are comfortable with his approach to solving your problem.

# Are You Resident or Non-resident for Tax Purposes?

The biggest single factor in determining how you will be treated by the tax authorities in any country is whether or not you are resident in that country for tax purposes. This concept of tax residence causes a great deal of confusion.

Tax residence can have different meanings in different countries. In Italy tax residence is known as *domicilio fiscale*. As a general proposition, Individuals are considered Italian residents if, for the greater part of the calendar year, they are either registered in the Italian civil registry or they have their residence or domicile in Italy, as defined by the civil law. According to the Italian Civil Code, 'residence' is the place of habitual abode; 'domicile' is the place where an individual has his/her main centre of interests ('centre of vital interests'). You will see that these definitions are very different from those in the UK.

They still give rise to quite a lot of confusion in the minds of foreigners and, in particular, British and US foreigners. Let us first look at what it does not mean. It is nothing to do with whether you have registered as resident in a country or obtained a residency permit or residency card (though a person who has a card will usually be tax resident). Nor does it have anything to do with whether or not you simply have a home (residence) in that country – although a person who is tax resident will normally have a home there. Nor is it much to do with your intentions.

Tax residence is a question of fact. The law lays down certain tests that will be used to decide whether you are tax resident or not. If you fall into the categories stipulated in the tests then you will be considered tax resident whether you want to be or not and whether it was your intention to be tax resident or not.

It is your responsibility to make your tax declarations each year. The decision as to whether or not you fall into the category of resident is, in the first instance, made by the tax office. If you disagree with the decision you can appeal through the courts.

Because people normally change their tax residence when they move from one country to another, the basis on which decisions are made tends to be regulated by international law and fairly, but not totally, consistent from country to country.

## The Rules that Determine Residence

You will have to consider two different questions concerning tax residence. The first is if you will be treated as tax resident in the UK and the second is if you will be treated as tax resident in Italy.

### UK

It is outside the scope of this book to go into any details about UK taxation but some basic points will have to be dealt with for the explanation of Italian taxation to make any sense.

In the UK there are two tests that will help determine where you pay tax. These assess your domicile and your residence.

#### Domicile

Your domicile is the place that is your real home. It is the place where you have your roots. For most people it is the place where they were born. You can change your domicile but it is often not easy to do so. Changes in domicile can have far-reaching tax consequences and can be a useful tax reduction tool.

#### Residence

Residence falls into two categories. Under English law there is a test of simple residence – actually living here other than on a purely temporary basis – and of ordinary residence.

A person will generally be treated as **resident** in the UK if he or she spends 183 or more days per year in the UK. A visitor will also be treated as resident if he or she comes to the UK regularly and spends significant time here. If he or she spends, on average over a period of four or more years, more than three months here, he or she will be treated as tax resident.

A person can continue to be **ordinarily resident** in the UK even after he or she has stopped actually being resident here. A person is ordinarily resident in the UK if his or her presence is a little more settled. The residence is an important part of his or her life. It will normally have gone on for some time.

The most important thing to understand is that, once you have been ordinarily resident in this country, the simple fact of going overseas will not automatically bring that residence to an end. If you leave this country in order to take up permanent residence elsewhere then, by concession, the Inland Revenue will treat you as ceasing to be resident on the day following your departure. However, they will not treat you as ceasing to be *ordinarily* resident if, after leaving, you spend an average of 91 or more days per year in this country over any four-year period.

In other words, they don't want you to escape too easily!

Until 1993 you were also classified as ordinarily resident in the UK if you had accommodation available for your use in the UK even though you may have spent 364 days of the year living abroad. This very unfair rule was cancelled but many people still worry about it. It is not necessary to do so provided you limit your visits to the UK to less than the 91 days referred to above.

## Italy

Tax residence in Italy – *domicilio fiscale* – is tested by a number of rules, the main ones of which are as follows:

- **If your main home is in Italy you will be classified as resident there however much – or little – time you spend there. If you have been classified as a resident in your *comune* – which gives you various tax advantages – you will be classified as resident for all tax purposes.**

- **If you spend more than 183 days in Italy in any tax year, you are tax resident in Italy. This time can be in one block or in bits and pieces through the year. The tax year runs from 1 January to 31 December.**

- **If your centre of economic interests is in Italy, you are tax resident in Italy. Your centre of economic interests is where you have your main investments or business or other sources of income and, usually, where you spend much of your money.**

- **If you work in Italy, except where that work is ancillary to work elsewhere, you will be tax resident in Italy.**

- **If you have an Italian residency card you will be *usually* be tax resident in Italy.**

- **If your family is resident in Italy you will be *assumed* to be resident in Italy unless you show the contrary. If you satisfy the taxman that you are not resident in Italy then you will pay tax on your income and assets as a non-resident but your husband/wife will pay taxes on their income and assets as a resident. *See* below for details.**

## Tax Residence in More than One Country

Remember that you can be tax resident in more than one country under the respective rules of those countries. For example, you might spend 230 days of the year in Italy and 135 days in the UK. In this case you could end up, under the rules of each country, being responsible for paying the same tax in two or more countries. This would be unfair so many countries have signed reciprocal 'Double Taxation Treaties'. The UK and Italy have such a treaty. It contains 'tie-breakers' and other provisions to decide, where there is the possibility of being required to pay tax twice, in which country any particular category of tax should be paid. *See* 'The Double Taxation Treaty', p.167.

## Decisions You Must Make

The most basic decision that you will have to make when planning your tax affairs is whether or not to cease to be resident in this country, whether or not to cease to be ordinarily resident in this country and whether or not to change your domicile to another country. Each of these has many consequences, many of which are not obvious.

The second consideration is when in the tax year to make these changes. Once again, that decision has many consequences.

For many ordinary people, getting these decisions wrong can cost them tens of thousands of pounds in totally unnecessary taxation and a great deal of irritation and inconvenience. It is vital that you seek proper professional advice before making these decisions. You will need advice from specialist lawyers, accountants or financial advisers, all of whom should be able to help you.

# Taxes Payable in the UK

The significance of these residence rules is that you will continue to be liable for some British taxes for as long as you are either ordinarily resident or domiciled in UK. Put far too simply, even once you have left the UK to live in Italy:

- **You will continue to have to pay tax in the UK on any capital gains you make anywhere in the world for as long as you are ordinarily resident and domiciled in United Kingdom.**

- **You will continue to be liable to British inheritance tax on all of your assets located anywhere in the world for as long as you remain domiciled in the UK. This will be subject to double taxation relief. Other, more complex rules also apply in certain circumstances.**

- **You will always pay UK income tax (Schedule A) on income arising from land and buildings in the UK – wherever your domicile, residence or ordinary residence.**

- You will pay UK income tax (Schedule D) on the following basis:

  - Income from 'self-employed' trade or profession carried out in the UK (Cases I and II) – normally taxed in the UK if income arises in the UK.

  - Income from interest, annuities or other annual payments from the UK (Case III) – normally taxed in the UK if income arises in the UK and you are ordinarily resident in the UK.

  - Income from investments and businesses outside the UK (Cases IV and V) – normally only taxed in the UK if you are UK domiciled and resident or ordinarily resident in the UK.

  - Income from government pensions (fire, police, army, civil servant, etc.) in all cases taxed in the UK.

  - Sundry profits not otherwise taxable arising out of land or building in the UK – always taxed in the UK.

- You will pay income tax on any income earned from salaried employment in the UK (Schedule E) only on any earnings from duties performed in the UK unless you are resident and ordinarily resident in the UK – in which case you will usually pay tax in the UK on your worldwide earnings.

If you are only buying a holiday home and will remain primarily resident in the UK, your tax position in the UK will not change very much. You will have to declare any income you make from your Italian property as part of your UK tax declaration. The calculation of tax due on that income will be made in accordance with UK rules, which will result in a different taxable sum form that used by the Italian authorities. The UK taxman will give you full credit for the taxes already paid in Italy. On the disposal of the property you should disclose the profit made to the UK taxman. He will, again, give full credit for Italian tax paid. Similarly, on your death the assets in Italy must be disclosed on the UK probate tax declaration but, once again, you will be given full credit for sums paid in Italy.

## Should You Pay Tax in Italy?

Under Italian law it is your responsibility to fill in a tax return in each year when you have any taxable income unless that income is:

- **taxed in full at source.**
- **outside the scope of Italian tax.**

There are three key points to remember:

- **Lots of Italian people don't pay the taxes they owe – and view with mild derision the fact that the British do so!**
- **The rules are applied more strictly every year.**

- **If you are caught not paying the taxes you owe, the penalties are substantial and the nuisance can be even more substantial.**

The **tax office** (*ufficio delle imposte*) provides a lot of help and advice over the internet. It is, not surprisingly, almost all in Italian, however.

It is probably simplest to arrange for an **accountant** (*commercialista*) to complete and file your various tax returns, as these are complicated and in Italian. There are many different deadlines for payment of the various taxes (though fewer than a few years ago since some taxes have been scrapped or amalgamated).

The Italian tax system is composed of two main types of taxes: **direct taxes** and **indirect taxes**. The distinction between the two is broadly the same as in the UK or USA. Non-residents will pay applicable indirect taxes in, generally, the same way as a resident, but they are treated very differently when it comes to direct taxation.

# Indriect Taxes: Local Italian Taxes

These taxes payable fall into various categories.

## Value Added Tax (VAT)

VAT is charged on any supply or service deemed to be made or rendered within the Italian territory. The ordinary VAT rate is set at 20 per cent. There are reduced rates of 4.5 per cent and 10 per cent on basic products.

## Transfer Tax (*Imposta di Registro*)

Transfer tax is due on specific contracts if made in Italy and on contracts, including those made abroad, regarding the transfer or leasing of businesses or immovable property (real estate) in Italy. The taxable base and the rates applicable depend on the nature of the contracts and on the status of the parties.

When transferring immovable property (real estate – including land, houses and apartments), **cadastral** and **mortgage taxes** also apply. These are in relation to the formal transfer or ownership in the public register.

Transfer tax, cadastral and mortgage taxes are a fixed sum of €129.11 on transfers of immovable properties subject to VAT. For non-VAT transfers there is transfer tax at rates from 4 per cent to 15 per cent, depending on the type of real property.

## ICI (*Imposta Comunale sugli Immobili*)

Any owner, resident or non-resident, of real properties located within Italian territory must pay this **annual municipal tax** on immovable property. The taxable base is the estimated value for the type and class of immovable property, as determined by the cadastral office. The municipality where the property is located sets the tax rate at not less than 0.04 per cent, and no more than 0.07 per cent of the base. The tax is raised and spent by the town hall (*municipio*) of the area where you live.

It is calculated on the basis of the notional rental value (*valore catastale*) of your property. You can appeal against the valuation decision, but the sums involved are usually so small it is not worthwhile.

These taxes are generally low, perhaps £100 for a country cottage or £300 for an apartment in an average area.

## Refuse Tax (*Tassa Rifiuti*)

Rubbish collection charges are, in some areas, raised separately; *see* p.192.

## Other Local Taxes

Town halls can also raise taxes for other projects and to cover shortfalls. You will also pay **car tax** (*bollo auto*), **scooter tax** (*bollo moto*) and a variety of other asset-focused taxes – including **TV tax** – if you possess these assets in Italy.

# Other Indirect Taxes

## Inheritance Tax

Inheritance tax was abolished in 2001. There is a strong feeling that this is a political gimmick – or that it can't be afforded – and that it may well be reinstated post-Berlusconi. It is therefore worth looking at the rules prevailing before October 2001.

If you were not domiciled in Italy, then inheritance tax was paid in Italy only on the value of any assets in Italy as at the date of your death. If you were domiciled in Italy, then inheritance tax was paid in Italy on the value of any assets that you owned anywhere in the world at the date of your death.

The tax was an inheritance tax rather than, as in the UK, an estate tax. That is, the tax was calculated by reference to each individual's inheritance rather than on the basis of the estate as a whole. Thus two people each inheriting part of the estate would each pay their own tax. Even if they each inherited the same amount, the tax they paid on the sum received might have been been different, depending on their personal circumstances.

The overall value of the part of the estate you inherited was calculated in accordance with guidelines laid down by the tax authorities. Assets were generally valued as at the date of the death. The value was declared by the person who inherited but was subject to challenge by the tax authorities.

Any debts (including mortgage or overdraft) were deducted from the asset values. Some gifts – mainly to the state and various charitable organisations – were partly tax-exempt.

The tax rates on the taxable amount of any gift to you depended on your relationship to the deceased and the amount you inherited.

The tax was calculated in slices. The basic tax was paid in every case. If there was more than one beneficiary, it was split between them pro rata to the value of their inheritance.

Also additional tax might have been be payable. The rate depended on your relationship to the deceased. No additional tax was payable if you were the spouse, child or parent of the deceased.

- Group A – brothers and sisters and direct relatives.

- Group B – relatives closer than the fourth degree.

- Group C – other more distant relatives and unrelated persons – including common law wives and gay partners.

E.g. a gift to a stranger (who was the sole beneficiary) of €70,000 used to bear tax at three different rates:

- First €5,000 – tax-free

- Next €45,000 – 6 per cent

- Balance to €70,000 – 8 per cent

You will see that large estates carried a high rate of tax – up to 60 per cent (27 per cent plus additional tax of 33 per cent) if left to people in Group C.

The tax was due at the time of accepting the inheritance by signing the deed of acceptance of inheritance.

## Inheritance Tax

| Gift from | Up to | Basic Tax | Group A | Group B | Group C |
|---|---|---|---|---|---|
| | | | | Additional Tax | |
| €0 | €5,000 | 0% | 0% | 0% | 0% |
| €5,000 | €50,000 | 0% | 0% | 3% | 6% |
| €50,000 | €125,000 | 0% | 3% | 3% | 8% |
| €125,000 | €175,000 | 0% | 6% | 9% | 12% |
| €175,000 | €250,000 | 7% | 10% | 13% | 18% |
| €250,000 | €400,000 | 10% | 15% | 19% | 23% |
| €400,000 | €775,000 | 15% | 20% | 24% | 28% |
| €775,000 | €1,550,000 | 22% | 24% | 26% | 28% |
| €1,550,000 | No limit | 27% | 25% | 27% | 33% |

Note: This table was prepared before any euro values for this tax existed. It has therefore been converted from the old lire values. It should therefore be checked.

**Note**: whatever the situation in Italy, if you are still UK-domiciled (*see* pp.151–4), all the assets will have to be declared for the purposes of UK taxation. Double taxation relief will apply, so you will not pay the same tax twice. UK tax is not further considered in this book.

## Gift Tax

Taxes on gifts were also, in general, abolished in 2001. Only gifts made to persons not having a close blood relationship with the donor and where the value of the gift is above €180,760 are subject to tax. *See* the section on the old inheritance tax for details.

## Withholding Taxes

There are three main withholding taxes deducted at source on certain payments: dividend withholding tax, withholding tax on interest, and withholding tax on royalties.

### Dividends

In principle, dividends paid to **Italian-resident individuals** from non-substantial (i.e. minority stake) participation in Italian corporations are subject to a 12.5 per cent final withholding tax. Dividends from substantial participations in Italian corporations are not subject to withholding tax.

Dividends paid to **Italian-resident corporations**, or to **Italian permanent establishments of non-resident corporations**, are not subject to withholding tax.

Dividends paid to **non-resident corporations** without an Italian permanent establishment are subject to a 27 per cent final withholding tax. The withholding tax rate is reduced to 12.5 per cent for dividends from saving shares. Reduced rates are possible under any double taxation treaties that Italy has concluded with the recipients' country of residence.

This withholding tax is *not* due, in line with the EU Parent-Subsidiary Directive, on **dividends paid by an Italian resident corporation to its EU parent company**. The benefit is subject to the parent's current ownership's dating back at least one year and to its holding no less than 25 per cent of the Italian subsidiary's share capital.

### Interest Payments

Interest from bank accounts and deposits, certain bonds and similar securities are subject to withholding tax at rates of 27 per cent or 12.5 per cent. These taxes, if any, on interest received by **Italian residents** generally consist of an advance payment of income tax due by the recipients. As such, gross interest must be included in the recipient's tax base and the withholding tax deducted from the aggregate taxable income.

If **non-Italian-residents** receive interest from bank accounts and deposits through an Italian permanent establishment, no withholding tax is due.

Interest and other profits from certain bonds issued by the state, by banks and by Italian-listed corporations are subject to a 12.5 per cent substitute tax.

If **Italian-resident corporations** receive interest from such bonds, no substitute tax is due. If residents in countries listed in the so-called 'White List', i.e. those with adequate exchanges of information with the Italian tax authorities, receive interest from such bonds, not through an Italian permanent establishment, no tax is due.

Interest from loans received by **residents other than business entities** is subject to a 12.5 per cent (27 per cent for recipients resident in countries listed in the so-called 'Black List', i.e. tax haven countries) advance withholding tax. If **non-residents** receive interest from loans, not through an Italian permanent establishment, the withholding tax is a final payment of tax – in other words, it exhausts your potential tax liability in respect of such payments. This can be a very useful planning tool.

The withholding tax rate may be reduced under the applicable double taxation treaty.

In line with the provisions of the EU Directive on Interest and Royalties, the withholding tax on interest payments is not levied if these payments are made by Italian-resident companies, or by Italian permanent establishments of EU-resident companies, to either affiliated companies or permanent establishments of companies resident for tax purposes in another EU Member State. In line with the Directive, the benefit also applies if certain shareholding requirements are satisfied.

### Royalties

Royalties paid to **Italian-resident corporations**, or to **Italian permanent establishments of non-resident corporations**, are not subject to withholding tax. Royalty payments to **non-Italian residents** are subject to a 30 per cent final withholding tax, sometimes on a tax base may discounted by 25 per cent.

The withholding tax rate may be reduced under the applicable double taxation treaty.

In line with the provisions of the EU Directive on Interest and Royalties, the withholding tax on royalty payments is not levied if these payments are made by Italian-resident companies, or by Italian permanent establishments of EU-resident companies, to companies or permanent establishments of companies resident for tax purposes in another EU Member State. In line with the Directive, the benefit also applies if certain shareholding requirements are satisfied.

## Direct Taxes Payable in Italy – Non-residents

In general a person who is non-resident for tax purposes has few contacts with the Italian tax system and they are fairly painless.

Please bear in mind the complexity of the Italian tax system. What follows can only be a very brief summary of the position.

## Personal Income Tax (*IRE*)

Personal income tax is regulated by the Consolidated Tax Code or CTC (*Testo Unico delle Imposte sui Redditi*). Italian-resident individuals are subject to *IRE* on their worldwide income but non-resident individuals are subject to *IRE* only on 'Italian' income.

As a non-resident you will generally only pay tax on the following:

- **income generated from land and buildings located in Italy. If you own a building in Italy and let it out, the Italian government collects the first wedge of tax from you. Note that if you are letting out your property you will usually have the normal deductions or allowances to set against your income.**
- **income from Italian securities and capital invested in Italy.**
- **income from business activities in Italy.**
- **earned income if you are employed or self-employed in Italy.**

You must file a tax return (available from the tax office's website). This must generally be filed by 30 June for the period ending 31 December of the previous year. Tax on your income for the year 1 January 2005 to 31 December 2005 is declared and paid in May/June 2006.

The Law of Reform, which came into force on 1 January 2005, provides for personal income tax rates as follows:

- **23 per cent for income up to €26,000, with some exemptions.**
- **33 per cent for income between €26,000 and €33,500.**
- **39 per cent for income over €33,500.**

In addition, a 4 per cent 'solidarity surcharge tax' is due on the portion of your income exceeding €100.000.

## Corporate Income Tax (*IRES*)

Corporate income tax is regulated by the Consolidated Tax Code (CTC). Italian-resident companies are subject to *IRES* on their worldwide income but non-resident companies are subject to *IRES* only on Italian source income. The flat tax rate on taxable income is 33 per cent. The tests of company residence and these taxes are not considered further here.

## Regional Tax on Business Activities (*IRAP*)

The regional tax on business activities (*imposta regionale sulle attività produttive; IRAP*) is a local tax applied to the production generated in each taxable period by persons carrying out business activities in a given Italian region. Non-Italian-resident corporations are subject to *IRAP* only on the production generated via their permanent establishments in Italy. It pays for healthcare for you and your employees. It is likely soon to be abolished or at least diminished in importance.

## Taxes on Capital Gains

Any gain is taxed as if it were income for the year in question. Payment of the tax on the gain can usually be spread over five years.

• **On the sale of real estate (***imposta comunale sull'incremento di immobili; INVIM***)**: Unless you bought your house before 1993 and sold it before 2003 there is no capital gains tax on the sale of real estate.

• **On stocks and shares**: The gain (the difference between the sale price and the purchase price adjusted to take account of inflation since the date of purchase) will usually be taxed at 12.5 per cent. You can offset any losses.

• **Other gains**: You will pay tax on the capital gain you make on the sale of any other capital asset, less various exempt items.

# Direct Taxes Payable in Italy – Residents

The Italian tax system is very complex. What follows can only be a very brief summary of the position. The detail is immensely complicated and is made worse because it is so different from what you are used to. This section is written with reference to the person retiring to Italy. Issues arising out of employment or self-employment are not considered in detail.

Remember that Italy is (taken overall, not just in relation to income tax) a high-tax society. Whether for this reason or out of an independence of spirit, many people suffer from selective amnesia as far as the taxman is concerned and significantly under-declare their income. Probably 30 per cent of Italian people and 50 per cent of foreign residents do this. This is dangerous. The penalties are severe. There are, however, quite legitimate tax-saving devices that you can use to reduce your liabilities. These issues are best addressed before you move to Italy, as there are then many more possibilities open to you.

## Personal Income Tax (*IRE*)

Personal income tax is regulated by the Consolidated Tax Code or CTC (*Testo Unico delle Imposte sui Redditi*). Italian-resident individuals are subject to *IRE* on their worldwide income – including benefits in kind – from most sources.

• income from real estate.
• income from capital, e.g. dividends and interest.

- income from employment, e.g. salaries and wages.

- income from independent work, e.g. professional fees.

- business income.

- miscellaneous income, e.g. capital gains from disposal of shares and securities.

Each of these categories of income has different rules for determining the amount of that income that is taxable. The overall taxable income equals the sum of the net income of each category. Exempt income and income subject to final withholding taxes, e.g. interest from bonds or dividends, fall outside the computation of the overall taxable income.

As far as **income from employment** is concerned, taxable income includes any compensation, in cash or in kind – including gifts – received during the taxable period in connection with the employment activity in question. Some fringe benefits for employees may not be considered taxable income. These include:

- **education and training provided by the employer and available as a benefit to all employees in a particular category.**

- **certain recreational activities.**

- **employers' or employees' contributions to funds for medical treatment, in accordance with collective work agreements and regulations of law, to an upper limit.**

- **voluntary payments to pension or insurance funds, to an upper limit of EUR 1291 (if signed before 1st January 2001).**

- **a refund to an employee in respect of travel and accommodation expenses incurred on business, subject to limit for travel inside Italy and for travel abroad.**

- **an employer's contribution to meals at work to an upper daily limit.**

- **shares offered to an employee at a price that is below the regular price if the shares have been held for at least 3 years from the date of purchase *and* the shares are offered to all employees *and* the profit on realising the shares does not exceed a limit in any one year.**

Certain types of income, such as compensation for the termination of employment, are taxed separately at reduced rates. In some cases, employment income deriving from an activity performed abroad is taxable, regardless of the actual salary received, on the basis of notional salaries determined annually by ministerial decree.

Progressive **tax rates** apply, with a minimum tax rate of 23 per cent and a maximum rate of 39 per cent. In addition a 4 per cent solidarity surcharge tax is due for the portion of income exceeding €100,000 (*see* table, overleaf). These rates are applied to the overall taxable income after subtracting certain types of

## Income Tax Rates – 2005 (payable 2006)

The tax payable is calculated using the following table.

The tax is calculated in tranches. That is, you calculate the tax payable on each complete slice in turn and then the tax at the highest applicable rate on any excess.

| Income from (€) | To (€) | Rate (%) |
|---|---|---|
| 0 | 26,000 | 23 |
| 26,000 | 33,500 | 33 |
| 33,500 | 100,000 | 39 |
| 100,000 | No upper limit | 43 |

income taxed separately, including (generally) any income taxed abroad. The resulting figure is the **gross IRE** tax payable.

The **net IRE** due to the tax man is obtained by subtracting certain additional tax deductions from the gross IRE (e.g. interest on loans for the purchase of your main dwelling, 19 per cent of specific medical expenses, maintenance payments for a dependent spouse or child, university tuition fees, allowances for a dependant spouse (€3,200) and dependant children (€2,700–3,400), health insurance premiums and burial expenses).

Strangely, if it is more favourable to do so, taxpayers can opt to apply the tax regime in force in 2002 or 2004 to the income tax due for the period 2005!

For the **salaried employee**, there is a type of **PAYE** in operation whereby your likely tax liability is collected in 12 equal instalments with a final annual adjustment either way.

A **self-employed person** must pre-pay income tax that will be offset against the actual liability shown on filing the annual return. The advance payment is determined on the basis of the return made for the previous year. In the event of a new business, the advance will be calculated on the basis of estimates made by the owner of the business.

## Social Security

As far as **employees** are concerned, the employer is obliged to deduct tax at source from an employee and to make additional contributions to social security. The employer's contribution is between 30–37 per cent of the salary and the employee's contribution is usually 9 per cent of the salary.

A **self-employed person** pays at a rate between 10–13 per cent, with an upper limit that changes from year to year.

A **foreign resident**, if self-employed in Italy, pays at the rate of 13 per cent.

# Corporate Income Tax (*IRES*)

As of January 1, 2004, corporations are subject to a new set of tax rules enacted by the government in compliance with the principles of the Law of Reform. Taxes payable include 'normal' items of profit and profit arising from the disposal of assets – i.e. capital gains. Capital gains are included in the tax base of the taxable period in which they are realised or, if the relevant assets have been held for at least three years, in equal instalments in the year of realisation and, in the following years, up to the fourth. The same rules apply to shares or participations, other than those qualifying for the participation exemption regime, entered into the last three balance sheets as financial assets.

Corporate income tax is regulated by the Consolidated Tax Code (CTC). Italian-resident corporations are subject to *IRES* on their worldwide income. The flat tax rate on taxable income is 33 per cent.

These taxes are not considered further here.

# Regional Tax on Business Activities (*IRAP*)

Regional tax on business activities (*imposta regionale sulle attività produttive; IRAP*), is a local tax applied on the value of the production generated in each taxable period by persons carrying out business activities in a given Italian region. It pays for healthcare for you and your employees. It is due for abolition.

# Taxes on Wealth

There is no Italian wealth tax.

# Taxes on Capital Gains

Any gain is taxed as if it were income for the year in question. Payment of the tax on the gain can usually be spread over five years.

• **On the sale of real estate (*imposta comunale sull'incremento di immobili; INVIM*)**: Unless you bought your house before 1993 and sold it before 2003 there is no capital gains tax on the sale of real estate.

• **On stocks and shares**: The gain (the difference between the sale price and the purchase price adjusted to take account of inflation since the date of purchase) will usually be taxed at 12.5 per cent. If the gain is from the sale of a company quoted on the stock exchange and you sell more than 2 per cent of the capital or the company is not quoted on the stock exchange and you sell more than 20 per cent of the capital, the rate is 27 per cent. You can offset any losses.

• **Other gains**: You will pay tax on the capital gain you make on the sale of any other capital asset, less various exempt items.

# New Residents

New residents will be liable to tax on their worldwide income and gains from the date they arrive in Italy.

Until that day they will only have to pay Italian tax on their income if it is derived from assets in Italy.

The most important thing to understand about taking up residence in Italy (and abandoning UK tax residence) is that it gives you superb opportunities for tax planning and, in particular, for restructuring your affairs to minimise what can otherwise be penal rates of taxation in Italy. To do this you need good advice at an early stage – preferably several months before you intend to move.

# Tax Returns and Payments

Taxpayers must report their annual income to the tax authorities. **Italian-resident corporations** must, generally, file their tax returns within 10 months of the end of the relevant financial year. **Italian-resident individuals** must file their tax returns within 10 months of the end of the tax period.

An **individual whose only income is from a salary** is not obliged to file an annual tax return. His employer deducts tax from the employee and transfers the payment immediately to the tax authorities on a monthly basis. The same rules apply for resident individuals and non-resident individuals.

A **self-employed Individual** is obliged to pay 100 per cent of the tax forecast for a year, or an amount that is the equivalent of 98 per cent of the tax paid in the previous year, whichever is the lower, This pre-payment is made in two instalments: 40 per cent of the total is paid by June 20th and the remaining 60 per cent is paid on November 30th.

The **date for filing an annual return** for an individual who is obliged to file – i.e. an individual with income other than just a salary – is July 31st. Fines are imposed for arrears in filing an annual return at the rate of 120–240 per cent of the tax, depending on the length of time that the return is in arrears.

A **limited company** is obliged to submit financial statements within 30 days of the date of approval of the statements. Up until the date of approval of the statements, the company is obliged to pay the tax due for the previous year *plus* 40 per cent on account of the tax forecast for the current year.

It is worth noting that, for income tax purposes, the **statutory period of limitation** is usually 4 years from the end of the year for which the income tax return is filed. The statutory period is extended by one year if no income tax return has been filed. The effect of the limitation period is that, if you don't file a tax return, your liability to pay the taxes due expires after 5 years.

# The Double Taxation Treaty

The detailed effect of double taxation treaties depends on the two countries involved. Whilst treaties may be similar in concept they can differ in detail. Only the effect of the Italy/UK treaty is considered here.

The main points of relevance to residents are these.

• **Any income from letting property in the UK will normally be outside the scope of Italian taxation and, instead, will be taxed in the UK.**

• **Pensions received from the UK – except for government pensions – will be taxed in Italy but not in the UK.**

• **Government pensions will continue to be taxed in the UK but are not taxed in Italy, nor do they count when assessing the level of your income or when calculating the rate of tax payable on your income.**

• **You will normally not be required to pay UK capital gains tax on gains made after you settle in Italy except in relation to real estate located in the UK.**

• **If you are taxed on a gift made outside Italy, then the tax paid will usually be offset against the gift tax due in Italy.**

• **If you pay tax on an inheritance outside Italy, the same will apply.**

Double tax treaties are detailed and need to be read in the light of your personal circumstances.

# Tax Planning Generally

Do it, and do it as soon as possible. Every day you delay will make it more difficult to get the results you are looking for.

There are many possibilities for tax planning for someone moving to Italy.

Here are some points worth considering.

• **Time your departure from the UK to get the best out of the UK tax system.**

• **Think, in particular, about when to make any capital gain if you are selling your business or other assets in the UK.**

• **Arrange your affairs so that there is a gap between leaving the UK (for tax purposes) and becoming resident in Italy. That gap can be used to make all sorts of beneficial changes to the structure of your finances.**

• **Think about trusts. They can be very effective tax-planning vehicles.**

• **Think about giving away some of your assets. You will not have to pay wealth tax on the value given away and the recipients will generally not have to pay either gift or inheritance tax on the gift.**

## Investment Incentives

It is worth remembering that, as in all high tax societies, there are substantial incentives available for people and businesses investing in Italy. The reason we mention them here is that they are a sort of 'negative taxation'.

The rules are complex – and change regularly – and the subject is beyond the scope of this book. Suffice it to say that, as a general rule, there is no discrimination between benefits granted to foreign investors and those granted to local investors. The benefits are given in the form of investment grants, loans at reduced interest or a state guarantee for exporters. Occasionally, the benefit is granted in the form of a combination of an investment grant and low-interest loans, depending on the geographical location of the investment and the size of the investing company. In areas hit by unemployment, particularly in the south, an exemption is granted, subject to certain conditions, from corporation tax and local tax for a period of 10 years. Companies that invest a sum in excess of the average investment for the 5 previous years are eligible for a deduction from taxable income to the limit of the excess investment. Subject to terms and the geographical area, an investment grant of up to 65 per cent of the investment may be obtained on investing in fixed assets. In no case shall the benefit exceed 50 per cent of the taxable income. Visit the excellent **www.InvestInItaly.com** website – in English – for up-to-date details.

# Inheritance

## The Italian Inheritance Rules

The Italians cannot do just as they please with their property when they die. Inheritance rules apply.

These rules for Italians are much more restrictive than the rules under English law. Certain groups of people have (almost) automatic rights to inherit a part of your property.

Fortunately, if you are not Italian you can dispose of your property in whatever way your national law allows. For British people this is, basically, as they please.

## Making a Will

It is always best to make an Italian will. If you do not, your UK will should be treated as valid in Italy and will be used to distribute your estate. This is a false economy, as the cost of implementing the UK will is much higher than the cost of implementing an Italian will, and the disposal of your estate set out in your UK will is often a tax disaster in Italy.

If you are not a resident in Italy, your Italian will should state that it only applies to immovable property in Italy. The rest of your property – including movable property in Italy – will be disposed of in accordance with English law and the provisions of your UK will. If you are domiciled in Italy (as to the meaning of which, *see* pp.151–4) you should make an Italian will disposing of all your assets wherever they are located. If you make an Italian will covering only immovable property in Italy, you should modify your UK will so as to exclude any immovable property located in Italy.

Always use a lawyer to advise as to the contents of your will and draft it. Lawyers love people who make home-made wills. They make a fortune from dealing with their estates because the wills are often inadequately drafted and produce lots of expensive problems.

### What if I Don't Make a Will of Any Kind?

A person who dies without a will dies intestate.

This gets complicated. Will the UK rules as to what happens in this event apply (because you are British) or will it be the Italian rules? This gives rise to many happy hours of argument by lawyers and tax officials. All at your (or your heirs') expense.

It is much cheaper to make a will.

# Investments

## The Need to Do Something

Most of us don't like making investment decisions. They make our heads hurt. They make us face up to unpleasant things – like taxes and death. We don't really understand what we are doing, what the options are or what is best. We don't know who we should trust to give us advice. We know we ought to do something, but it will wait until next week – or maybe the week after. Until then our present arrangements will have to do.

If you are moving to live overseas you must review your investments. Your current arrangements are likely to be financially disastrous – and may even be illegal.

## What Are You Worth?

Most of us are, in financial terms, worth more than we think. When we come to move abroad and have to think about these things it can come as a shock.

Take a piece of paper and list your actual and potential assets (*see* checklist overleaf).

## Checklist: What Are You Worth?

|  | Value € | Value £s |
|---|---|---|
| **Current Assets** | | |
| Main home | | |
| Holiday home | | |
| Contents of main home | | |
| Contents of holiday home | | |
| Car | | |
| Boat | | |
| Bank accounts | | |
| Other cash-type investments | | |
| Bonds, etc. | | |
| Stocks and shares | | |
| PEPs | | |
| Tessas | | |
| ISAs | | |
| SIPPs | | |
| Other | | |
| Value of your business | | |
| Value of share options | | |
| | | |
| **Future Assets** | | |
| Value of share options | | |
| Personal/company pension – likely lump sum | | |
| Potential inheritances or other accretions | | |
| Value of endowment mortgages on maturity | | |
| Other | | |

This will give you an idea as to the amount you are worth now and, just as importantly, what you are likely to be worth in the future. Your investment plans should take into account both figures.

## Who Should Look After Your Investments?

You may already have an investment adviser. You may be very happy with the service you have received. They are unlikely to be able to help you once you have gone to live in Italy. They will almost certainly not have the knowledge to do so.

They will know about neither the Italian investment that might be of interest to you or, probably, of many of the 'offshore' products that might be of interest to someone no longer resident in the UK. Even if they have some knowledge of these things, they are likely to be thousands of miles from where you will be living.

Nor is it a simple question of selecting a new local (Italian) adviser once you have moved. They will usually know little about the UK aspects of your case or about the UK tax and inheritance rules that could still have some importance for you.

Choosing an investment adviser competent to deal with you once you are in Italy is not easy. By all means seek guidance from your existing adviser. Ask for guidance from others who have already made the move. Do some research. Meet the potential candidates. Are you comfortable with them? Do they share your approach to life? Do they have the necessary experience? Is their performance record good? How are they regulated? What security/bonding/guarantees can they offer you? How will they be paid for their work – fees or commission? If commission, what will that formula mean they are making from you in 'real money' rather than percentages?

Above all be careful. There are lots of very dubious 'financial advisers' operating in the popular tourist areas of Italy. Some are totally incompetent. Some are crooks, seeking simply to separate you from your money as cleanly as possible. Fortunately there are also some excellent and highly professional advisers with good track records. Make sure you choose one of these.

## Where Should You Invest?

For British people the big issue is whether they should keep their sterling investments.

Most British people will have investments that are largely sterling-based. Even if they are, for example, a Far Eastern fund they will probably be denominated in sterling and they will pay out dividends, etc., in sterling.

You will be spending euros.

As the value of the euro fluctuates against sterling, the value of your investments will go up and down. That, of itself, isn't too important because the value won't crystallise unless you sell. What does matter is that the revenue you generate from those investments (rent, interest, dividends, etc.) will fluctuate in value. Take, for example, an investment that generated you £10,000 a year. Then think of that income in spending power. In the last three years the euro has varied in value from €1 = £0.53 to €1 = £0.73. Sometimes, therefore, your income in euros would have been around €18,900 a year and at others it would have been around €13,700 a year. This makes a huge difference to your standard of living *based solely on exchange rate variations*.

This is unacceptable, particularly as you will inevitably have to accept this problem in so far as your pension is concerned.

In general terms, investments paying out in euros are preferable if you live in a euro country.

# Trusts

Trusts are an important weapon in the hands of a person or people going to live in Italy.

Trusts offer the following potential benefits.

- **They allow you to put part of your assets in the hands of trustees so that they no longer belong to you for wealth tax or inheritance tax purposes.**

- **They allow you to receive only the income you need (rather than all the income generated by those assets) so keeping the extra income out of sight for income tax purposes.**

- **They allow a very flexible vehicle for investment purposes.**

So how do they work?

After leaving the UK (and before moving to Italy) you reorganise your affairs by giving a large part of your assets to 'trustees'. These are normally a professional trust company located in a low-tax regime. Needless to say, the choice of a reliable trustee is critical.

Those trustees hold the asset not for their own benefit but 'in trust' for whatever purposes you established when you made the gift. It could, for example, be to benefit a local hospital or, more likely, school or it could be to benefit you and your family. If the trust is set up properly in the light of the requirements of Italian law, then those assets will no longer be treated as yours for tax purposes.

On your death the assets are not yours to leave to your children (or whoever) and so do not (subject to any local anti-avoidance legislation) carry inheritance tax. Similarly, the income from those assets is not your income. If some of it is given to you it may be taxed as your income, but the income that is not given to you will not be taxed in Italy and, because the trust will be located in a nil or low-tax regime, it will not be taxed elsewhere either.

The detail of the arrangements is vitally important. They must be set up precisely to comply with Italian tax law. If you do not do this they will not work as intended.

Trustees can manage your investments in (virtually) whatever way you stipulate when you set up the trust. You can give the trustees full discretion to do as they please or you can specify precisely how your money is to be used. There are particular types of trusts and special types of investments that trusts can make that can be especially beneficial in Italy.

Trusts can be beneficial even to Italian resident people of modest means – say £350,000. It is certainly worth investing a little money to see if they can be of use to you, as the tax savings can run to many thousands of pounds. If you are thinking of trusts as an investment vehicle and tax-planning measure you must take advice early – months before you are thinking of moving to Italy. Otherwise it will be too late.

## Keeping Track of Your Investments

Whatever you decide to do about investments – put them in a trust, appoint investment managers to manage them in your own name or manage them yourself – you should always keep an up-to-date list of your assets and investments *and tell your family where to find it*. Make a file. By all means have a computer file but print off a good old-fashioned paper copy. Keep it in an obvious place known to your family. Keep it with your will and the deeds to your house. Also keep in it either the originals of bank account books, share certificates, etc., or a note of where they are to be found.

As a lawyer it is very frustrating – and expensive for the client – when, after the parents' death, the children come in with a suitcase full of correspondence and old cheque books. It all has to be gone through and all those old banks contacted lest there should be £1,000,000 lurking in a forgotten account. There never is and it wastes a lot of time and money.

# Conclusion

Buying a home in Italy – whether to use as a holiday home, as an investment or to live in permanently – is as safe as buying one in the UK.

The rules may appear complicated. Our rules would if you were an Italian person coming to this country. That apparent complexity is often no more than lack of familiarity.

There are tens of thousands of British people who have bought homes in Italy. Most have had no real problems. Most have enjoyed years of holidays in Italy. Many have seen their property rise substantially in value. Many are now thinking of retiring to Italy.

For a trouble-free time you simply need to keep your head and to seek advice from experts who can help you make the four basic decisions.

- **Who should own the property?**
- **What am I going to do about inheritance?**
- **What am I going to do about controlling my potential tax liabilities?**
- **If I am going to live in Italy, what do I do about my investments?**

If you don't like lawyers, remember that they make far more money out of sorting out the problems you get into by not doing these things than by giving you this basic advice!

# Settling In

07

Now that you own a piece of Italian property, you can start to enjoy what so many people call *la dolce vita*. Life is certainly sweet in Italy, generally, but the saccharine content definitely increases once you understand the ins and outs of Italian services, institutions and society. Not understanding the basics can quickly lead to a very sour existence.

The best, and only, way to fully understand is through the gift of communication. Learn Italian. Once you have learned the language, or can at least converse on a basic level, the country's charm, intricacies and riches will be yours for the picking. This romantic language is a delight to study and its melodic syllables will soothe your lips like ice cream on a hot summer day. Unlike the French, who have an infamous aversion to mispronunciation and twisted grammar, there is no bigger compliment to an Italian than a foreigner who makes the effort to speak in their tongue. Not knowing the language will be a dead weight carried around until you do. Knowing it will set the seal on your settling-in process.

# Making the Move

As you pack your boxes, close up your house in Britain and prepare to make the move to Italy, make sure you have considered the following.

- Is your paperwork in order, including visas and stay permits if required (*see* pp.16–28)?

- Is your passport valid throughout your intended stay in Italy? Keep photocopies of your passport at home and with you, as they are often required when compiling official documentation and will be invaluable in getting a quick replacement should your passport go missing at any time.

- Pets should be accompanied by a Certificate of Good Health supplied by your local vet and translated into Italian (although officials are familiar with English-language ones and rarely put up a fuss). Your pet should also have had a rabies vaccination at least one month prior to departure (but no longer than one year prior). However, *see* pp.221–3 for details of the legal requirements should you wish to take your pet back to the UK.

- If you bring a computer from England, make sure it has the correct plug adapters. You can sign up with an Internet service provider once you get to Italy (*see* pp.196–8) but, if you choose to stay with your current provider, check that you won't incur the painfully high surcharge often associated with connecting from abroad.

- If you are moving permanently, notify your credit card companies and mailing lists of your change of address.

- Also contact the post office, to forward your mail to your new address.

• If you intend to bring large amounts of money – for the restoration of your new house, for example – you should consider opening a *conto estero* with an Italian bank branch office at home. A *conto estero* allows you to keep your savings in sterling and euros.

• If you have regular debts to pay in England, such as a mortgage, arrange to prepay them or request that payments be made automatically on your behalf by your bank.

• Make sure you have access to your British tax forms before they are due.

• Terminate or suspend your utility contracts back home.

• Set up a British account with an overseas courier service if you plan on doing a lot of shipping. It will cost you less than an Italian account and is easier to set up.

• Bring books or sheets of British postage stamps with you. You will need them if you have to send self-addressed stamped envelopes to the UK.

• Check that your insurance company covers you overseas and, if you will be away for some time, arrange a last round of dentist and medical appointments before your departure.

• Make a list of any medical conditions from which you suffer, such as diabetes or allergies. Have this translated into Italian.

• Take ample supplies of prescription medicine – from painkillers to the Pill – that you will not be able to fill in Italy before you have signed on with an Italian doctor. Or arrange with your UK doctor for repeat prescriptions and for someone to fill them and send them to you while you are away.

• If you are particularly attached to any beauty or other products you can't find in Italy, stock up before leaving.

• Bring plug adapters and power surge protectors that fit your appliances. Don't bring a television set, as it won't work in Italy.

• Stock up on English-language software since it is difficult to find in Italy, and bring your English computer keyboard since Italian ones have all the letters in the wrong places, and you'll discover the true meaning of cyber-torture.

# Removal Companies

As a British or other European Union citizen you will be able to take your possessions with you to Italy without paying taxes or customs duties. All foreigners should have certain documents in order before they can move their household goods to Italy, such as a *codice fiscale* and a valid *permesso di soggiorno* (*see* pp.16–28). Non-EU citizens may also be asked for a *nulla osta* (no obstacle document) if they intend to import electronic goods like a stereo.

## Customs

European Union nationals can import an unlimited amount of goods for personal use. Non-EU nationals must pass through Italian customs at the airport (there are customs stops on road and rail borders but, since the Schengen Convention came into effect, these are usually unmanned), and you may not bring more than 200 cigarettes, 100 cigars, a litre of spirits or three bottles of wine into Italy. Customs officials are more watchful for electronic goods in large quantities that they suspect may be for commercial use or resale. You are only allowed to bring a couple of cameras, a movie camera, 10 rolls of film for each, a taperecorder, radio, CD player (customs notices still read 'record players'), one canoe less than 5.5m in length, sports equipment for personal use and one television set (although, as mentioned above, the latter won't work anyway).

You will also be required to produce a full inventory list. You should give the moving company a photocopy of your passport, your *codice fiscale*, your *permesso di soggiorno* and the inventory. If you are a non-EU resident, give them the original *nulla osta*. If you can produce all of the above, the mover will get your goods through customs with no import duty.

If you cannot produce the above documentation, some moving companies can negotiate the payment of a bond to clear customs. Make sure you appoint a removal company that is an accredited customs clearing agent. All items you import to Italy must be for personal, not commercial use. That means you should not plan on selling them once in Italy.

For a list of removal firms, storage facilities and freight forwarders serving Italy, *see* **References**, p.264. For updates on new companies, consult the English *Yellow Pages* (**www.intoitaly.it**). This excellent phone book also has detailed listings for Rome, Florence, Genoa, Catania, Palermo, Bologna, Milan and Naples.

The alternative to a removal company is to move your goods yourself. You could pack everything into a truck or van and, with the Schengen Convention in place, you wouldn't have to produce any documentation whatsoever at the Italian border. If you are making a light move, you might be able to squeeze your belongings into suitcases for air travel and bring a bit over with each trip.

# Learning and Speaking Italian

Learning to speak Italian is a pleasure, not a chore. It's a seductive language with soft vowels and musical intonations that soften even the ugliest verbal exchanges. The grammar is not especially difficult if you know the basics of French or Spanish. Spelling is based on phonetics, so words are written just as they sound. Besides its appeal, Italian may be the world's most fun language.

You can illustrate colourful expressions with acrobatic arm gestures and circus-like facial expressions. Native speakers are thrilled when you speak to them in Italian and always respond with compliments or a gentle correction if needed. English is a much more difficult language to learn from scratch, as Italians are well aware, but if you make the effort, chances are you will inspire them to do the same. Italian is also a language that you will never stop learning. There are so many dialects, expressions and pronunciations that, even when you think you are totally fluent, you will chance on a word that seems total gibberish. The fun is in deciphering it all.

Some innocent mistakes do raise eyebrows. In general, English-speakers have a hard time mastering male versus female genders (remarking, for example, that something *non vale il pene* instead of *la pena* changes 'it's not worth the effort' into 'it's not worth a penis'). Double consonants are also difficult for many foreigners to decipher as is the awkward *'gli'* hissing sound created by contorting your tongue at the very back of your mouth. One foreign woman in Rome announced cheerfully at her neighbourhood bar that she would very much like to be served a *cappuccino e un cornuto* ('a cappuccino and a cuckold'). She meant *cornetto* for 'brioche' and, after providing the barmen with entertainment value for the morning, was served what she wanted (her breakfast, that is).

Dante Alighieri is credited as the father of modern, or standard, Italian because he was the first to put it in writing by penning his masterpiece *Divine Comedy*. That's why, today, people from Florence claim they speak the purest version of the language, but to people outside the Renaissance City, the Florentine inability to pronounce the letter 'c' is a linguistic deformation like all the others. Romans have a tendency to make double consonants sound like triple consonants – *cafffè* instead of *caffè*. People in Milan sound as though they're always whining, while those in Emilia–Romagna have a slight lisp. Venetians sound as if they will break into a falsetto before the end of their sentence and Neapolitans pepper their speech with an abundance of 'shh-shh' sounds. Sardinians speak slowly, enunciating each syllable over a painfully long period of time, while Sicilians, who also speak slowly, speed up the tempo by violently truncating consonants.

Besides varying pronunciations, Italy is home to thousands of dialects – some so unrecognisable that television broadcasts in them provide the rest of the nation with subtitles. There are towns within a few dozen kilometres of each other that literally communicate in different languages. Although television has done much to homogenise Italian, each region has its own dialect with its own cadence, vocabulary and sometimes different grammatical rules. Italy has also been heavily influenced by centuries of foreign invasions and immigration from distant lands. There are Spanish, French, German, Albanian and Arab words, depending on where you are. English has also had a profound influence

## Speak Arbëreshe?

Now you can learn this archaic form of Albanian in Sicily. The decision to include the language spoken across the Adriatic Sea and in parts of Sicily, Calabria and Puglia in academic curricula ends a decades-long battle to keep the language, with its singular phonetics and syntax structure, alive. 'I couldn't be happier,' says Nicolà Petta, who owns the Bar Kalinikta in the 7,000-inhabitant town of Piana degli Albanesi, about 20km (12 miles) from Palermo. The father of two children aged five and eight explains, 'We have always spoken our language at home but no one knows how to read or write it. Now they will.'

Indeed, Piana degli Albanesi is decorated with banners reading *po të mbahij Arbëreshë e të ruani gluhën tënë*, meaning 'keep Albanian roots strong and preserve our language'. Although teaching of the language in public schools was previously allowed on an experimental level, it is only since a 1999 law, passed to protect Italy's linguistic minorities, that resources for schoolrooms, teachers and books have become available. Five towns, all near Palermo and representing 15,000 Italo-Albanians, qualified for state funding. Citizens not only speak Arbëreshe, reflected in local last names and written on street signs, but many observe Byzantine rites based on the Christian Orthodox church. 'History has been kind to us, and our culture was never suppressed to the point of extinction during the past 600 years,' says historian Giuseppe Schiró di Modika, who has written the only Italian–Arbëreshe dictionary in existence.

Piana degli Albanesi, originally known as Hora e Arbëreshëvet, was founded in 1488 by a group of refugees from central-southern Albania fleeing a Turkish invasion. During Italy's Risorgimento, the Arbëreshë, or ethnic Albanians, in Sicily offered food and shelter to Giuseppe Garibaldi's troops. Over the centuries, Piana degli Albanesi has produced noted poets and writers, but one of its most famous sons became the nation's most secretive powerbroker. The late Enrico Cuccia, the man behind Milan's merchant bank Mediobanca, came from the Kuqi family, a very common surname that means 'red'. Another famous Cuccia was Chicco Cuccia, an alleged Mafia kingpin who wielded his power over dictator Benito Mussolini in 1939 by warning him 'not even a leaf moves here if I don't let it'.

on the modern language, as Italians voraciously borrow words to make themselves sound more authoritative and competent – even if the words are not exactly used the way they were intended. For example, television viewers are measured in units of *audience* and *fare il footing* is 'jogging.' Other English words have seeped into boardroom speech, such as *il manager*, *l'innovation* and *il know-how*. In all, Italy is home to six sub-languages, and some 30 linguistic minorities are protected under Italian law including Ladino (a language mixing Celtic roots and pure Latin, spoken in the far north). More obscure languages exist in the south.

Learning Italian is best done on the move, in conversations with your local shopkeepers and friends, but if you are looking for a more structured learning environment you could choose from one of the hundreds of Italian-language schools scattered throughout the peninsula from Catania to Como. Look at **www.intoitaly.it** for a list of schools nearest you. Many of these offer specialised courses for 'business Italian' or 'medical Italian'. Alternatively you could sign on with a private tutor in the UK for 'buying-a-house-in-Italy Italian' in advance of your home purchase plans. Many foreigners arrange conversation lessons with Italian friends. For example, you could sit on a park bench with an Italian and speak for 30 minutes in Italian followed by 30 minutes in English, or you could organise a language exchange after a cinema visit or as you collaborate to prepare a meal.

The nation's best language schools are located in Siena and Perugia. Both the Università per Stranieri di Siena and the Università per Stranieri di Perugia offer total-immersion courses that last three months. The courses cost about €800 and do not include accommodation. There are similar schools in Florence, Bologna, Bergamo, Genoa, Parma, Trento, Urbino and Rome. These schools also issue Italy's most prestigious diploma, called the **Certificate of Italian as a Second Language**. There are four levels of CILS: *principiante* for beginners, two levels of *intermedio* (intermediate), and an *avanzato* (advanced) certificate. Most other schools advertise their own diplomas, awarded at the end of their courses, but if you need to demonstrate fluency for any official reason, the CILS is the most respected. Other good schools with branches all over the country are the Dante Alighieri, the Leonardo da Vinci and the Galileo Galilei. These are sponsored by the state.

# Shopping

You may remember from the beginning of this book that Italians prefer slow to fast and quality to quantity. Nothing illustrates those tendencies better than Italy's shopping and retail scene. This mundane exercise is different in every way from what we are accustomed to at home. Shopping is not about speed. It's not about convenience. And it's not about stocking your cupboards with enough supplies to last throughout the winter. It's about finding the perfect head of broccoli, haggling with the vendor over price, and examining the specimen for a few minutes longer to confirm that it is the one marked by destiny to be united with your hob. It's about going to as many stores as items on your shopping list: one for milk, one for bread and one for cheese. It's about paying €40 for a golf-ball-sized bottle of balsamic vinegar and jealously conserving its precious contents for as long as your child is at university.

# Types of Shop

## Grocers and Other Food Shops

The king of food shops is the *alimentari*, where you will find cold meats, cheeses, canned and dried goods and some detergents and beauty supplies. This is the postcard-perfect Italian shop, with legs of *prosciutto* hanging overhead and a glass display of mouthwatering treats. One gourmet *alimentari*, in Milan near the Duomo, can only be described as a shrine to Italian food. At Peck you will find 3,500 different kinds of cheese, wild boar sausages and chocolate truffles. You will spend a lot of time at your neighbourhood *alimentari*, not only for shopping but also to catch up on the latest gossip. Some towns also have a *pizzicheria* that specialises solely in cured meats. A *fornaio* sells oven-fresh bread; don't go there if you are looking for anything not made of flour. Other stores include the *latteria* for milk, the *enoteca* for wine, the *macelleria* for meat, the *gelateria* for ice cream (but you already knew that), and the *pasticceria* for sweets and pastries. The *fruttivendolo*, which sells fruits and vegetables, is open longer than the outdoor markets that start to dismantle by late morning.

### The 'Poet Butcher'

He's known as the 'poet butcher' because he can recite the entire 'Inferno' section of Dante Alighieri's *Divine Comedy* by heart – as he often does while hacking away at cartilage or extracting chicken innards with his fist. To keep the theme, his 200-year-old family-run shop in Panzano (south of Florence) is decorated with devils and angels, and gilded flames protrude from behind the flesh-filled counter.

But Dario Cecchini's eccentric antics and prosaic talents weren't what catapulted this butcher to national stardom. 'Mad cow' disease did.

When the BSE (bovine spongiform encephalopathy) crisis spread in 2001, Italy frantically started checking its seven million head of cattle. Some animals tested positive for the disease, and government officials decided to ban the *Fiorentina* – the phone-book-thick T-bone steak that is one of Tuscany's most loved gastronomic specialities. To Cecchini, the Fiorentina ban was more than bad business. It was a calling.

In defiant violation, he organised protest barbecues and handed out free steaks and red wine to pedestrians. He staged a T-bone steak funeral in which a *Fiorentina* was placed in a coffin and paraded around town accompanied by a marching band. He invited people from as far away as Rome and Milan to attend the funeral service and requested that they dress appropriately in black clothing. His mission, perhaps, was greater than simply lifting the ban; it had to do with saving sinners. 'Tuscans like to celebrate gluttony and lust, and the *Fiorentina* is all about those things.' The 'poet butcher' succeeded in his divine duty, as the ban was eventually lifted.

Not to take away from the fun of shopping at the local grocery, it must be said that Italy also has numerous **supermarket chains**. Each city has its own, such as Pam, GS, Standa and Esselunga. Here you can buy all the goods described above in one go, and most offer home delivery. Many discount and foreign stores, such as France's gargantuan Carrefour hypermarket, are also found on the outskirts of cities such as Milan.

When you are in a food shop, you are usually expected to order first, pay at the *cassa* and then pick up your order. This is so that the person who handles your food is not also touching your money.

## Outdoor Food Markets

Large squares in every town are converted into outdoor fruit and vegetable markets where the selection is vast, produce is freshest and prices usually low. Rome's has the tourist-swamped Campo de' Fiori market, as well as the fabulous Piazza Vittorio one (which, until recently, was located in the square but has now moved to nearby Via Principe Amedeo, in an indoor space). At the second market, you can not only find Italian staples like *broccoletti di rapa* and *cicoria* but also, because of the large immigrant population in the area, spices for curries, fresh coriander for Mexican food, and seldom-seen limes.

To avoid an embarrassing *faux pas* (as bad as ordering a *cappuccino* after dinner), never buy produce out of season. An Italian wouldn't touch a watermelon before July or nibble at a porcini mushroom any time after November.

## Other Markets

It is not only food that is sold at open-air markets. Many cities have their own speciality markets. San Remo has the perfumed Mercato dei Fiori for flowers, and Florence is home to a famous leather market. Many other *mercati* sell everything from clothing to bric-a-brac to houseware items. If you're looking for junk, don't miss the Porta Portese flea market held every Sunday morning in Rome. Here you can find Second World War surplus military helmets, 'authentic' ancient Roman artefacts (fakes for sure) and anything else you probably don't really need. There are tales of shoppers with a keen eye who have walked away from Porta Portese with a genuine Raphael bought for pocket change, but these urban legends are about as authentic as the assortment of ancient Roman art that you'll see.

If you are looking for furniture, stop by Milan's Navigli antiques market, held once a month, or any other *mercato dell'antiquariato*. The most famous is the one held in Arezzo's Piazza Grande on the last weekend of each month, but you can also visit Pisa's Ponte di Mezzo market, Lucca's San Martino market or Naples' Piazza Bellini antiques fair.

## Newspaper Kiosks (*Edicole*)

Because the distribution of published media is controlled by the state, only *edicole* sell newsprint. Here you will find myriad Italian dailies, weeklies and monthlies, as well as a host of international reading such as *The Economist*, the *Guardian*, the *International Herald Tribune* (with the English-language insert *Italy Daily*) and *Le Monde*. Because they hold a monopoly on distribution, when the *edicole* go on strike – as they often do – the whole country experiences a printed news blackout. Yet very few Italians subscribe to newspapers, as they prefer to buy the one that speaks to their political temperament each morning at the kiosk. You will also see tons of 'gadgets', or music CDs and videos, for sale. These are offered at low prices with newspapers as an incentive by publishing companies to attract more readers. In addition to papers, the *edicola* sells bus tickets and sometimes mobile phone top-up cards or normal phone cards.

## Tobacconists

Impossible to miss, *tabacchi* are marked with a big black (or sometimes dark blue) 'T' outside their entrance, but don't be fooled into thinking that only smokers shop there. Because owning a licence to sell tobacco is an important state role, these little shops act as miniature public service offices. You can buy bus tickets, lottery tickets, tax stamps and all kinds of pre-paid phone cards for both mobiles and landline phones.

If you have come for cigarettes, you could try the decidedly unsophisticated MS – Monopolio dello Stato – brand. Once under government monopoly as the name suggests, Italy's cigarette company is now partially privatised.

## Discount, Department and DIY Shops

These have been popping up like mushrooms in areas immediately outside the urban centres. **Budget supermarkets**, called *i discount*, stock cheap non-brand name products that are usually imported (sometimes from Greece or Spain). The products are just as good as the ones you will find in an Italian supermarket, but costs up to 20 per cent less. Discount shops are great if you have a car or want to establish your lifetime supply of toilet paper, washing-up liquid or mineral water.

Within cities you will find *grandi magazzini* (**department stores**) such as Standa, COIN and UPIM, that have wonderful home decoration departments, cheap kitchen goods and extra goodies like garden furniture. There are plenty of *fai-da-te* (**do-it-yourself**) shops with masonry supplies, gardening tools and all the other materials you need for home repairs. For example, the Gigli commercial centre outside Florence includes a huge *fai-da-te* retailer.

## Other Shops

Then there are the *ferramenta* (hardware shops), the *tipografia* (print shop), *tintoria* or *lavanderia* (dry cleaner/launderette), the *farmacia* (pharmacy or chemist, always identified by a green cross over the entrance), the *profumeria* (perfumery), the *cartoleria* (stationery supplies), the *gioielleria* (jewellers) and the *libreria* (bookshop).

## Clothing

Unless you shop at department stores, shopping for clothes can be a quite unpleasant experience. You are expected to know what you want when you enter the store (say, a medium-sized white sweater) and the concept of browsing or 'just looking' is not embraced. You will be met with enthusiasm of dubious sincerity. Shirts will be neatly stacked and socks packed into drawers behind the counter. The only way to see them is by asking the *commessa*, or salesperson, to pull them out. As a result of that kind of effort, you may feel pressured to buy, but if you do purchase something that later you decide you don't want, you cannot return it; at best you will be given a credit note.

# When and How to Shop

Once you know where to go, the tricky part is knowing when to go. Opening times do not follow rules of logic. Most shops are open from 9am to 1.30pm and 3.30 or 4pm to 7.30 or 8pm. This schedule changes depending on what part of the country you are in. The working day is structured around lunch, and most offices and shops shut down, making it impossible to run errands when you have free time. However, as the *pausa* (or lunch break) tradition is quickly disappearing in the north, some owners opt not to leave for lunch and might close a bit earlier in the early evening – these have an *orario continuato* (continuous schedule). A handful of *tabacchi, farmacie* and *benzinai* (petrol stations) stay open at night.

You'll also need to know which shops take a rest day and on which day, since these are not uniform either. It was once safe to assume all shops were closed on Sunday, as ordered by law and church, but rules have been relaxed and those in high pedestrian traffic areas remain open for business seven days a week. A few smaller boutiques take Saturday afternoons off as well as Sunday, and many shops (clothing, shoes and household items) are closed on Monday morning. The *alimentari* are usually shut one afternoon in the middle of the week, either on Wednesday or Thursday. Outdoor markets are only open in the morning and dismantle by 2pm. Restaurants and bars have a designated *giorno di riposo*, or rest day, when they are shut. The majority take off Sunday or Monday (making restaurant plans for a Monday night is not always easy).

Count on all businesses being closed during the *ferragosto* break in mid-August, including essential ones like pharmacies and tobacconists. Cinemas also turn off their projectors that month. Most businesses take off a few days when there is a *ponte*, or 'bridge', of a holiday next to a weekend. In the case of a medical emergency in August, look in your local phone book to see where the nearest open pharmacy is located. They stay open in shifts, so at least one in your general vicinity should be able to help you. Pharmacies also take turns to stay open during the night.

Remember to get a *scontrino*, or fiscal receipt, because it is just as illegal for you not to request it as it is for the shopkeeper not to give it. The *scontrino* is the only means by which tax authorities can keep tabs on store earnings, but shopkeepers are hit with such high taxes that it's no wonder so many 'forget' to give receipts. If you turn a blind eye when this happens, it is customary to receive a *sconticino*, or 'little discount' on your purchase.

If you are a non-EU citizen, remember that you can be refunded the 20 per cent IVA (VAT) tax on large purchases if you present the 'tax-free-cheque', given to you at the shop, to customs officials on your departure.

# Home Utilities and Services

Former state monopolies have been or are in the process of being privatised; these are the main ones of which you should be aware:

- **Electricity**     **ENEL or AEM Elettricità**
- **Gas**     **Italgas or AEM Energia**
- **Water**     **ACEA**
- **Telephone**     **Telecom Italia**

As a result of phone deregulation, there are other land-line phone companies that charge less than Telecom Italia, but you still have to set up your phone service with this company. Afterwards, you can dial into cheaper fixed-line phone companies from Telecom Italia's infrastructure. For more on the phone service, *see* pp.193–6.

You should also be aware that sometimes ACEA provides electricity, and in other areas the water company has a different name.

When installing your electricity, water and gas, make sure you know where the meter, or *contatore*, is located.

Most utility bills look the same. They are folded into quarters: the top half contains your personal data, account number and the amount due, while the bottom, detachable half is your remittance slip for making payments. Some utility bills, or *bollette*, now come with a computer-generated letter explaining what you owe in a much clearer fashion than previously, but the remittance slip still looks the same. The *numero utente* is your account number, the *importo* is the amount owed, the *scadenza* is the due date and the *conto corrente* is the utility's bank information needed for making payments. Keep in mind that many bills are not itemised (including the phone bill) unless you specifically request it, sometimes for a small extra fee. Other bills are calculated by your 'estimated' consumption, not your real usage. You are expected to wait for a refund if you've overpaid and a supplementary bill if you've underpaid (a more likely scenario).

To set up a new service you should contact each utility and be able to produce documentation such as proof of residency, a photocopy of your passport and your bank account details. You can consult the Italian phone book under *numeri di pubblica utilità* to find the companies you are looking for, then call and ask for the *nuovo contratto* department.

# Payment

There are four main ways to pay your utilities, and unfortunately none of them involves sending off a cheque. Instead, a good amount of footwork may be required. Bills usually come every two months or quarterly depending on the service. Utilities are paid in cash or by bank transfer. No other financial instruments are accepted.

• **Pay at the utility company**: This is highly inconvenient because it usually means trekking across town at dawn to wait in a queue with everybody else.

• **Pay at the post office**: This is the way most Italians pay their bills. Bring your remittance slip from the utility company and the amount due in cash and wait in line at one of the *sportelli* (service windows) to make your payment. Based on the *conto corrente* number on your slip, the post office knows where to send your money. Keep your receipt handy as proof of payment. The post office is not only where you pay household bills; you can also pay taxes and even magazine subscriptions there. However, you cannot pay more than four bills at a time. If you have more than that, pay the first batch and head back to the end of the queue for a second round. Most post offices also accept payment by *bancomat*, or debit card (not a credit card).

• **Pay through your bank**: The easiest way to handle utility bills, especially if you do not live in Italy year-round, is to have your Italian bank pay them for you via automatic *bonifico bancario* or wire transfer. You pay a few euros in fees each time a bill is processed, but it saves you having to go to the post office every few months. The bank will keep track of payments on your statement and the utility company will also send you a receipt for payment. Make sure to always keep enough money in your account, however, as utility companies are very quick to pull the plug on services if a payment request is refused due to lack of funds. They will first send you a warning letter, but if you are not in the country to read it you won't be warned.

• **Internet**: Since 2003, if you open an account at Poste Italiane (the so-called 'BancoPosta'), it has been possible to pay bills on **www.poste.it**. You can also pay the bills using the online services set up by Italian banks, providing you have an account (in addition, you can keep track of your expenditure and account online). You can check your electricity usage on the well-designed **www.enel.it**, by clicking on '*sportello online*', then '*paga la bolletta*', where you can also pay the bills by credit card. The website for water (and also sometimes electricity), **www.aceaspa.it**, is not as user-friendly, but you can send your meter readings to them electronically. This site offers a full English translation, too. The website **www. italgas.it** (or the more direct **www.italgaspiu.it**) also lets you check usage and bills online. Many foreigners set up automatic payment through their bank and check that it has gone through from abroad via the Internet. You will need to register with all the above web pages with a user ID and password, and will need the account information found on your bill and your *codice fiscale* number (*see* pp.28–9) to set this up.

If you need to dispute a bill, don't count on an easy ride. The best thing to do is never get to this point by regularly and religiously checking your meter and comparing notes with what you are billed by the utility company. If you leave Italy for a few months and return to find a €500 water bill, bring the bill and your air ticket (as proof that you were not in the country) to ACEA's nearest office. You will probably be told you left the tap on while you were away, but if it is acknowledged that you were overcharged, you should receive a refund or credit. A few years ago it was discovered that ENEL had mistakenly overcharged its customers less than one euro cent each over many years. Thanks to the oversight, they pocketed €1 billion. Since the ensuing scandal, utility companies have been more careful.

# Electricity

Italy's electricity company is the Ente Nazionale per l'Energia Elettrica or ENEL, now often replaced by AEM. It provides contracts that range from 1.5 to 6 kilowatts for private homes, or more if you have a business. Most Italian homes run on 3 kilowatts, which isn't very much at all: don't attempt to vacuum your floors and toast bread at the same time; you will almost certainly blow a fuse. If you don't want to be left in the dark looking for the circuit box, make sure you know how to reset your system before you overload it. If you have a home in the country, it might be worthwhile to upgrade to 6 kilowatts.

When you buy property, make sure ENEL staff take an official reading of your meter so that you don't inherit the old owner's bills. However, when a new contract is taken out, a reading is mandatory (often you can do this yourself and phone them with the numbers). If your house is not connected to a source of

### Air-conditioning

Air-conditioning is considered a luxury item in Italy and is consequently expensive to install and operate (this will be reflected in your electricity bills). However, once you have spent a sleepless night in Milan at the end of July (you can't open windows to cool down otherwise vicious mosquitoes will turn you into a bloody pulp) you'll run to the nearest electrical appliance shop. It is highly recommended that you install air-conditioning, especially if you are buying a home for retirement or expect to have elderly visitors.

electricity, check the cost of bringing in lines before you buy the property. They are so steep that it may force you to reconsider. Once your contract is set, ENEL will bill you every second month based on an estimate of consumption. Even if you leave the country for a month and don't use any electricity at all, your bill will not reflect zero consumption. At the end of the billing cycle, ENEL will send a statement with your exact usage, with either a credit or an extra charge.

Italian wiring is different from that of the UK, so you should not bring an electrician from home to do work in Italy. Their work probably won't comply with Italian standards and fiddling with incompatible wiring is downright dangerous. Almost all property in Italy is connected at 220 volts. Any property still connected at 125 volts can be converted.

Because of old wiring, power outages and surges are frequent. Get a UPS (uninterruptible power supply) and a surge protector to safeguard your television sets, video recorders and computers.

## Gas

Italy doesn't have many natural resources, but it does have reserves of methane gas. This gas is used for heating water and cooking and is billed by Italgas, Italy's main gas company, owned by petrol giant ENI since 2005. There are two systems for regulating the gas you consume. The first is through *riscaldamento autonomo* (independent heating). That means you have your own *caldaia*, or boiler, and can turn it on or off when you please. When it breaks, you must fix it. You should also be prepared to pay for annual servicing to make sure it is running correctly. Alternatively, if you are in an apartment, your building may have *riscaldamento centrale* (central heating). In this case, your building administrator turns the heat on or off following a predetermined schedule set by regional authorities, and the costs are divided between neighbours.

You might be surprised at how many homes are not connected to mains gas and run on expensive electricity instead, but many home-owners in the country rely on *bomboloni*, refillable gas tanks tucked away behind their house. There are companies that will deliver the bottled gas to your door and check on your appliances before allowing you to sign a contract. If you don't want to pay for frequent home delivery – and you have the space – you can buy large volumes of the gas and store it yourself. Italgas will supply you with information regarding regional branches so that you can order more gas when needed. If you are especially keen to cook or heat with gas, or if you don't want to pay high electricity bills, then this is a much more viable option than the huge expense of linking up with a distant gas main.

# Water

Water holds special importance in Italy. Fountains are architectural centre-pieces and thermal baths are considered a cure for a long list of illnesses. Supermarket shoppers compare mineral water brands as if they were choosing

## Case Study: Water, Water...

Mary Salmon bought a house in Umbria seven years ago from a *contadino*, or farmer, who probably never foresaw that his once humble abode (with no running water but plenty of lazy donkeys napping nearby) could be trans-formed as beautifully as it has been. Following years of renovation and battling it out with the local planning authorities, this English woman and her family have created a holiday home that they happily return to year after year. But despite the house's proximity to Lake Trasimeno, Mary says the only glitch she experienced had to do with water, or the lack thereof.

'I remember a huge lorry filled with water from the lake making it up our long driveway to fill our swimming pool one July day,' she recalls. That might seem extreme but, in arid areas of Italy, you take water from whatever source you can. Even when the Salmon family embarked on drilling a well for domestic use, they were forced to reach some 100m (330ft) into the earth before hitting the precious liquid they sought. 'I must say it is some of the most beautiful-tasting water I've tried.'

But it wasn't until forest fires edged dangerously close to their home a few years back that Mary realised her water problem wasn't limited to filling the pool or the bath. She called the forest rangers to enquire about their fire-combating strategies and was duly informed that her area suffered from insufficient water, even where their needs are concerned. The next step she took was to call her insurance company to take out a policy against fires. 'I was told that I wouldn't qualify unless all the trees up to 50 metres away from our home were cleared.' No sooner had she received that information than she was told that she could face stiff fines or even prison for cutting down the ancient oaks on her property (some of which are well within that distance of the house). Unsure of what to do next, she called back the fire rangers. 'They came to take a look and identified certain trees that could go,' she says. 'Then they told me not to worry because oaks take a long time to burn.'

between a Barbaresco and a Barolo. As a result, water comes at a high price (as much as €70 per month for a medium-sized house). Each *comune* determines pricing for water with ACEA (Azienda Comunale Energia e Ambiente, but note that your local water company might not go by this name) and prices vary according to reserves, rainfall and how much water is used. For example, if you live in an area with many swimming pools to fill, you will have a higher water tariff per cubic metre. Each individual house or apartment complex has a *contatore* that measures consumption. If you share a meter with neighbours, you will be billed equally, even if someone else takes 12 showers a day.

Most water companies bill quarterly or twice a year. When you go on holiday, be sure to turn off your water, as much Italian plumbing is old and leaks are frequent. Pipe bursts are especially common in August, when the mass exodus of holidaymakers dramatically influences water pressure . If you live in a rural area, you should also expect water shortages. The result is restrictions on supply, particularly in summer months, so it's a good idea to think ahead and fill a storage tank to meet your needs, especially if you have a garden.

Here are some other watery issues.

- **Boilers**: If you have a *caldaia* in a *riscaldamento autonomo* property, make sure it is big enough to meet your needs. A small boiler only holds enough warm water for one quick shower.

- **Wells**: Even if you don't intend to obtain drinking water from your well, it is a useful and cheap way of watering your garden or filling your swimming pool. However, some wells dry up in the summer and others develop such a high salt content that they can't be used for irrigation. You should check the well carefully before buying a property, and check that the water rights belong to you. If you do intend to use it for drinking, contact the local health department to certify that the water is fit for human consumption (that it is *acqua potabile*).

- **Septic tanks**: Most rural properties depend on a septic tank for drainage and sewage disposal. A septic tank acts as a filter, and treats sewage by breaking it down with bacteria before discharging relatively harmless treated water into the environment. Older models only deal with toilets, which leaves waste and soapy water from sinks and baths to be released without treatment. Modern equipment treats all the waste you produce and discharges it safely. Septic tanks have a natural lifespan, and when you need to replace one you will need planning permission to do so. If you are putting in a new one, make sure you get the right size (a 3,000-litre tank should be fine for a small- to medium-sized home but a 4,000-litre tank is better for a larger one. If your tank is too small for your needs, you will spend more time and money emptying it.

- **Swimming pools**: If you live in an arid area with frequent water shortages, your *comune* probably won't give you a permit to build a swimming pool.

But if you do want to put one in, remember that they are expensive to build (up to €15,000) and expensive to maintain (up to €2,000 a year). You will have to hire someone to clean it and treat it once or twice a week in summer months. You will see hundreds of prefabricated above-ground swimming pools for sale on the side of the *autostrada*. That could be one alternative – granted, not a very attractive one. No planning permit is needed, but it will still be very expensive to fill.

## Condominium Fees

If you live in an apartment complex, you will be charged *spese del condominio* to cover costs such as cleaning the hallway, paying the *portinaio* or *portiere* (porter) and keeping the lift running.

The *portiere* should also be tipped at Christmas or whenever extra services are rendered. He or she sits in a booth at the building entrance to watch that strangers don't enter, and also does light cleaning, collects mail and signs for large packages when you're not at home. I

f your building has a lift and you live on the top floor, expect to pay a higher condominium fee than those on the ground floor. Sometimes water fees (ACEA) are included in the condominium fee. Prices are determined by the building administrator and are charged quarterly or twice a year.

For more on the *condominio*, *see* **Making the Purchase**, pp.129–30.

## Rubbish Tax

You might think it's a joke, but it's not. The *tassa comunale dei rifiuti* (refuse, or rubbish, tax) is one tenacious tax. It will follow you everywhere and there's no way to escape it. Even if you move away from Italy for years, your local *comune* will have your unpaid rubbish bill in safe keeping for your return. The money you pay is for the removal of your rubbish but, since prices vary according to how big or small your property is (the idea being that people who live in small houses produce less rubbish), many see it as a disguised evil twin of the property tax. The rubbish tax is paid in four instalments throughout the year, or you can pay it all at once at the beginning of the year. And, since it is a tax, you can only pay it at the post office (no bank transfers for this one).

Rubbish is collected by different companies according to region. For example, in Milan it is AMSA (Azienda Municipale Servizi Ambientali) and in Rome it is AMA (Azienda Municipale Ambiente). If you have large items that you want disposed of, these companies will collect them. If you live in the historic centre of Rome or Milan, be careful not to dispose of refuse illegally. On top of paying the rubbish tax you'll get a fine, that you can't just throw in the bin.

## Television Tax and Satellite Television

There has been talk of phasing it out but, for now, Italians pay a mandatory **television tax** known as the *pagamento canone RAI*. Each year the price increases and it is already about €100 per annum (*see* 'TV and Radio', p.200, to get a better understanding of what you are paying for). When you buy a new television set, you are required to register it with the authorities and pay the tax. However, there are so many ways around this – from buying a used TV set to officially declaring yours 'broken' – that few do. Italy spends a fortune on a publicly funded televised campaign to urge people to pay their TV tax. In one town in Puglia, out of 3,000 inhabitants, not a single resident owns a TV set, according to tax officials.

If you want to pay for more channels you can sign up with Italy's satellite **Sky Italia** television, the recent acquisition in Rupert Murdoch's global expansion strategy. The packages and channels are very similar to those of UK Sky, but of course feature Italian contents. With one of their decoder boxes, you can receive movie channels and get a plethora of football channels covering everything from the Italian leagues to the World Cup. With a satellite dish you can pick hundreds of free channels, such as one that broadcasts Italian variety shows in Islamic countries and 'Sicilia International', which features a lot of pagan rites in off-the-beaten-track parts of Sicily. Soccer programmes are scrambled for those without a pay-TV subscription, as are the majority of movie channels.

Please note that, if you are a Sky user, your UK card does not authorise you to receive pictures in Italy because Sky does not have a licence to operate outside Britain. But look again. Hundreds of holidaymakers and British residents in Italy happily use their British cards anyway. If you go to a specialist satellite serviceman, he can even arrange for a card for those who never had one in England. (This book does not, of course, condone this course of action.) Just don't bring your television set – it won't work in Italy.

In 2005, **digital terrestrial television (DTT)** started broadcasting in most cities; the decoder permits you to watch many free channels, in high definition if you have an HDTV set, plus, if you pay a charge, the Italian football league matches. As in the UK, the government intends that digital television will replace analogue from 2009, but it is difficult to foresee whether the Italians will be persuaded to change their habits in so short a time.

## Telephones and Faxes

The biggest Italian phone company is Telecom Italia (**www.telecomitalia.it** or **www.187.it**). Although Italy's telecommunications industry is open to competition, they still run the show because most of the nation's wiring and infrastructure belongs to them. This means that rates have not come down as far as you would expect; however, more and more ways to avoid high tariffs are becoming available.

If you want to set up a fixed-line phone service (that is, a phone in your home as opposed to a mobile phone), dial **t** 187 from any phone. Setting up a service takes about five days (but keep calling **t** 187 if it takes longer!) and will cost approximately €200. Also call **t** 187 if you wish to install a second phone line or an ADSL (called 'Alice') line for your fax or modem.

Telecom Italia **bills** come every second month and are not itemised (unless you request it and pay a surcharge) and are paid in the same way as other Italian utilities (*see* pp.187–8). Phone tariffs are calculated by *scatti*, which is a unit of time that has a fixed price. The more time you spend on the phone, the more *scatti* you use. If you dial long-distance, the *scatti* add up faster than when you call a local number.

The phone company offers the same range of services that you are familiar with at home, such as call waiting, call forwarding, caller identification and automatic answering services. These will add a bit more to your phone bill. If you buy a fax machine, remember that slower band rates in urban areas mean hundreds of extra *scatti*.

There are a few ways to steer clear of Telecom Italia. You could use a British calling card for long distance or you can hook into cheaper phone companies by dialling a prefix and then the number you want. For more information on competitors' rates, contact Fastweb (**www.fastweb.it**), Tele2 (**www.tele2.it**) or Libero (**www.libero.it**). These companies offer special package deals if you sign up for fixed and Internet service together, as does Telecom Italia.

One last way to tiptoe around high phone bills is to buy one of the many pre-paid phone cards available at the *tabaccaio* or the *edicola*. Few people know about these, but you can save so much money that these cards will soon surely represent a threat to Italy's traditional phone companies. There are many cards to choose from, and they come in different denominations (of €5–100). For example, if you buy a Europa card (sold by a company called Vectone) you get 300 minutes of phone time to the United States for only €15. A €5 card will buy you almost as many minutes to Great Britain. Think about it: €5 for five hours! The drawback is that you must dial a tiresome series of numbers and codes (provided when you purchase the card) to access the system; but one good thing is that you dial into a freephone number, so you can use the card either from a payphone or from your home phone with no additional cost. Keep in mind that many of these companies are fly-by-night, so it's better not to invest in cards with huge denominations.

## Mobile Phones

If you could select a single symbol of Italy today, it would no longer be a pizza or a gondola. It would be a mobile phone, or *telefonino*. Italians are mad about

## Mobile Madness

When Italy auctioned off five UMTS licences a few years ago it envisaged flooding the treasury with so much cash that part of the national debt would be wiped away, but the bidding war for third-generation mobile phone technology turned into a national melodrama and an outstanding failure. UMTS auctions raised €38 billion in Britain and a record €51 billion in Germany. Italy raked in a measly €13 billion.

What went wrong? Six bidders entered the race for five licences. Tight controls and secrecy surrounded the proceedings. Teams of three representing each bidder were installed in bunker-like rooms inside Rome's Communications Ministry so that no team would have knowledge of the others' strategies, but a few days into the bidding, Blu (a consortium led by Benetton's Autostrade and British Telecom) abruptly dropped out of the race, leaving five bidders with five licenses acquired at bargain basement prices. Some analysts called it 'suicide', others said Blu would benefit from the 'gratitude factor' by leaving the race when bidding prices were low and could ask favours in the future from operators with whom it shares roaming networks. An official inquiry was opened to determine if Blu's intentionally left the running.

UMTS, or Universal Mobile Telecommunications System, allows for Internet access at 384 Kb/s, 10 times faster then GPRS, and allows mobile phone users to download images, music and videos. At the time of writing, over 60 per cent of Italians use a mobile phone – equalling 40 million subscribers – compared with 52 per cent in Britain and 40 per cent in Germany.

mobiles, and instant text messaging, or SMS, is a national obsession – if Darwin's theory of evolution is right, Italian motor skills will be phased out in favour of quick digiting. The *telefonino* is seen as the ultimate way of radiating the *bella figura* (or good impression) because it tells those within earshot that you are important. Being cool no longer has to do with expensive watches or brand-name loafers; it's having the catchy *Mission Impossible* theme tune as your ringtone.

Like them or not, if you don't have one already you should buy a mobile phone as soon as you arrive on Italian soil. Not having one is a major liability – you will be shunned by everyone from estate agents to friends for whom primitive forms of communication are no longer an option.

Italy is Europe's largest mobile phone market, and two companies, **Vodafone** (**www.vodafone.it**) and **TIM** (for Telecom Italia Mobile; **www.tim.it**) control most of it, but **Tre** (**www.tre.it**) is fast moving up in rank and **Wind** (**www.wind.it**) follows as the fourth provider. All four offer competitive rates and similar services. To sign up for mobile services, visit one of the thousands of telecommunications shops spread through the nation. You will need identification and a *codice fiscale* (*see* pp.28–9). If you don't have a *codice fiscale*, some companies will sign you up anyway, although they're not supposed to.

As far as the phone is concerned, you can choose from the same models you will recognise in England. GSM is the standard technology, so don't get talked into older systems like TACS. Newer UMTS models (*see* box, previous page) let you surf the Internet from your phone faster than ever.

As far as your service is concerned, you have two options. You can either sign up for a **contract** (you pay every two months when your bill arrives) or you can sign up to use pre-paid cards and **pay as you go**. Most foreigners find the second method more convenient (since there are no phone bills involved) and all four companies offer both these alternatives. Each company has its own prefixes. For example, TIM numbers start with 333, 334, 335, 338, 339,363 or 366; Vodafone numbers generally start with 340, 343 or 347, 348 or 349; Tre with 390, 391, 392, 393; and Wind with 320, 323, 328 or 329. Having said this, remember that portability allows your original number to be 'ported' to a different operator.

If you go with the pay-as-you-go system you can purchase pre-paid 'recharge' (*ricarica*) cards at any *tabaccaio* or phone shop and at some *edicole* (newspaper kiosks) or supermarkets. If you have an Italian bank account, you can recharge your card at most *bancomat* (ATM) machines. Most companies also let you charge your card via the Internet with a credit card. Remember that when your money runs out, you can no longer make or receive calls when you are abroad. If you are in Italy you can still receive calls with zero credit.

If you bring your existing mobile phone with you to Italy you could, in the short term, keep your British SIM card (and therefore phone number) but you will be paying truly exorbitant rates for both making *and* receiving calls and text messages, as will the sender or receiver at the other end. If you are staying for any length of time but don't want to buy a new mobile phone, it would be a good idea to purchase an Italian SIM card to put into your existing phone (keeping your other one safely stored for use back in the UK). It will give you an Italian number and calls will cost somewhat less to and from the UK, and far less to other Italian numbers. You will need to have your phone 'unlocked' from its UK network first, unless you purchased it SIM-free in the first place.

## The Internet

Whereas mobile phones took off like wildfire in Italy, the Internet had a slow start. A lower percentage of Italian homes have a computer than European averages, and it is not unheard of to meet people who don't have an e-mail address, although they are in a minority. Within the last few years, most public institutions, universities and small businesses have set up comprehensive and informative websites (albeit a bit flashy and slow to load because of heavy graphics). Italy missed out on the 'new economy' glory years that sparked the rapid rise and fall of so many companies, but that may be a reason for its enthusiasm about the Internet today.

## Sites to See

You are sure to find others, but here are six useful Internet sites for British home-owners in Italy. For more, *see* **References**.

**www.italydaily.com**: Offers an outline of the sites of the most important local and daily Italian newspapers, only on the web.

**www.intoitaly.it**: A wealth of information and a brilliant database. You can access the entire English *Yellow Pages* online. EYP is the annual phone directory for Italy's English-speaking community, covering Rome, Florence, Genoa, Catania, Palermo, Bologna, Milan and Naples. In English.

**www.informer.it**: This is a subscription site but it is the key to understanding Italy's red tape – from housing planning permission to changing ownership of a car. In English.

**www.trenitalia.it**: This website represents one of the single most revolutionary events in Italy. Everything you need to know about train travel (when they leave, where they go and whether you can eat on board) is available. To buy tickets online you must register with the site. In Italian and English.

**www.italia.gov.it**: One site with everything you need to know about laws, immigration, public offices, visas and permits and transport. In Italian.

**www.ebay.it**: Not as popular as its branches abroad, but you can find authentic bargains for decorating your home. Sometimes you are the only bidder. In Italian.

Italy, like France, has free Internet service providers (although this probably won't last forever). Tiscali, a start-up from Sardinia (*see* p.59) that rapidly grew to become one of Europe's best-performing stock companies, was the first to offer Italians free Internet access in the mid-1990s. Since then, many more have followed. Because local phone calls are not free, your Internet expenses will probably be linked to the phone company rather than your ISP. Many companies, such as Telecom Italia, Fastweb, Tele2 and Libero, offer special package deals including e-mail addresses at reasonable rates. Italy's free ISPs offer good service and there's little reason to pay for one, although subscription services are also available. Like in the UK, there is an option to pay a flat monthly subscription that offers a freephone line to avoid call charges.

To set up an account with an Italian ISP, you will definitely need a *codice fiscale* (*see* pp.28–9). It's also best to have the actual *codice fiscale* card in front of you as you complete the procedure, as your ISP will check your *codice fiscale* information online before giving you an account. For example, if you go by the name of 'John Smith' but your *codice fiscale* card reads 'John N. Smith', your request will be denied until you add the 'N'.

The following are the main Italian portals, search engines and ISPs.

- **Agora (www.agora.it)**: This portal was created by the Radical Party, but has since passed into private hands.

• **Caltanet (www.caltanet.it)**: Portal with free web access, e-mail, weather, sports and lots of local news.

• **Ciao Web (www.ciaoweb.it)**: This is a free ISP with 10MB for your mailbox or 200MB if you pay a fee. It is financed by the Fiat industrial group.

• **Infinito (www.infinito.it)**: This ISP was bought by British Telecom. It offers access to the Internet, unlimited e-mail addresses and 100MB of web space for free.

• **Jumpy (www.jumpy.it)**: A child of Silvio Berlusconi's Mediaset empire, this is a free ISP with access to 32,000 newsgroups. It has a handy function that allows surfers to see how much they are spending on phone calls.

• **Kataweb (www.kataweb.it)**: Part of the La Repubblica and L'Espresso group, it is both an ISP and one of Italy's biggest portals. It also lets you send free SMS messages to mobile phones.

• **Libero-Wind (www.libero.it)**: A portal with free SMS to mobile phones if you log in through Libero ISP, as well as news, weather and more.

• **McLink (www.mclink.it)**: An ISP that mostly services businesses.

• **Pippo (www.pippo.it)**: A fun start-up portal with several search engines.

• **SuperEva (www.supereva.it)**: Not only a portal but also a search engine with web space, e-mail and free access to the Internet.

• **TIN (Telecom Italia Net; www.tin.it)**: Part of the Telecom Italia group, this is a portal and an ISP. You have to buy your modem at a TIN store.

• **Tiscali (www.tiscali.it)**: The pioneer of free ISPs, Tiscali was founded by a young businessman in Sardinia.

• **Virgilio (www.virgilio.it)**: One of the oldest Italian search engines, owned by Telecom. It offers many services free, as dictionaries, job advertisements, news, road maps and an e-mail box.

• **Yahoo (www.yahoo.it)**: Now in Italy, this portal gives you free e-mail.

To avoid slow Internet access, you can have ISDN or ADSL installed. Alternatively, your home could be wired for **Fastweb** (**www.fastweb.it**), which has laid down kilometres of fibre-optic cable in the main cities for faster Internet access. These services are usually not available in rural areas.

If you decide to stay with your British ISP, make sure they have an access number near you in Italy. Also check that they don't charge extra fees when you log on from abroad. To connect, you might need to click on 'ignore dial tone' if your modem has difficulty communicating with Italian phones.

# Major Media

The media are unusual in Italy because they all belong to the same group of people. As a result, you may have a sneaking suspicion that newspapers aren't exactly 'objective' and television is not 'unbiased'. It's more than suspicion – it's fact. Major print media and television are the mouthpiece of government and industry. A newspaper owned by Italy's largest car-maker won't publish a scoop about shoddy mechanics. Similarly, a television network operated by the former Communist Party might broadcast more anti-Fascist Second World War documentaries than normal. Lawmakers have been trying to straighten the media out for years, but with little success. They have even charged an institute with counting how many minutes of airtime each politician gets. If it is discovered that one from a left-wing party got two hours more over the course of a year than his right-wing equivalent, scandal ensues.

Of course, what balance might have been reached was completely disrupted when the owner of Italy's biggest private television network became prime minister, thus controlling Italy's public television too. Lawmakers scratched their heads and went back to the drawing board.

Part of the phenomenon is that the profession of journalism is practised differently in Italy. Anglo-Saxon journalism is supposed to let the readers draw their own conclusions based on the facts. Italian media loves to draw the conclusion for you. If, for some reason, the death of an eight-year-old boy doesn't strike you as a horrible tragedy, you will face an onslaught of emotive adjectives and tear-jerking metaphors until you come around.

## Newspapers

The largest-circulation newspaper is *Corriere della Sera*, headquartered in Milan. It has a centre-left stance and is considered to have the best foreign coverage. *La Repubblica*, founded in the late 1970s by a group of young journalists, leans more to the left and is the country's second-largest daily. It is published in tabloid format and has great local news, a good culture section and many fun inserts. *La Stampa* is part of the Fiat empire and has good political coverage and a great arts section. *Il Giornale* is further to the right, while *L'Unità* (*see* box, overleaf) was founded by Communists. *Il Sole 24 Ore* is the nation's financial daily and is regarded as Italy's best newspaper. The English-language *Italy Daily* is included when you buy the *International Herald Tribune*.

## Magazines

Weekly magazines include *L'Espresso* (part of the *La Repubblica* group), which is left-leaning and has in-depth coverage of national politics and mainstream

### L'Unità *We Stand*

The bible of the left, *L'Unità*, evokes Communist nostalgia, proletariat doctrine and workers' rights. Ideology might not sell newspapers, but capitalising on a brand-name product will.

*L'Unità* first hit news-stands in 1924 and was begun by Antonio Gramsci, the founder of Italy's Communist Party. The paper soared in circulation peaking at more than 300,000 copies a day. Its celebrated May Day editions sold as many as one million copies.

But the fall of the Berlin Wall meant hard times for *L'Unità*. Editors tried to boost circulation artificially by giving away free videos and music cassettes, or *i gadget*, to attract readers. Political benefactors pumped in as much as €40,000 per day to keep its presses running. In a fiercely competitive sector, *L'Unità* eventually went into liquidation. Staff layoffs were particularly painful for the paper that was a champion of worker's rights, and its passing marked the end of an era.

Enter a group of investors and *L'Unità*'s back-from-bankruptcy tale begins. Aware of the paper's brand-name potential, a new budget was drawn up and an Internet project launched to help *L'Unità* stand on its own feet through sales and advertising revenues. 'It's a story that, for many, makes the heart beat faster,' says one journalist who has written for the paper for more than 20 years. It's a story that may make Gramsci turn in his grave.

business and culture. Its main competition is *Panorama*. *Oggi* and *Gente* have less news and lots of gossip and a regular supply of photos of celebrities caught topless at the beach.

## TV and Radio

The government-run broadcaster is collectively known as RAI (Radio-televisione Italiana) and is divided into three main channels: *Raiuno, Raidue* and *Raitre*. Depending on which government is in power, the first is considered the most mainstream and the last is considered furthest to the left. *Raitre* is largely dedicated to educational programmes and documentaries. RAI's radio programming follows a similar set-up.

Italy's three biggest private television networks (*Canale 5, Rete 4* and *Italia Uno*) were all founded by Silvio Berlusconi and are part of the Mediaset empire. Those six channels make up the core market. However, there are other smaller national networks such as *La Sette* (in rapid growth) and *Sportialia* (a new sport channel), plus music channels *MTV* and *ALL Music*. There are also hundreds of regional channels that are only useful to watch from a sociological standpoint or for weather updates. The availability completely changes if you subscribe to satellite television (*see* p.193).

# Money and Banking

Anybody can open a bank account if they are over 18, have proof of identity, an address in Italy and a *codice fiscale* (*see* pp.28–9) The type of account you open will ultimately depend on whether you are resident or non-resident in Italy. Banking needs vary dramatically from person to person. If you are retiring to Italy or running a business, you may require fairly sophisticated banking services. If, however, you are a tourist with a holiday home then your banking needs are likely to be very simple. Most British people fall into this category and their only real concerns are finding a bank nearby for convenience and finding one with English-speaking staff. Easy. You should bank locally – it will make you feel part of a community and, more importantly, will make the community feel that you want to be part of it.

The biggest convenience of having an Italian account is that you can arrange for your bank to take care of telephone bills and utility expenses while you are away. Most institutions offer Internet banking for a small surcharge that allows clients to keep track of deposits and deductions. If you are choosing between various banks, select the one that has the most affordable charging structure for receiving money. Italian banks charge for absolutely everything and some charge quite a lot for the simple task of receiving funds sent from England.

If you choose to use a British bank, remember that their services will not differ much from an Italian bank. There is no reason why you should close your existing account bank home.

Italian **banking hours** are generally 8.30am–1pm and 2.30–4pm or 3–4.30pm Monday to Friday. Some are also open for a few hours on a Saturday morning.

## Types of Account

The *conto corrente* is a basic bank account and your *estratto conto*, or bank statement, will be sent to your home every month, or every three months depending on the bank. You can open a savings account with a *libretto di conto* (passbook savings account) or a current account with a *libretto di assegni* (cheque book). You should also request a *bancomat*, or ATM card. These can be a

### Quick Banking Tips

• Get used to writing the date in Italian. The 7th November 2003 is 7/11/03. Remember to cross the '7' so that it is not confused with a '1'.

• Remember that, in Italy, a comma replaces a full stop and vice versa. We write €2,500.00. An Italian would write €2.500,00.

• When you write a cheque, put your location before the date, as in 'Roma, 7/11/03'.

## On the Cards

Italy is still, after several years. experimenting with a new calling card: the long-anticipated Smart Card, or high-tech hybrid that assumes the functions of both an identification card and a *bancomat*.

Encrypted on the photo-identification card will be electronic information containing a citizen's basic vital statistics, as recorded at the state census bureau. In addition, the card will be capable of performing simple electronic functions such as buying tickets at museums and paying automated parking and highway tolls. It will also be plugged into the national health care system, useful for pulling up the holder's medical records and blood type in the event of an accident. And, in the future, it will be linked to your bank so you can use it as a debit or credit card.

simple debit card or a combination debit and credit card. You cannot withdraw more than €500 per day at the *bancomat* machine.

If you plan to open a joint account, you have two options. The first is a *conto corrente a firme congiunte*, where both signatures are needed for transactions, and the second is the *conto corrente cointestato* that allows either party to make a transaction independently.

Note that, with any account, funds that you wire from abroad will be converted automatically into euros based on the day's exchange rate. If you don't want to have your funds automatically converted into euros, as a non-resident in Italy you have the option of opening a *conto estero* (Italian citizens can do this too with a *conto in valuta*). In all other ways, the account works just like a normal *conto corrente*.

Italian banks generally pay very little interest on current accounts. It is therefore sensible to also open a deposit account. Most banks will arrange for a sum from the current account to be automatically transferred into an interest-bearing account.

Do not even think about writing a cheque on your Italian bank account if there are insufficient funds. This is a criminal offence. Bounced cheques also lead to substantial bank charges. There are no cheque guarantee cards in Italy, yet cheques are widely – if somewhat reluctantly – accepted.

Some people think that, by having an offshore bank account, they do not have to pay tax in Italy. This is not the case. The only way not to pay tax is by illegally hiding the existence of the bank account from Italian tax authorities.

# Working and Employment

Italy's unemployment rate is now about 8 per cent (7.7 per cent in the third quarter of 2005), but, in some areas of the south, a frightening 50 per cent of recent school leavers are completely without work. Lately a higher percentage of under-employed people has been recorded, too. For that reason, finding employment is difficult, especially if you are looking for a position that an out-of-work Italian could occupy. If an employer can offer a job with full benefits and a contract, he or she might feel a moral as well as a legal obligation to hire an Italian over a foreign citizen of the EU.

That said, very few foreigners come to Italy to compete for Italian jobs in the first place. When foreigners come to Italy for work, they usually bring skills with them that Italians don't have. These could be language skills, or technical abilities. And they usually come with a company that sponsors them, or as independent contractors who set up their own business using contacts and resources they acquired at home.

# Job-hunting

The process of looking for a job follows what are now universal rules. You should make a list of target opportunities and mail or e-mail a CV and covering letter. Make sure you use the formal *lei* tense in Italian, not the *tu* form, unless you are specifically asked to. Your **covering letter** should be addressed to either *Egregio Signore* or *Gentilissima Signora*, or *Spettabile Ditta*, in the polite tense.

Italian **CVs** tend to be longer than one page and include details we would never dream of putting on ours in the UK (unless it were specifically relevant to the job), like a photograph, but a one-page, succinct résumé with brief descriptions of experience, in the Anglo-Saxon tradition, is always appreciated. Make sure to translate it into accurate Italian. You can also fill the standard European CV, increasingly used in the last few years (*see* **www.europass-italia.it**, for information and CV download).

Job interviews can be very informal, over a meal or in an outdoor café, and don't be surprised if a vague promise of employment is made immediately after first impressions have settled in. Regardless, you should be well informed about Italy (read a few issues of the newspapers listed on *Italy Daily*, **www.italy daily.com**) in advance and expect questions about where you come from. A favourite question that always stumps foreigners is, 'What is the population of your home town?' You might want to check, just in case.

# Contracts and Benefits

There are many types of work contract, and legislative changes currently under way should add more flexibility and more opportunity to what is a very rigid labour market. The two principal contracts are the *contratto a termine* or *a tempo determinato* (fixed-duration contract) and the *contratto a tempo indeterminato* (open-ended). One sets a time limit on your employment and the other is permanent, which in Italy means that you can never be fired unless you do something really, really bad.

> ### Working 'Underground'
> Around a quarter of Italy's economy, and around a third of its labour, is part of a vast underground economy where the taxman does not tread, according to the International Monetary Fund. Between 30 and 48 per cent of the national workforce is engaged in what Italians call the 'submerged' economy. It accounts for 27 per cent of GDP, or roughly twice the 21-nation OSCE average.

These open-ended contracts have been the source of much friction in Italy, because employers who would like to rid their offices of dead wood cannot fire unproductive employees. The employers say that unemployment would diminish if more part-time jobs and temporary employment possibilities were created. Labour unions, on the other hand, feel that if employers were allowed to fire at will, workers' rights would be violated. Both have a point and, for this reason, labour reforms are still being debated.

Labour is also incredibly expensive. The employer must pay social security benefits (*contributi*) in addition to bonuses and other benefits. These represent 40 to 45 per cent on top of the worker's salary. Each employee receives a *busta paga*, or pay slip, at the end of the month that tracks salary, benefits and automatic income tax deductions.

- **Pay**: Salary (*lo stipendio*) is based on the category into which the worker falls. The main ones are *operai* (manual workers), *impiegati* (office workers) and *dirigenti* (managers).

- **Pay rises**: All workers can expect a rise every two years. This is called *scatti di anzianità*.

- **Working hours and overtime**: Most contracts call for 38 hours of work per week, and you can earn 115–130 per cent of your pay in overtime. Working at night or during holidays earns 120–175 per cent of your basic pay. Usually employees belonging to the higher categories (*funzionari, dirigenti*) are not eligible to receive overtime payments.

- **Holidays**: Employees get 12 national holidays each year plus the saint's day of their home town (*see* **References**, pp.268–9). Paid holiday ranges from four to six weeks per year.

- **Bonuses**: Employees annually receive a bonus known as the *tredicesima* ('13th month's pay') which, as its name suggests, is equal to one month's pay. A lucky few also get a *quattordicesima*, or 14 pay cheques per year.

- **Health cover**: All employees get free health benefits.

- **Maternity leave**: A woman is entitled to five months of paid leave, two before giving birth and three following. The father can ask permission for a *congedo parentale*, a period lasting up to six months to support this wife, providing she is working during the father's leave. This parental leave can be prolonged to up to ten months if the father becomes single (death, or serious infirmity or abandonment of the mother), or if for some other reason the primary care of the child is entrusted to the father. Note that the first option is usually applied at the company's discretion. For information, *see* **www.welfare.gov.it/Sociale/famiglia/congedi+parentali/default.htm** (in Italian only).

• **Sickness and disability**: Sick employees receive their full salary for up to 180 days of absence per year. If they go over that, they are considered permanently injured and qualify for a pension.

• **Pensions**: The retirement age is 65 for men and 60 for women. Following 15 years of paying contributions, employees can receive a partial pension and a full one comes after 35 years.

• **Dismissal policies**: An employee can only be fired if 'just cause' is proven, and he or she has two months to contest the dismissal.

• **Termination indemnity**: If an employee leaves his or her post, a *trattamento di fine rapporto* is paid. This usually comes to one month's pay per number of years employed.

# Self-employment

Italy has a special appeal for freelancers and self-employed individuals. Its artistic heritage, gastronomy and reliance on the tourist industry make it the perfect environment for art restorers, painters, travel writers, fashion designers, graphic designers, tour guides, chefs, historians, web designers and a vast number of other professions suited to independent contractors. Many foreigners move to Italy precisely because they are able to work for themselves in ways they cannot at home. With a modem, a laptop and a property in Italy, they have an office. And with all the riches immediately outside their door they can carve out a niche market. Some open online estate agencies to help others find a dream home. Others freelance for a public relations firm and put their English skills to use on press releases and company pamphlets. Some become translators and interpreters, and some teach English as a foreign language. Others write books and some are involved with art restoration projects. More still work in the expatriate community at one of the English-language schools, publications or companies.

If you want to work for yourself, the only paperwork you need is a *codice fiscale* and possibly a *partita IVA* (*see* pp.28–30) to issue invoices and receive payment. Or you could open your own business.

# Starting Your Own Business

If you are interested in setting up for yourself and expanding your entrepreneurial talents, you will need a *codice fiscale* and a *partita IVA* and you will have to register with your local chamber of commerce (*camera di commercio*). The main business types are representative offices, branch offices, sole proprietorships, partnerships and corporations.

- **Representative office**: An *ufficio di rappresentanza* is for those who come to do research, distribute information or promote the image of a home office back home. They do not sell services or goods. For example, a newspaper's foreign bureau is a representative office. It is not subject to Italian taxes.

- **Branch office**: A *sede secondaria* is an Italian branch of a foreign company doing business in Italy. It is subject to Italian corporate law and taxation. You will need the help of a *notaio* (*see* p.126) to register this type of business with the tax authorities.

- **Sole proprietorship**: A *ditta individuale* is the simplest business structure to set up because there is no capital requirement. The owner must have a *partita IVA* and be registered with the *camera di commercio* within one month of starting the activity. As the sole proprietor, you bear all the tax consequences and liability of the company.

- **Partnership**: There are two types of partnership, or *società di persone*. There is no capital requirement and profits and losses are passed on to the partners. The first is a general partnership or a *società* in *nome colletivo* (general partnership) or S.n.c. All partners are liable without limit for the debt. The second is a *società in accomandita semplice* (limited partnership) or S.a.s. The liability of each partner is determined by his or her original investment. Partnerships are subject to tax and IVA in addition to the personal income tax of the partners. You will need a *notaio* (*see* p.126) to set one up, as well as court approval.

- **Corporation**: By forming a corporation (*società di capitali*) you are protected against liabilities, except where the initial investment is concerned. There are two types of corporation, and each has its own capital requirement. Both can be managed by a single director or by a board of directors and both can be fully foreign-owned. Both are subject to income tax, IVA and corporate tax (IRES). The first is a limited liability company or *società a responsabilità limitata* (S.r.l.). It requires a minimum quota capital of €10,000. It cannot be listed on the stock exchange and has quotas instead of shares. The size of the quota determines the liability and the voting right of the quota-holder. It may require an annual audit. The second, and more complex, type of corporation is the joint stock company or *società per Azioni* (S.p.A.). It must have minimum capital of €120,000. This type of corporation is usually set up by businesses that want to be traded on the stock exchange, or *borsa*. It is required to submit its accounts to outside auditors. The *notaio* fees involved with setting up a S.r.l. or S.p.A. can run up to €5,000.

You will require outside help when setting up running your own business. A *notaio* (*see* p.126) can help you do the following:

- **Ask the court for approval of your business.**
- **Register with the Ufficio Registro (Tax Registrar's Office).**
- **Register with the Registro delle Imprese (Registrar of Businesses).**
- **Register with the Registro dell Ditte (Registrar of Companies) at the nearest camera di commercio.**
- **Register with the Registro delle Imposte (Register of Taxes).**
- **List your business in the official bulletin of companies, called BUSARL.**

As Italian tax laws are very complicated, you will also rely on the services of a *commercialista*, or accountant, to prepare your tax returns and keep your books in order. All books should be kept for ten years. Make sure you also seek the advice of a solicitor. The British chamber of commerce or the commercial section of the British Embassy should have more information on opening a business.

Because each *comune* and its *circoscrizioni* regulate business enterprises under its domain, you will have to go to them to apply for a permit and licence for your business. Permits are issued after an inspection for sanitation and labour. A licence determines the kind of business you have. For example, a grocer's has one kind of licence and a news-stand another; these licences enable the state to limit the density of a particular type of business. For example, if your area has too many restaurants, you won't be able to get a licence for another. Look into the availability of your licence before spending large amounts of money on your business plan.

Every area of the country has its own chamber of commerce (*camera di commercio*) that keeps track of local businesses. You will have to register yours with them. To find out more about their services, visit **www.camcom.it** or **www.cameradicommercio.it**.

# Education

If you move to Italy with children, you have a number of choices to make regarding their education. You can either send them to an Italian school (private or public) or you can enrol them in one of the many private British schools located throughout the country.

An Italian's education starts with the *scuola dell'infanzia*, or **pres-chool**, for ages three to six. Attendance is free of charge but parents are asked to contribute to transport fees and the charges for the meals provided by the *comune*. Children aged five or six (parents have now the option to send them earlier if the birth date falls into the first year of attendance) are then sent to

**primary school**, or *scuola elementare*, until age 11. The next step is *scuola media*, or **lower secondary** education. This lasts three years. Italian students then enrol in *liceo*, or **upper secondary** education. This lasts four or five years, but the compulsory stage of the country's education system ends at age 15. At the end of this they may continue on to higher education or begin an apprenticeship for a job up to age 18.

There are three main kinds of **secondary education schools** from which to choose: *liceo classico* (classical high school), *liceo scientifico* (scientific high school) and *liceo artistico* (artistic high school). Otherwise, teens can opt to continue with a technical education (*istituti tecnici*) or a vocational school (*istituti professionali*). The *liceo classico* offers a course of study in the humanities with a focus on culture and the classics, while the goal of the *liceo scientifico* is to prepare students who intend to study science at university level. These schools offer a five-year course that terminates on completion of the exam that every Italian child dreads, called *la maturità*. *Liceo artistico* students get an education orientated towards the visual arts; studies last four years and end with the *maturità artistica* exam. On completion, they can apply to enter a fine arts academy or the architecture department of a university.

The last step is university, where a student earns a *diploma universitario di primo livello* (*laurea breve*: two or three years), or a *diploma di laurea* (four years), or specialist degree. Some go on to earn a *dottorato di ricerca o scuola di specializzazione* (doctorate).

## *Are You a* Dottore?

It's the moment university graduates wait for, and is more meaningful than holding the freshly minted degree itself. It's when a student goes from being an anonymous 'anybody' and becomes a *dottore*.

Now the days of the *dottore*, or title of 'doctor', bestowed on all university graduates, are numbered. Part of a packet of educational reforms is a proposal to ban what is seen as an inflationary use of the title; *dottore* will be limited to doctors, surgeons and physicians.

For many, earning the right to be called *dottore* is an Italian rite of passage, with roots in a time when class lines were drawn by noble titles. Titles still exist, and key business executives have been permanently branded by theirs. Gianni Agnelli, the honorary chairman of Fiat, is simply known as *l'Avvocato*, or 'the lawyer'. Carlo De Benedetti, the former CEO of Olivetti, is referred to as *l'Ingegnere*, or 'the engineer', and Silvio Berlusconi carries the distinctive title of *il Cavaliere* – 'the knight'.

'My father told me a story of his friend who gave good hunting tips to the king of Italy,' says Giampaolo Rossi, who heads the commission pushing for the *dottore* ban. 'As a reward, the king asked him to choose between a noble title and a new gun. He was smart, he took the gun.'

If you would prefer that your children continue with a British education, consult **www.intoitaly.it** for a list of the English-language schools nearest you. For more information on education in Italy, visit **www.britishcouncil.it**. Schools from which to choose include the following.

- **Britannia International School of Rome (britanniainternational@hotmail. com)**. Offers a curriculum based on primary school practice in Britain.

- **St George's British International School (www.stgeorge.school.it)**. In Rome; this has a 95 per cent British staff, teaching a curriculum leading to the International Baccalaureate.

- **The New School (www.newschoolrome.com)**. Also in Rome, is similar.

- **Sir James Henderson British School (www.sjhschool.com)**. In Milan.

# Health and Emergencies

State-run healthcare in Italy, or SSN (*servizio sanitario nazionale*), is generally good and free to residents or available at a low annual fee for non-residents, but, since much of the funding for healthcare is accessed regionally, expect to get better service in richer areas and less so in poorer ones. There is always the option of seeing a doctor in a private hospital if you are wary of the public system. However, if you decide to rely on Italy's state healthcare, get to know your doctors and options in advance of an emergency to avoid problems or unpleasant surprises – vital where your health is concerned.

The English *Yellow Pages* (**www.intoitaly.it**) has a complete list of English-speaking dentists, doctors, therapists, surgeons and hospitals.

If you are only visiting a holiday home for short periods each year, and are still paying UK National Insurance and tax-reident in the UK, you should obtain a **European Health Insurance Card (EHIC)**, which replaced the old E111 form in January 2006. You can apply for it at post offices, online at **www.dh.gov.uk/ travellers** or by phone, **t** 0845 606 2030. It gives all EU citizens access to the same national state healthcare as citizens of each member state or EEA country, and thus can reduce the cost of, or allow free, health service when you travel. The card is valid for 3–5 years and covers expenses in case of illness, accident (if the latter occurs, you will be given the same assistance as an Italian citizen living in the country), and assistance for treatment due to chronic disease. The card is not valid if your trip to Italy is made with the principal intention of receiving medical treatment.

For further information, see **www.ehic.org.uk**, or obtain a copy of the free NHS booklet *Health Advice for Travellers*. When going to the pharmacy or to see a specialist or to hospital, remember to carry the EHIC with you.

If you become employed or self-employed in Italy for up to a year, and continue to be liable for UK National Insurance contributions, your UK-issued EHIC is valid. If the employment continues for longer than a year, you will probably then be paying social security contributions locally and will be eligible for healthcare as an Italian resident (*see* below) – at which point you will need to apply for an Italian-issued EHIC to cover you for trips to countries *outside* Italy.

EU pensioners are entitled to free healthcare as if they were Italian citizens; obtain form E121 from the pensions office before you leave the UK.

Visitors from non-EU countries have no such entitlements and will need comprehensive health insurance. There may, however, be bilateral agreements between your country and Italy that will give you limited benefits (ask at your local ASL office).

Everyone living in the country should register with a local doctor (GP) in Italy. All visits to your local doctor will be free. He or she can issue prescriptions and make onward referrals to specialists. You may choose treatment from any doctor, dentist or authorised hospital registered with the state health scheme (*servizio sanitario nazionale; SSN*). Certain types of treatment need prior consent from your local health service administrators or a prescription from your local doctor. Do remember that many dentists in Italy work as private doctors; to find those operating with the national health service, ask your local ASL (*see* below).

Care received is free, but you pay part of the cost of medicines and a ticket for specialist treatment at hospital. In emergencies or cases of hardship there can be exceptions to this rule, according to the region you have settled in. If you choose to be treated in a private hospital, you will have to pay all of the costs and then, possibly, reclaim part repayment.

The **Azienda Sanitaria Locale (ASL)** is the government agency responsible for running Italy's vast network of health services. You can locate the nearest ASL office by looking in the Italian phone book under Azienda Sanitaria Locale or ASL. The requirements for national healthcare coverage depend on your status; for example, a non-EU resident in Italy on a student visa is eligible for some services. Freelance employees are often required to register with the local **INPS** (Italian social security office) when they sign on with the ASL.

In general, anyone in Italy, even those who would not automatically be entitled, such as those economically inactive but still below retirement age, can have state health coverage if they pay an annual fee that starts at €600 per year. They will be registered for the *mutua* (medical coverage) and will be assigned a *medico mutualistico*, or general practitioner.

If you opt not to sign on with state healthcare, you will be expected to pay for treatment, either directly via a medical insurer's charge card or from your own resources. In the latter case you can reclaim the cost from your insurers. In general, you will have to pay part of the cost of medicines. Many people carry supplementary insurance to cover these expenses. These policies are usually quite inexpensive.

If you are interested in coverage with an Italian health insurer, the largest company is INA (Istituto Nazionale delle Assicurazioni; **www.inaassitalia.it**).

Private policies are also offered by Sanicard, Filo Diretto, Europa Assistance and Pronto Assistance. Contact information is listed in your local phone book under *assicurazioni* for insurance companies.

In the case of an **emergency**, go directly to the nearest hospital or call **t** 118 for an ambulance or for emergency medical assistance. This number can be reached from any phone in Italy (landline or mobile) and there is no charge for calling.

# Social Services and Welfare Benefits

You can qualify for welfare benefits in one of three ways: by enforced reciprocal EU/EEA rules; under the rules of the country where you pay social security contributions; or under the rules of the country where you are living.

## The General EU Rules

The basic idea behind the EU/EEA rules is that persons exercising their right to move from one EU or EEA state to another should not lose out on their welfare benefit rights by doing so.

The people covered by the EU/EEA rules are:

- **employed and self-employed nationals of EU/EEA states**
- **pensioners who are nationals of EU/EEA states**
- **subject to certain restrictions, members of the families of the above, whatever their nationality**
- **civil servants of EU/EEA states and members of their families, provided they are not covered by an enhanced scheme for civil servants in their own country (this is generally not a problem for UK civil servants)**

Note that the EU/EEA rules do not cover the economically inactive (people retired early, students, etc.). In other cases, they cover:

- **health benefits**
- **accidents at work**
- **occupational maladies**
- **invalidity benefits**
- **old-age pensions**
- **widows' and other survivors' benefits**
- **death grants**
- **unemployment benefits**
- **family benefits**

The rules do not replace the national benefits to which you may be entitled. Rather, they co-ordinate varying national schemes and decide in which of several possible countries a person should make a claim and which country should pay the cost. Apart from the basic principle that you should not lose out on benefits simply by moving to another EU country like Italy, the other basic principle to keep in mind is that you should only be subject to the rules of one country at a time. The laws of one EU member state cannot – except in the case of unemployment benefits – take away or reduce your entitlement to benefit just because you live in another member state.

If you remain entitled to a UK benefit while living in Italy, payment of benefit to which you were entitled in your original member state can be made in different ways, depending on the country and benefit concerned. It can be paid by authorities in the member state in which you now live, on behalf of the authorities of your home country, or it can be paid to you directly in your new country by the benefit authorities in your home country.

If you remain entitled to a UK benefit or one from another EU country while living in Italy, payment of benefit to which your were entitled in your original member state can be paid in a number of different ways, depending on the state and benefit concerned. It can be paid:

• **by the benefit authorities in the member state in which you now live, acting on behalf of the benefit authorities in your original country.**

• **to you directly in your new country by the benefit authorities in your old country.**

## How Do You Decide Which Rules Apply to You?

The rules that apply to you depend on which country insures you and the country in which you live.

• **Which country insures you?**

You are insured in the country where you carry out your **work**. If you work regularly in more than one member state you are insured in the country where you live. Short-term postings (of less than one year) to another country will be ignored.

**Retired people** who have only worked in one member state will remain 'attached' to that state for pension and other purposes for the rest of their lives. People who have worked in several states will have built up pension entitlements in each member state in which they worked for more than one year.

• **In which country do you live?**

Some benefits flow from your presence in a country. Each potential benefit, in Britain and in Italy, has associated rules stipulating which categories of people are entitled to benefit from it.

# Italian Benefits

If you need to claim benefits in Italy, your entitlement will be determined by the social security payments you have made in Italy, as well as any relevant contributions made in the UK.

## Health Benefits

These were covered in the healthcare section, above. To summarise, you can qualify for free healthcare or, if you are a non-EU resident, you may pay a subscription fee to access the system.

## Accidents at Work, Occupational Maladies and Invalidity and Disability Benefits

Unless you have worked in Italy at some time you are not likely to benefit from this kind of pension. For more information, *see* 'Working and Employment', pp.203–205.

## Pensions

Unless you have worked in Italy at some time you are not likely to benefit from an Italian pension, but you will continue to receive your UK pension. Pensions in EU countries are paid on the basis of 'totalisation'. This means that if you have lived in various countries, all of your contributions in any EU country will be added together to calculate your pension entitlement. For example, if Italy pays a minimum pension after 15 years' contributions and a full pension after 35 years', if you have paid enough contributions – anywhere in the EU – to qualify, you will get a pension. If you have worked for 5 years out of 35 in Italy and the balance elsewhere, the Italian government will pay 5/35ths of your pension at the rates applicable in Italy. If you had worked for 10 years in the UK, the British government would pay 10/35ths, and so on. In Italy, the retirement age is 65 for a man and 60 for a woman.

## Unemployment Benefits

f you lose your job, the Italian unemployment benefit authority must take into account any periods of employment or NI contributions paid in other EU countries when calculating your entitlement to benefits in Italy. You must, however, have paid at least some insurance payments in Italy prior to claiming unemployment benefits in Italy. That means you cannot go to Italy for the purpose of claiming benefit. You should obtain form E301 from the UK benefit authorities before going to Italy.

If you travel to Italy to seek employment there are restrictions on your entitlement to benefit, and you must comply with all Italian procedural requirements.

You must have been unemployed and available for work in your home country for at least four weeks before going to Italy. You must contact your 'home' unemployment benefit authority and obtain a form E303 before leaving for Italy. You must register for work in Italy within seven days of arrival. You will be entitled to benefit for a maximum of three months. If you cannot find a job during that period you will only be entitled to continuing unemployment benefit in your home country if you return within the three-month period. If you do not, you can lose all entitlement to benefits. You are only entitled to one three-month payment between two periods of employment.

## Family Benefits

If the members of your family live in the same country as that in which you are insured, then that country pays the benefits. You are entitled to the same benefits as nationals of that state. If your family does not live in the same country as that where you are insured, if you are entitled to benefits under the rules of more than one country, they will receive the highest amount to which they would have been entitled in any of the relevant states. Pensioners normally receive family benefits from the EU member state that pays their pension.

# UK Benefits

Despite living in Italy, you are still eligible to claim many UK benefits.

Welfare benefits in the UK are divided into two categories: 'contributory' and 'non-contributory'. The former are benefits to which you are only entitled if you have paid (or been credited with) sufficient National Insurance contributions to qualify. The latter do not depend on paying any National Insurance contributions.

In the UK there are various classes of National Insurance contributions. Not all rank equally for benefits purposes and some types of National Insurance contributions cannot be used to qualify for payments of certain benefits.

The categories are:

- **Class 1**: paid by employees and their employers and consisting of a percentage of income.
- **Class 2**: a flat-rate payment paid by self-employed people.
- **Class 3**: voluntary payments made by people no longer paying Class 1 or Class 2; their rights are protected for a limited range of benefits.
- **Class 4**: compulsory 'profit-related' additional contributions paid by self-employed people.

These differing types of NI payments qualify you for various benefits:

## NI Contributions and Entitlement to UK Benefits

|                               | Class 1 | Class 2/4 | Class 3 |
| ----------------------------- | ------- | --------- | ------- |
| Maternity allowances          | Yes     | Yes       | No      |
| Unemployment benefit          | Yes     | No        | No      |
| Incapacity benefit            | Yes     | Yes       | No      |
| Widow's benefit               | Yes     | Yes       | Yes     |
| Basic retirement pension      | Yes     | Yes       | Yes     |
| Additional retirement pension | Yes     | No        | No      |

In addition to being categorised as 'contributory' and 'non-contributory', benefits are also divided into 'means-tested' and 'non-means-tested'. The former are paid only if you qualify under the eligibility criteria for the benefit in question and are poor enough to qualify on financial grounds. The latter are paid to anyone who meets the eligibility criteria, irrespective of their wealth. (Means-tested UK benefits are likely to be of little interest to the resident in Italy.)

## Health Benefits

These were covered in the healthcare section, pp.209–11.

## Accidents at Work

Any benefits you presently receive from the UK benefits system as a result of an accident at work should remain payable to you in Italy.

## Occupational Maladies

Any benefits you receive from the UK benefits system as a result of an occupational disease should remain payable to you despite the fact that you have moved to Italy.

## Invalidity Benefits

Any National Insurance benefits you receive from the UK benefits system as a result of invalidity should remain payable to you in Italy. Attendance Allowance, SDA and DLA are not usually payable if you go to live abroad permanently.

## Pensions

If you are already retired and you only ever paid National Insurance contributions in the UK, you will receive your UK retirement pension wherever you choose to live within the EU/EEA. You will be paid without deduction (except remittance charges) and your pension will be updated whenever pensions in the UK are revised.

If you have established an entitlement to a retirement pension in several EU countries by virtue of working in them, all of the pensions will be payable to you in Italy. Once again, they will be paid without deduction (except remittance charges) and your pension will be updated whenever the pensions in those countries are revised.

If you have not yet retired and moved to Italy (whether you intend to work in Italy or not), your entitlement to your UK pension will be frozen and the pension to which you are entitled will be paid to you at UK retirement age. This freezing of your pension can be a disadvantage, especially if you are still relatively young when you move to Italy. This is because you need to have made a minimum number of NI contributions in order to qualify for a full UK state pension. If you have not yet done this but are not far off, it may be worth making additional payments while you are resident overseas.

You may choose to pay either continuing Class 2 or Class 3 contributions. You may pay **Class 2** contributions if:

- **you are working abroad.**
- **you have lived in the UK for a continuous period of at least three years during which you paid NI contributions and you have already paid a set minimum amount of NI contributions.**
- **you were normally employed or self-employed in the UK before going abroad.**

You may pay **Class 3** contributions if:

- **you have at any time lived in the UK for a continuous period of at least three years.**
- **you have already paid a minimum amount in NI contributions in the UK.**

Class 2 contributions are more expensive but potentially cover you for maternity allowance and incapacity benefits. Class 3 contributions do not. In both cases you should apply in the UK using form CF83 from the DSS.

## Widow's and Other Survivor's Benefits

Any benefits you receive from the UK benefits system as a result of your being a widow should remain payable to you despite the fact that you have moved to Italy.

## Unemployment Benefits

You may be able to get contribution-based Jobseeker's Allowance in the EU/EEA for up to 13 weeks if you:

- **are entitled to a contribution-based Jobseeker's Allowance on the day you go abroad.**
- **have registered as a jobseeker for at least four weeks before you leave (this can be less in special circumstances).**

- are available for work and actively seeking work in Great Britain up to the day you leave.

- are going abroad to look for work.

- register for work at the equivalent of a Jobcentre in the country to which you are going, within seven days of last claiming Jobseeker's Allowance in the UK (if you do not, you may lose benefit).

- follow the other country's system for claiming benefit.

- follow the other country's benefit rules, such as being available for and actively seeking work, that would have applied had you stayed in the UK.

# Retirement

A large number of the foreigners who move to Italy do so in their retirement years. The section above describes pension benefits, both Italian and UK ones that are applied in Italy, in detail. To summarise, income from state or private UK pensions can be paid in Italy without a problem. Unless you have worked in Italy at some time you are not likely to benefit from a Italian pension. Earlier in this chapter, you will also find information regarding healthcare options for the elderly in Italy. The following section, on the other hand, highlights some of the other questions you may face when retiring to Italy.

## Receiving Pension Payments

If you have a company pension, it will be paid wherever the pension scheme rules dictate. Some plans allow the administrators to pay the money into any bank in the world and others, ostensibly for security reasons, insist the money be paid into a UK bank account. If your plan will pay into your Italian bank, this is the most convenient option, but keep in mind that you will pay for bank transfers so it is probably best if this happens no more than four times per year. You should also keep an eye on fluctuating exchange rates. Some pensioners make arrangements with currency dealers who send the money at an exchange rate that applies for the whole year. If you have a government pension (army, civil service, police, etc.) your pension will still be taxed in the UK. Otherwise the pension should be paid gross (tax-free) and it will be taxed in Italy.

## Death

A death in Italy must be registered within 24 hours. This, like many other bureaucratic procedures, is done at the town hall or *comune*. As a British person, you should also record the death with the British consulate. Burial is much more common in Italy than is cremation. Crematoria are usually only found in larger towns and cities and 'burial' is often in a filing cabinet-type vault. Funerals are as exceedingly expensive in Italy as they are in the UK, and taking a body home is also very costly. (*See also* pp.157–9.)

## Inheritance

Inheritance law for Italians is much more restrictive than the rules under English law. Certain groups of people have (almost) automatic rights to inherit all or a part of your property, such as spouses and offspring. Fortunately, if you are not Italian you can dispose of your property according to your national law. For British people this is, basically, as they please. (*See also* pp.168–9.)

### Making a Will

*See* pp.168–9.

# Cars and Other Private Transport

The rules of the road and driving in Italy were covered in **Selecting a Property**, but there are also many considerations around ownership of a car in Italy: insurance, drivers' licences and the differences between buying a car in Italy and bringing your car from the UK.

Starting with the last point, it must be noted that, curiously, it is still technically illegal for non-Italian-residents to own a car in Italy. Yet, since this is almost certainly a breach of EU law, some dealers will provide you with conflicting information, and some will sell you a car anyway, leaving you with problems when you try to register it. Nonetheless, Italian law is bound to change soon, making it easier for foreigners to purchase and register vehicles there.

If you are an Italian resident and an EU national, it makes more sense for you to **buy a car in Italy**, despite the fact that prices are on average slightly higher. It is much safer, when driving on the right, to do so in a car with the steering

### A City on a Plate

In the past, licence plates showed which city the car was from. For example, 'MI' is for Milano and 'CA' for Catania, but, because lawmakers argued that racist acts were being committed against drivers from the south (an increase in 'car-keying' was seen at the height of secessionist sentiments in the 1990s), the names of the cities were removed from licence plates. However, a few years ago, a wave of nostalgia moved lawmakers to reinstate the city codes. As a result, Italian roads are a mish-mash of different plates, some of which don't even resemble Italian ones. There are white plates, black ones, ones with blue EU shading and older ones with orange lettering.

wheel on the left-hand side, and you will find that it is easier to get spare parts. Parts can differ on UK models, even if that same vehicle is sold throughout Europe. Also, having an Italian car will make you stand out less in the eyes of thieves who scan car parks and motorway service stations for foreign licence plates that they mistakenly believe denote valuable treasures hidden within.

If you are a non-EU citizen, you can purchase a car in Italy without paying the 20 per cent VAT, but this special privilege has its limits. If you qualify, go to your local town hall, or *comune*, and ask for an *atto sostitutivo*, which states that you are not an EU national. Once you have obtained that you can get EE (*escursionisti esteri*) licence plates that are valid for one year and can be renewed once for a second year. At the end of that time, you must take your vehicle out of the country (paying the 20 per cent VAT), or give back the EE plates (and pay the 20 per cent tax).

EU nationals must **register their vehicles** (*immatricolare*) like anyone else, and pay the tax. You will then be given national licence plates (*targhe nazionali*).

If you buy a used car, you must complete a transfer of ownership (*passaggio di proprietà*) and might have to wait several months (sometimes a year) until the registration papers (*libretto di cirolazione*) are in your name. While you wait for the *libretto*, you must obtain a temporary one called the *foglio sostitutivo*, which can be renewed every three months at the Ufficio di Motorizzazione, or Department of Motor Vehicles. In addition, all owners must pay an annual *bollo*, or tax, determined by the size of the car's engine. It can be paid at the ACI (Automobile Club d'Italia) at the end of January or February each year (depending on the type of vehicle).

If you **bring your car from the UK**, technically you are supposed to register it with the Italian authorities, thus obtaining Italian plates, after one year. Although it is illegal not to do so, few foreigners bother. Some drive around in British cars for years, even decades, beaming with delight because they know that no parking ticket (*multa*) or other violation will ever contaminate their blissful existence on the road. (This is a fantastic loophole in Italian law, whereby parking violations must come by registered mail to your home, but city officials won't send registered mail abroad so, if your car is registered in England, those tickets never materialise.) Italian parking police have started to fight back by clamping foreign cars and demanding cash payment from owners before freeing them from the shackles.

If you are not sure what nationality to give your car, there is a middle ground. You can use a British car on Italian roads for a maximum of six months per year without converting it into an Italian car. If you intend to keep the vehicle in Italy for more than six months in any year (or if you keep it longer than one year) you must officially import the vehicle into Italy, which involves it being tested and re-registered in Italy to get Italian plates.

If you are resident in Italy and bought the vehicle in another EU country you should be able to import it free of VAT. If you bought the vehicle tax-free or in a non-EU country you will have to pay the VAT immediately on arrival in Italy. In either case, you will need a customs certificate confirming that the vehicle is free of Italian VAT, or that the VAT has been paid. You will also have to pay the Italian registration fees and tax.

Whether you buy a car in Italy or import your own, you will have to decide what to do about your **driving licence**. Until recently, Italian law demanded that all foreigners living in Italy convert their licences into Italian ones. There was a certain amount of paperwork involved (mostly official translations) but it did not involve taking an Italian driving test. Following the latest EU directive on the mutual recognition of driving licences this is no longer required for EU nationals. That means you are allowed to drive in Italy on a valid British licence.

To obtain an **Italian driver's licence**, you must register for both the written test and the practical one at the nearest office of the ACI (**www.aci.it**), the Automobile Club d'Italia, which also registers cars and offers driving lessons and 24-hour roadside assistance for members. The test is taken at the Ufficio di Motorizzazione and is based on European standards (including kilometres instead of miles). It can be taken in English but, nonetheless, the test is still hard, including questions on the length of truck axles and first-aid knowledge. ACI can provide you with a 200-page booklet with sample questions. In addition to passing both the written and practical exams, you must take an eye test, provide photos, and pay an application fee. You will get a *foglio rosa* (learner's permit) first and will have to drive around with a large 'P' (for *principante* or 'beginner') on the back of your car. Once you have obtained the driver's licence you must keep it valid by paying an expensive *marca da bollo* tax each year. This is a driver's licence tax, and is paid in addition to the car tax.

Always make sure your **car insurance** is current, as driving without insurance can lead to a hefty fine, and roadside checks for insurance violations are common. Remember that it is illegal to drive in Italy without insurance, a drivers' licence and a *libretto di circolazione* (registration document). Photocopies are not acceptable. If you are insured in England, make sure you have been given a *carta verde* (Green Card), which demonstrates coverage in other European countries. Third-party insurance is a basic requirement in Italy.

If you plan on buying Italian insurance, there are two kinds. The first is the so-called *bonus-malus* whereby you pay a premium depending on the number of accidents in which you are involved. Payments are low for those who manage to avoid regularly hitting other moving targets. The second is the *assicurazione con franchigia fissa ed assoluta*. In this case, you pay a set excess before the insurance company will cover damages. There are three main companies: Sai, Riunione Adriatica di Sicurità (Allianz Ras) and Assitalia (Generali).

If you have an **accident**, make sure you get the *numero di targa* (licence plate number), *marca e tipo di macchina* (make and model description of the vehicle), the *numero di patente* (driver's licence number), address, name and phone number of the other driver. If you and the other driver agree on what happened, fill out a *constatazione amichevole-denuncia di sinistro* form, which means the case will be settled between insurance companies. If you and the other driver don't have matching versions of events, you will be requested to submit a letter with your side of the story, and might be asked to furnish witnesses.

If you need **roadside assistance**, call **t** 116 from any phone, free of charge.

**Parking** is a serious problem in Italy and, if you can afford it, it makes sense to find a dedicated parking space. Cities like Rome – in which there are 300,000 official parking spaces for the city's two million registered cars – are parking no man's land for frustrated drivers. Pay parking spaces are marked by a blue line and any other open space you find is undoubtedly illegal. An army of parking police, *vigili urbani*, regularly make the rounds and hand out tickets. Some spaces are guarded by 'self-nominated parking guardians' who will offer to 'protect' your car while you are away and ask a small donation for their efforts. You're better off paying than discovering what happens if you don't. Also remember that the historic centres of most big cities are closed to cars without special entry permits. You can only qualify to receive such a permit if you can demonstrate that you live within the historic centre and have Italian plates. Authorities will not give a *centro storico* pass to a car with British plates even if the owners can prove that they live in the centre. Many big cities, such as Rome, divide the pass by neighbourhood so that, for example, a driver with a pass for Zone A still can't drive in Zone B, and vice versa. At times of high pollution, alternate days of access to city centres (*targhe alterne*) are allocated to odd – and even-numbered licence plates. This applies to all traffic.

If you buy a moped or scooter, make sure the seller gives you the *libretto di circolazione* (registration papers) and that the serial number (*numero di telaio*) matches the one on the registration. Stolen mopeds are a hot commodity on the black market. You will also need to get a *targa*, or licence plate, which is issued in your name. If you sell the vehicle, you should remove the plate and put it on your new one. Insurance for damages on others is mandatory, and so is wearing a helmet. When it went into effect, Italy's two million *motorino* owners complained about the helmet law, although those in Rome and the north have now grown accustomed to headgear. Evidently no one told people in Naples the law had gone into effect, and there it is incredibly rare to see a moped driver wearing a helmet, just as it is incredibly common to see three or four family members (father, mother and kids) hanging on to the seat of a single Vespa.

# Taking Your Pet to Italy

The rules regarding the transportation of pets to and from Italy have changed over the last few years, so it's best to contact authorities at the British and Italian Ministries of Agriculture in advance of your trip. In general, you are welcome to bring most domestic pets into Italy, but if you own something

## Case Study: The Case of the Cow

'What else could I do?,' asks John Lasant. 'I called my office and said I wouldn't be making it to work that day because there was a dead cow floating in my swimming pool.' This 40-year-old business executive bought a farmhouse in inland Sicily five years ago with his Sicilian wife and his two children. With offices in Rome and London, he makes the vertical commute down the Italian peninsula almost every weekend simply because he can't get enough of southern living. 'But this incident was enough to break the camel's back – only in this case it was a cow.'

The Lasant estate is located in a rural area, where cows graze nearby and shepherds herd goats to rest under shady trees during the hottest hours of the Sicilian sun. Apparently, on one very hot day in the summer of 2002, a thirsty cow meandered over to his swimming pool and leaned over just a bit too far while trying to steal a sip. 'We had to bring in a crane to hoist it out and it took something like 15 people to perform the operation.'

But, according to Lasant, the worst was yet to come. 'About a month later, I got a letter saying I was being sued for damages by the cow's owner for failing to put up a fence around my property,' he muses. 'And it looks as if I'll have to pay.'

exotic you should definitely check first. Animals other than ordinary pets (for example, South American birds and African reptiles) require a special importation certificate from the Italian Ministry of Agriculture, which may well have a lengthy list of conditions attached to it.

The most important decision to make is whether or not you intend to bring the pet back to England again, as the United Kingdom has notoriously stringent rules for the importation of animals. If your pet is booked for a round trip, you will need a British 'Pet Passport'. To obtain one, see your vet at least six months before your departure and expect to pay about £250. You will not receive one at the last minute, for reasons outlined below, so it's best to make arrangements well in advance. It will allow your pet to return to its native ground without enduring the six-month quarantine period that incoming pets have been subject to in the past.

You will be required to do the following, with a government-authorised vet in any country covered under the Pet Travel Scheme (known as PETS), including Italy:

- Have your pet microchipped, so that it can be conclusively identified.
- Have your pet vaccinated against rabies.
- Arrange for a blood test that confirms a satisfactory level of protection against rabies (note: your pet may not enter the UK until a full six months have passed since a successful blood test result).
- After the successful test result, get a PETS certificate from the vet.

Further to this, before your pet enters the UK you must also do the following.

• **Have it treated for ticks and tapeworm. This must take place between 24 and 48 hours before it is checked in for its journey to the UK. Any qualified vet can carry out this procedure, and must issue an official certificate of treatment. If this is dated longer than 48 hours before check-in, your pet will not be allowed into the UK.**

• **Sign a declaration of residency, which states that your pet has not been outside any of the PETS qualifying countries in the previous six months.**

Note that the PETS scheme only applies to cats and dogs, and only operates on certain sea, air and rail routes to England. Because conditions may change, and for further information, see the British government web page about PETS (**www.defra.gov.uk/animalh/quarantine/index.htm**), or order a PETS information pack from PETS Helpline (**t** 08702 411 710).

If you know you are not going to want to bring your pet back to Britain, then all you need is an export certificate from the British Ministry of Agriculture and a health certificate issued within 15 days of your departure by a state-approved vet. If the animal is susceptible to rabies, it will require a rabies vaccination certificate. You are only allowed to take two animals into Italy at any time. This is for each traveller and does not prevent you from returning with more animals later. Once you and your pet have settled into Italy, you should see an Italian vet for a general check-up and to make sure your cat or dog has been vaccinated against all the appropriate maladies. Diseases carried by rabies, ticks and animal bites are obviously a concern to all pet-owners and, since your pet could be less resistant to some 'alien' ones not common in the UK, this will be money well spent.

# Crime and the Police

Where there is money, there are thieves. Security is an issue in Italy – especially if your Italian home is empty much of the year. There are nightmare stories of home-owners who return after a trip abroad to find that their home has been stripped clean. In one case, robbers even tore down walls and made off with valuable copper pipes used for plumbing. In another, bandits removed a one-ton safe that was fixed to the property's support beams and carried it down four flights of stairs.

Mass hysteria concerning crime rates has kept Italy on its toes for some years but, in fact, the numbers have not moved significantly in recent times. Some data suggests that crime is actually diminishing. Most people believe that the south is far more dangerous than the north. While this is true, the latest statistics suggest that the south is getting safer just as quickly as the north becomes more of a target.

## The Medieval Way

There aren't many reasons to visit San Genesio, a nondescript town lying between soggy rice paddies in the expanses of Lombardy, but, if the mayor gets his way, even chance visitors will be prohibited from entering at all, at least at certain times. San Genesio's first citizen is pushing a plan to lock in residents and lock out robbers. He has freed up money to install iron gates on three of the town's four entry points, that will be open during the day but will shut at dusk. An overnight guardian will be posted at each entrance to prohibit passage. Only San Genesiani will know where the fourth, ungated entrance is.

Why gates? Because this town of just 3,300 people has been hit hard by what locals describe as a 'crime wave'. A Jeep Cherokee, a Volkswagen Golf and a Mitsubishi have vanished. A Mercedes-Benz was even stolen from its garage as its owners ate dinner in the room above. Although gated communities are par for the course in many country club-type neighbourhoods, Italy hasn't seen a *città chiusa*, or closed city, since fortified bastions and castle moats kept out rivals, brigands and bandits. 'It's not as if we're going to throw boiling oil on people,' said the mayor; 'we're being compared to a medieval town, but there's nothing wrong with legitimate defence.' That may be, but, as one inquisitive resident ventured, 'What if the thieves are hiding inside?'

There are no special precautions that you should take in Italy that you wouldn't take at home. You can install iron bars on your windows or fit *serrande*, metal curtains, on your doors. These make your home almost impenetrable. You can fit electric alarms or hire the services of a private patrol or guardian. Some owners install a fake security camera as a deterrent. The best thing is to know your neighbours and local shopkeepers, and be active in your community. Don't leave obvious signs that your home is empty. A pile of unopened mail in front of your door or an overgrown garden could attracted unwanted attention. Remember the expression *occasione fa ladro* ('opportunity makes the thief') and don't put temptation in anyone's way. Also bear in mind that more than 50 per cent of home robberies occur in the summer months when most Italian homeowners are on vacation.

If you need **emergency assistance** at any time dial **t** 113. You can also get in touch with the police on your mobile phone even if your pre-paid phone is out of credit or you are outside your provider's roaming zone.

There are four branches of Italian police with which you should become familiar. Each has a special jurisdiction and operates independently of the others. These forces were put in place to deter any one police force from growing too strong (following Italy's deadly flirtation with Fascism), and each is controlled by a separate ministry. And, last, each has its own fashion designer. Giorgio Armani designed the *carabinieri*'s uniform and Fendi created the one for the *vigili urbani*.

• **Carabinieri**: They work for the Ministry of Defence and, in the past, have been implicated in shady operations such as attempting to overthrow the government, as in 1964. The *carabinieri* are an all-male military police force, although women may soon be allowed to volunteer. There are currently about 100,000 active members and their headquarters are the *caserma* or *commando*. You'll see these elegant officers, with a red stripe on their trouser legs, arresting pornography kingpins and drug dealers as their jurisdiction is nationwide. Television shows featuring these officers are prime-time favourites.

• **Polizia**: Notorious competitors of the *carabinieri* (as the many bad jokes regarding the two will tell: 'Why did the *polizia* officer shoot the witness to the Mafia killing? Because he knew too much.'). They are regulated by the Ministry of the Interior and their headquarters are the *questura*. There are female officers (popular on another kind of late-night TV programming). If they want to get your attention, they will wave a lollipop-like paddle at you.

• **Guardia di finanza**: They are responsible for combating tax evasion (needless to say, a big problem in Italy) and smuggling, as they also serve as the nation's coastguard. Their roots go back to the ancient police forces that watched borders between warring principalities before Italian unification. They are regulated by the Ministry of Finance and you will often see their gallant efforts on TV as they save illegal immigrants from ruthless human traffickers in the south.

• **Vigili urbani**: They do not carry guns like all the others (although some municipalities have recently allowed them to carry pepper spray) and are not after major criminals. They are after you, especially if you park in an illegal spot or dispose of your household refuse in the wrong bin. They are like a neighbourhood police force and have even been spotted handing out tickets to shirtless male tourists (an indecent exposure offence).

# Italian Politics

The Republic of Italy is just over a century old, despite roots in antiquity. Before 1861, the country was a collection of regional principalities with independent states, dialects, currencies and even different standards for weights and measures. Each spent a good amount of time on the battlefield but, despite their contrasts, Italy was proclaimed a united nation following the Risorgimento, when Giuseppe Garibaldi and his army of Redshirts united the territories in the name of King Vittorio Emanuele II and the Italian monarchy. In 1870, Rome was conquered and Italy as we know it was born.

Even once under the single *tricolore* flag, Italy remained a loosely assembled collection of regions. Benito Mussolini, who led the nation into the Second

World War, had fantasies of the victorious conquests of an Italian empire with colonies in Africa, but an empire was never born and, even today, many of the problems of the past, such as regionalism, continue. The fact that Italy has such a short history explains many of the contradictions inherent today. It has long been commented that Italy is only unified during World Cup football matches, when Italians push aside regional differences to support their team. Some have noted that Italy is no more than a 'geographic expression' – or a land held together by mountains and water but not by a sense of identity.

Italy emerged from Fascism with a desire to rebuild a unified nation. In 1946, the Italian Republic was formed following a popular referendum in which voters ousted the monarchy that had ruled them for 70 years. A year later, the Italian constitution was approved and Italy became a democratic republic divided into 20 regions made up of *province* (provinces) and *comuni* (municipalities). A political structure was implemented so that no one party or individual could gain too much power, as Mussolini had. Ultimately, that system has been partly responsible for the country's subsequent lack of political stability.

The government consists of two Houses of Parliament (a Chamber of Deputies and a Senate), the president (*presidente della repubblica*) and the prime minister (*presidente del consiglio*). The president is elected by the Parliament and functions as the official head of state, though he or she does not set the political agenda. Instead, the prime minister, chosen by the president based on election results, runs the nation. The prime minister is also responsible for forming the actual government by selecting from members of his or her coalition and appointing heads of ministries. Overseeing all of this is the Constitutional Court, which consists of 15 judges (five appointed by the president, five elected by Parliament and five elected by the ordinary and administrative Supreme Courts), who define the power of the state.

While Italy's political system has many built-in safety measures, it actually amounts to a structure so weak that Italian governments fall on average every nine months. About 60 governments have been in place since the founding of the Republic. With as many as 40 political parties at one time, few ever gain a high enough percentage of votes to make a difference. As a result, the only way that governments stay in power is by putting various parties together in poorly defined political alliances. In 1993, the electoral process was reformed by popular referendum to give more direct voting power to the people, but the resulting 'mixed system' based on two electoral principles (proportional and majority representation) is so confusing that lawmakers have repeatedly failed to come up with anything better.

Despite weakened government, the industrial post-war period brought enormous wealth to Italy. The decades of the 1950s and 1960s are known as the period of the 'Italian Miracle', as businesses in the north flourished, catapulting Italy into the same economic bracket as its prosperous northern European neighbours. Turin, the main industrial hub, saw the rise of Fiat, Italy's number

## The Mafia

In 1992, anti-Mafia prosecutor Giovanni Falcone and his wife were murdered, along with three police officers, when his car drove over a remote-controlled mine packed with 500kg (1,100lbs) of explosives on a stretch of highway outside Palermo. A few months later, Falcone's successor and friend Paolo Borsellino was murdered in front of his mother's house in downtown Palermo by another powerful bomb. The explosion killed him and five bodyguards and left virtually no trace of bodily remains.

The Mafia is like the Hydra, the monster from Greek mythology with dozens of heads. If one of its heads is chopped off, two new ones replace it. Hercules and his partner Iolaus discovered that if fire was applied to the wound, Hydra's new heads would not grow, and, with this knowledge, the heroes defeated the monster. Magistrates Falcone and Borsellino are regarded as a modern-day monster-fighting team as they put the heat on the Mafia (they staged the first 'maxi-trials', with hundreds of defendants at a time), but, in the real world, the heroes were defeated by the monster.

After the assassinations, commentators ventured to say that the Mafia had been weakened because those and later attacks were interpreted as acts of desperation to restore the Mafia's diminishing influence. The timing was also suspicious as the bombings were staged in the midst of the 'Clean Hands' investigations, when organised crime lost its influential friends in government. Indeed, a tidal wave of *pentiti*, or turncoats, surfaced leading to the arrests of an unprecedented number of *mafiosi*, including the 'Boss of all Bosses', Totò Riina, who is said to have ordered the Falcone and Borsellino murders. Even today, *pentiti* continue to squeal, brushing aside their allegiance to *omertà*, or the code of silence, which served as a protective shield in the past.

Whether the Mafia has been weakened is still to be seen. Without a doubt it still holds a death grip on parts of the south. The 'Super Mafia', as it was known in the 1970s, infested the country and lurked in every shadow, thanks to isolation and underdevelopment. And, while a centralised Super Mafia is supposedly dismantled, there are regional branches that control large territories. These are the Cosa Nostra in Sicily, the Camorra around Naples, the Ndrangheta in Calabria and the Sacra Corona Unità in Puglia. The latter is said to be gaining rapidly in power and strength thanks to its proximity to the Balkans and its cut of lucrative trafficking in cigarettes, arms, drugs and human beings. Many worry that the state's fight against the Mafia has not succeeded and some suspect that the older generation of *mafiosi*, now sitting in jail cells, is already replaced by a new, younger breed that is more violent and ruthless than its predecessor. If that is so, Hydra's decapitated head may have multiplied.

one car-maker and its single most important company. During the Cold War, Italy served as an axis between the East and West, and was home to the largest Communist party in the Western world. On the other side of the political spectrum, extreme right-wing groups with roots in Fascism began to reappear. To keep the extreme right and left at bay, centrist political alliances held a virtual monopoly on power during those years. The common denominator was the Christian Democratic Party, which had strong ties to the Catholic Church and the United States, both with interests in limiting the spread of Communism. Tensions exploded on 16 March 1978, when former prime minister Aldo Moro was kidnapped by the extreme left-wing Red Brigade. His bullet-ridden body was discovered months later stuffed into a car boot in Rome. The so-called 'Years of Lead', the era of Italian terrorism, mark a turning point in Italian history. The enthusiasm once connected to new wealth halted. Italian governments continued to operate on the 'revolving-door' principle. The same group of people went in to and out of power and, as with anything that stays in one place for too long, a climate ripe for corruption emerged.

With the fall of the Berlin Wall, the division between the East and West became muddled and Italy began a process of self-evaluation so intense that it has been called the 'Second Italian Republic'. A group of judges, led by Antonio di Pietro, exposed the corruption that had tarnished almost all political parties during the 'revolving-door' governments, most especially the Christian Democrats and the Socialists. The judges forced Italians to acknowledge that their nation was rotten at its very core. Di Pietro created computerised files on politicians and businesspeople, logging their incomes and expenses and then cross-referencing the information to uncover massive discrepancies. The evidence became the basis of the anti-corruption probe 'Operation Clean Hands'. It started in around 1992 and, within three years, more than 5,000 businesspeople and politicians, as well as three former prime ministers, had been

## *North and South*

Former separatist Umberto Bossi basked in the limelight when he argued that the prosperous north, including Lombardy, Piemonte and the Veneto, become its own nation named Padania. In 1996, he declared Padania's 'independence' from Italy and pledged that it would have its own parliament and police force. Although Bossi soon switched his focus away from his failed secessionist movement, it became clear that he had exposed a nerve in Italian society that pits north against south.

The north is nine times richer than the south, and is taxed eight times as much. Yet much of the revenue goes to fund reconstruction and development programmes in the impoverished *Mezzogiorno*. Italians live with an enormous feeling of injustice: the northerners because their wealth is not recycled, and the southerners because they are forced to rely on government handouts. The tension borders on racism, with the southerners calling northerners *polentoni* after the cornmeal (*polenta*) they eat. Southerners are branded *terroni*, a pejorative term for 'earth, or dirty, people'. Steps have been taken to decentralise government and award more autonomy to regions.

implicated (including the late Bettino Craxi and seven-times prime minister Giulio Andreotti, once nicknamed 'Eternal Giulio'). Much of the corruption consisted of kickbacks paid in exchange for public works contracts. Italy's financial capital, Milan, became known as *Tangentopoli*, or 'Bribesville', because so many of its citizens were under investigation.

One result was polarised politics, or more defined left- and right-wing groups that cut out many of the in-between parties. Yet many firmly believe that Italy is really governed by interest lobbies, not politicians. All politically affiliated, the most powerful labour unions are the Confederazione Generale Italiano del Lavoro (CGIL), the Confederazione Italiana Sindacati Lavoratori (CISL) and the Unione Italiana dei Lavoratori (UIL). These unions, along with the business lobby Confindustria, might well be Italy's real policymakers.

Don't try to sell that idea to Italy's richest man, though. A former cruise-boat crooner turned media mogul named Silvio Berlusconi campaigned for the prime minister's seat in 1994 and won, bringing his Forza Italia party (named after a soccer chant) to the pinnacle of power. His first mandate lasted a mere eight months and failed partly because of the assorted coalition partners he engaged (including former separatist Umberto Bossi and Gianfranco Fini, formerly the leader of the Movimento Sociale Italiano founded by the Fascists). However, Berlusconi aligned himself with the same people when he became prime minister again in May 2001. Between his governments, the centre-left ruled and, led by Romano Prodi, claimed victory for getting Italy ready for the European Monetary Union (a very difficult task that forced Italy to re-evaluate its role as one of the founding fathers of the European Union). After Prodi, and without a popular mandate, another centre-left leader, Massimo d'Alema (actually further to the left, with ties to the old Communists), took the helm. His government faced the tricky task of joining NATO forces during the Kosovo conflict. Since then, Berlusconi's government, complete with Gianfranco Fini as his number-two man, has held power, while the centre-left opposition struggles to overcome the painful splintering that so many of its parties experienced, as they try to redefine their role in the new millennium.

The right wing led by Berlusconi has undertaken several reforms concerning the labour market, the education system, the law and even the constitution. Yet, for many, the personal interests of the entrepreneur prevailed once more on the subject of national welfare. The government's politics worsened the economic situation of families, who found themselves fighting a progressively decreasing spending power at the same time as the increasing cost of living due to the introduction of the euro. Its strategy caused greater uncertainty for young people in the labour market: they hardly ever, as before, succeed in getting advantageous contracts. A great deal of criticism of foreign policy also came from the opposition, with Italy playing the role of a loyal US and UK ally at times when international terrorism represents a major concern to most of the common people. In the latest regional administrative elections, Forza Italia and friends were, with a few exceptions, deafeningly defeated in most regions of the country, and at the time of writing Italy is heading towards new national elections, taking place in April 2006; many think that the centre-left wing, featuring a great favourite in the person of Romano Prodi, will easily succeed.

# Religion

Italy is a Roman Catholic nation, with Rome home to the Pope, the Vatican, and St Peter's Basilica, the largest church on the planet. However, Italy's religious identity is rapidly changing. Immigration has brought many faiths to Italian soil. Only a few miles away from the Vatican is one of the biggest Islamic mosques in the Western world. A thriving, but small, Italian-Jewish community flourishes, and influences everything from modern intellectual philosophy to cuisine. Sects of Buddhism have appeared, regularly holding conferences that attract members from all over the world. It often surprises foreigners to learn that many Italians are not practising Catholics. In the north, church attendance has dwindled and some only feel 'religious' when businesses shut down to celebrate local saints' days.

## Case Study: The Course of True Love

Here is a story of love found, love lost and a house in Umbria. Cliona, a young artist from Dublin, and her boyfriend, a painter, went on holiday to Italy seven years ago and stumbled across what she describes as a 'barn' near Città di Castello and the Tuscan border at Cortona. 'We just saw it and fell in love,' says the soft-spoken 34-year-old.

Telling themselves they would make an appointment with an estate agent 'for a laugh', Cliona and her partner discovered the property was cheaper than they had anticipated and temptation soon turned into acquisition. 'We thought it would be difficult to buy from abroad, but it really wasn't.' Having a home in Italy made sense to the artistic couple, who foresaw spending a good portion of the year working in Italy. Cliona found conscientious and earnest people to restore her barn and turn it into a home. 'The cost of labour is cheaper but I think there is a higher standard in Italy,' she says. 'The people we worked with were perfectionists, more like craftsmen or artisans than contractors.'

Some way into the project a problem arose. 'We learned that our barn was not zoned to be a residence,' she says. 'We're not sure if our estate agent neglected to tell us or if we were told and our Italian wasn't good enough to understand. Then, my boyfriend and I broke up,' she says, 'and I bought his share of the property, but that's another story.' Cliona remains optimistic that the zoning problem will be resolved and that she will soon be able to work from the home she still loves.

# Italian Food and Drink

What a better way to celebrate your purchase of a new home, and end this chapter, than by toasting with a glass of wine and contemplating Italy's gastronomic tradition. Of course, there is not enough space here to delve deep into the vast heritage that nourishes Italians and feeds their psyche. You will discover – in fact you probably already have – how much importance Italy places on what it eats, and how vast and varying the food-fest is. The good news is that, no matter how long you live in Italy you will never tire of tasting it.

From the deep south, where fresh fish is hauled in on small wooden boats and steamed, fried and baked, to the far north, where cinnamon, spice and everything nice is added to red wine to take winter's chill away, Italy speaks to your inner epicurean. *La cucina italiana* is not just about nutrition. Many dishes, like seafood, are regarded as potent aphrodisiacs, and herbs like basil are credited with magical powers. Every dish, from guitar-string pasta to bean soup, has a story to tell. For example, legend says *tortellini* were invented by a tavern-owner deeply in love with a countess who often stayed overnight as a guest. One night, the man peeked into her bedroom through the keyhole to catch only a glimpse of her bellybutton. That fleeting image was enough to send him back to the kitchen where he shaped pasta dough to resemble what he saw. *Lardo di Colonata*, a wax-like lard, was once chewed by miners in the Carrara marble quarries as a quick energy-booster. Today it is served in the chicest eateries around the world. Italian wines have also outpaced and out-scored many of France's best bottles. From Barolo in the north to Nero d'Avola in Sicily, you'll always find something good to cleanse your palate. For more information on regional gastronomic specialities, *see* the regional food boxes throughout **Profiles of the Regions**.

## Uncorking the History of Italian Wine

Archaeologists recently unearthed evidence in Tuscany that suggests that the wine trade in ancient times was more sophisticated and extensive than previously believed. The findings also confirm that neighbouring France's most distinguished vintages are distant descendants of a massive industry of popular 'plonk' from Italy.

The key to this discovery is in the amphorae, or the large two-handled jars with narrow necks, used by the ancient Romans and Greeks to transport oil and wine. The heavy vessels were designed with pointed bottoms to be used as a third 'handle' to facilitate pouring. Chips and fragments of these clay containers litter the outer rim of the Mediterranean basin, reflecting the breadth of the ancient wine market. Experts determined that an overwhelming number of amphorae – especially those discovered in France – originate from the ancient

## Hollywood's Grape Expectations

Sting, Sean Connery, Anthony Hopkins, Michael Douglas and wife Catherine Zeta Jones are said to be partial to Tuscan vintages – especially wines produced by the Frescobaldi estate. Douglas is even reported to have sent scouts to the region for barrel sampling before investing. Russell Crowe bought a house in Tuscany but has a taste for Piemonte's Barolo. Robert de Niro has a thirst for Brunello di Montalcino. Madonna prefers to wind down with a glass of Bolgheri Sassicaia and Johnny Depp with Terre Alte Felluga.

The list goes on: Daniel Day-Lewis drinks Ornellaia; George Clooney likes Rosso da Nipozzano; Chardonnay Planeta cools Naomi Campbell; and Montepulciano d'Abruzzo warms Cameron Diaz.

port town of Albinia, near Orbetello in southern Tuscany. The consistency of the clay used to make these pots, as well as identifying marks embossed on the vessels by merchants, confirms this. 'This is a very important discovery,' says Daniele Manacorda of the University of Siena's archaeology department. 'To trace ancient trade routes, finding distribution points, is not enough. You must find the production site.' The presence of just such a large site suggests that Tuscany was home to one of the biggest wine industries since the beginning of civilisation.

Carefully cushioned by straw and packed in wooden braces, wine amphorae were shipped to the port city of Massalia, founded by the ancient Greeks and now Marseille. Each container held one cubic Roman foot of wine, or about 26 litres (over 5½ gallons). The wine was ferried up the Rhône to the ancient city of Bibracte, once capital of Gaul, in what is today Burgundy. Despite suggestions from classical literature that ancient Italian wine was undrinkable, historians claim the Gauls had an unabashed thirst for the stuff. The less-than-appetising flavours of pine resin, used to render the amphorae's insides waterproof, and dried mud, used as a stopper, probably did little to improve the nectar's subtle nuances. Nonetheless, the Gauls happily traded human slaves and other common currency with the Romans to acquire massive quantities of the beverage that evolved into what we call 'Super Tuscans'. Rich Celtic chieftains drank prodigious quantities of Italian wine because it distinguished them from peasants, who drank beer.

Why didn't Gaul compete with Rome by producing its own wine? Because the Empire's expansionistic policies gave it firm control of the industry; but, as the name Burgundy testifies today, this ancient monopoly couldn't last forever.

For more about the regional Italian wines of today, *see* **Profiles of the Regions**.

# Letting Your Property

08

Around 45 per cent of British people who buy houses in Italy also let them at some time or another. They divide roughly into two groups. The first are people who see the property exclusively or very significantly as an investment proposition, and want to let it out seriously – that is, they want to make money by letting their property and will try to find the maximum number of tenants each year. The second group consists of people who are primarily buying a holiday home and are not so much looking to make a profit from letting as simply hoping to cover some or all of the costs of their new purchase through rental income, sometimes just by letting casually to family and friends.

There are fundamental differences in the ways these two groups should approach the house-buying process. For the first group this is a business. Just as in any business, the decisions they make about where and what to buy, whether and how to restore the property and what facilities to provide will be governed by the wish to maximise profit. They should put themselves in the position of the person to whom they want to let their property, and consider which part of the market they expect to appeal to – whether, for example, they might be couples wanting to enjoy Italian culture and cuisine or families wanting a cheap beach holiday – and anticipate what features clients like these would expect. They should choose an area, buy a property, convert it and equip it solely with their prospective tenants in mind.

The second group will have to bear in mind some or most of the same considerations, but overall can make far fewer concessions to their tenants. Theirs is first and foremost a holiday home for their own use, and they will be ready to compromise on the more 'businesslike' aspects of house-buying (and so reduce potential income) in order to maximise their own enjoyment of it. They will have to make some changes to accommodate visitors – extra bedding, setting aside some wardrobe space where they can lock away their own things while the house is let out – but these should be as few as possible. Where they draw the line will be determined by just how much income they need to get out of the property.

The section that follows relates mainly to the first group. If you identify more with the second category, you can pick and choose from the ideas within it, and there are also some points that are more directly relevant to your situation. And, whichever group that you feel you fall into, there is a very important point to remember: in either case, you are most unlikely to cover all of your expenses and both capital and interest repayments on a large mortgage from letting your property, however efficiently you do so.

# Location, Choice of Property and Letting Potential

The choice of the area in which to buy your rental property is by far the most important decision that you will make. There are many parts of Italy in which it is fairly easy to let a property regularly enough to make it a commercially viable proposition. On the other hand, there are thousands of properties around the country that are, commercially speaking, almost impossible to let. A rustic house in a rural backwater may find a few tenants each year, but there will not be anywhere near enough to generate a real commercial return on your investment. If you are interested in a house like this you will probably have taken this on board, and should view any rental income as a bonus that may help with some of your expenses, rather than any kind of nest-egg.

The factors to take into consideration when deciding on an area are slightly different from those you might look at when just thinking about buying a place for yourself. They will also vary depending on your target clientele and your preferred way of administering the property. Most are related, as one would expect, to the tourist traffic of an area, its attractions and services, and also to the practical services it has available that you can call on to help manage the letting.

If you advertise any property well, you will always get some tenants. But you will only begin to get repeat customers and a spreading circle of recommendations from previous tenants – one of the best ways of building up your customer base, since it saves on repeat advertising – if the house or flat itself, the area around it and the things there are to do really satisfy or, better still, exceed people's expectations of an enjoyable time.

## The Right Location

### Climate

Climate is, naturally, a major factor (*see* pp.76–7 and p.270). Of course, anywhere around the Italian coast and the islands can usually be relied on to have good, sunny weather during the prime summer holiday season from June to September, but for letting purposes you will have much greater flexibility if you are in an area where you can also expect blue skies in April, May and October, and mild weather through the winter. For one thing, you may want to use the house yourself in summer, and so will need to let it at other times of the year (alternatively, if you want to maximise your rents, you will let it in summer, and use it yourselves in December–February). There is also a relatively small market for longer-term winter lets in areas with particularly mild climates or which are socially desirable. In northern Italy, also bear in mind that a property within reach of the skiing areas can have a separate winter market, while an apartment in Milan, Venice or Rome could be a year-round draw, regardless of the type of weather.

## Attractions

Of equal importance are the attractions of the area, both natural features such as spectacular landscape, and 'tourist attractions' – a term that in itself covers a multitude of things. The most obvious of them on the coast is, of course, access to a good beach, but it helps if there are other activities available, such as sailing, diving and other sports facilities. For some clients, proximity to a charming, historic town would be a major asset, while for families it might be being near a water park or other child-orientated attraction. On a far smaller scale, a local attraction might consist of a craft centre in the nearest village. The point is that there must be something to bring people to your area so that they will need to use your accommodation. The mere fact that the house is located in the countryside will not, of itself, be enough to attract a significant number of tenants.

Added to these 'activities' are the more everyday attractions of an area which, for most people, loom as large as the more spectacular features in their enjoyment of a holiday let. Most people who rent self-catering accommodation will want to be able to stock up on food, drink and other necessities without too much trouble, and, since they won't want to cook all the time, will also want to be able to eat out. They will appreciate it greatly – and your property will be much easier to let – if your house is within easy distance (preferably walking distance) of at least a few shops and a choice of bars and restaurants.

## Access

As important as climate and the charms of the locality is the ability of tenants to get to your property. This has two sides to it. The area where your flat or house is located must be reasonably accessible from the places where your prospective tenants live, and the property itself must be easy to find.

For most British visitors, convenient access means how easy it is to get there from a local airport with direct flights from a UK airport reasonably close to where they live (for details of airports and routes to Italy, *see* **Selecting a Property**, pp.64–8). It is worth repeating here the travel industry figures that show that 25 per cent of all potential visitors will not come if it involves travelling for more than one hour from a local airport at either end of their journey, and that, if the travelling time rises to 1½ hours, this will deter around 50 per cent. Of course, this does not mean that if your home is over an hour's drive from an airport you will never let it – with characterful rural houses, for example, a different set of rules applies, and their very remoteness can be an attraction. For more conventional homes, though, there is no doubt that finding interested tenants will be simpler if you are within the magic hour's distance of an airport.

Owners should not underestimate, either, the importance of being able to find the property easily. Navigation in the depths of rural Italy can be trying: there are few people to ask for directions (especially if you don't speak Italian) and few signposts of much help in locating a single villa or farm. The situation is not much better if you are trying to locate an apartment in Naples. Giving tenants decent maps and guidance notes on getting there is essential.

## Letting Agencies

Strange as it may seem, the decision as to how you are going to let your property is one of the first that you are going to have to make, before you actually buy it. This is because if you decide to use a professional management or letting agency it will alter your target market and therefore the area in which you ought to be buying (*see* 'Management Agencies', pp.244–5). If you are going to let your property through a professional agency then it is worth contacting a few before you make a final choice of a location, to see what they believe they can offer in the way of rental returns. They will also be able to advise you on what type of property is likely to be most successful for letting in that area.

If, on the other hand, you expect to find tenants yourself, then you need to decide on your primary market. Most British people who let their property themselves in Italy do so mainly to other British people or other foreigners, chiefly because of a lack of language skills.

# The Right Property

Picking the right property is just behind choosing the right area in terms of letting potential. Not all properties let to the same extent – villas and flats that most potential clients find attractive let up to five times more frequently than others that do not stand out for any reason. New properties are generally cheaper to maintain than older ones; however, they are not likely to be as attractive to potential tenants. Most people going on holiday to rural Italy are looking for a character property (preferably with a pool), while most going to coastal Italy are looking for proximity to facilities and the beach.

It's very useful, therefore, to pick a home that's pretty (if it isn't one of those big enough to count as spectacular) if you intend to let it. Most people will decide whether to rent a holiday home after they have seen only a brief description and a photograph, and of these two the photo is by far the more important. When buying a house for letting purposes, it is vital to make sure that it 'takes a good picture'.

The number of bedrooms is also important. In cities, you will generally get a better return on your investment in properties with fewer (one or two) bedrooms – a good deal cheaper to buy – than on bigger apartments. On the coast or in the countryside, where the majority of your guests may well be families, a three-bedroom property is probably the most popular.

## The Right Price

When buying a property as a business you will be concerned to pay as little as possible for the property consistent with getting the right level of rental return. If you are only buying the property as a business proposition, this price – rental balance (or return on investment), together with your judgement of the extent to which the property will rise in value over the years, are the main criteria on which you should base your decision which property to buy.

If you are going to use the property not just as a rental property but also as a holiday home there is an additional factor to take into account: the amount of time that you will be able to use the property yourself consistent with getting a certain level of rental return. For example, if you bought a one-bedroom property in Rome, that property might be let for 25 weeks a year and produce a return after expenses of, say, 6 per cent; however, if you bought a two-bedroom property in rural Italy (for a similar price) and let that for just 15 weeks per year you might also generate 6 per cent on your investment. Both would be performing equally well, but the rural property would allow you and your family to use it for a much greater part of each year. This and the fact that it had a second bedroom could make it a more attractive proposition. These figures are simply examples, rather than indications as to what will be actually obtainable at any particular moment.

Whichever way you look at it, though, paying the minimum necessary for the property is the key to maximising investment performance.

# Equipping the Property

After the selection of an area and a property comes the fitting-out of the villa or flat with all the features that tenants will expect. If you advertise the property well, you will get tenants. You will only get repeat tenants and recommendations from existing tenants if the property meets or exceeds their expectations in terms of the facilities it offers and its cleanliness.

It should, of course, be well maintained at all times, and the external decoration and garden and/or pool area should be kept in good condition – apart from anything else, these are the parts that create the first impression as your guests arrive. Other than that, the facilities required will depend to some extent on the target audience that you are trying to attract. If, for example, you are trying to attract mountain walkers or sailors, they will appreciate somewhere to dry their clothes quickly so that they can be ready to get wet again the following day.

The following is a quick checklist of the main points to be taken care of when preparing any property for holiday tenants.

• **Documents**: Make sure that all guests are sent a pre-visit pack. This should include notes about the area and local attractions and a map of the immediate area (all usually available free from your local tourist office), notes explaining how to get to the house, emergency contact numbers and instructions as to what to do if the visitors are for any reason delayed.

Inside the property there should also be a house book. This should give much more information and recommendations about local attractions, restaurants and so on – collect as many local leaflets as you can – and a comprehensive list of contact numbers for use in the case of any conceivable emergency. The more personal recommendations you can give (best bakery, best café, etc.), the more people will appreciate it. Provide some space in it too, or in a separate book, to be used as a visitors' book. As well as being a useful vehicle for obtaining feedback, this builds up positive feelings about your home, and can also be a means of making future direct contact with visitors who might have been supplied by an agency.

• **Welcome**: It is best if someone is present, either at the property or at a nearby house, to welcome your guests when they arrive. They can sort out any minor problems or any particular requirements of the guests. You should also consider leaving a **welcome pack**: make sure that basic groceries such as bread, milk, teabags, coffee, sugar and a bowl of fruit are left in the house to welcome your guests on arrival. A bottle of local wine always goes down well, too!

• **Cleanliness**: The property must be spotlessly clean, above all in the kitchen and bathroom. You will probably employ a local cleaner, to whom you may well need to give some training and/or a detailed schedule, as people's expectations of rented accommodation are often higher than their expectations in an ordinary home.

• **Kitchen**: This must be modern, even if traditional in style, and everything should (of course) work. The fridge should be as large as you can manage since, in hot weather, your tenants will need to keep a wide range of things chilled. The kitchen should have a microwave, and you should check regularly that there is sufficient cutlery and cooking equipment and that it is all in good condition. A cookbook giving local recipes is a nice extra touch.

• **Bathroom**: Or, these days, more usually bathrooms, plural – en-suite bathrooms for each bedroom are the ideal. Spanish bathrooms will usually have a bidet. Make sure there is soap in the bathrooms, and guests will also much prefer it if you provide towels as part of the service.

• **Laundry facilities**: A washing machine and drier are now fairly standard.

• **Bedrooms**: These should have adequate storage space. Most importantly, they should also have clean and comfortable beds, as nothing except dirtiness produces more complaints than uncomfortable beds. The only beds that last well in a regularly used property, in which the people sleeping will be all sorts of different sizes and weights, are expensive beds such as those used in the hotel industry. Beds should be protected from obvious soiling by the use of removable mattress covers, which should be changed with each change of tenant. All clients will much prefer it if you supply bedding as part of your service rather than expecting them to bring their own.

• **Living areas**: Furniture and upholstery should be comfortable and in good condition; the style is a matter of personal preference, but a 'local' style is often attractive. Also make sure that sofa covers, etc. are fairly hard wearing and easily washable. There should be adequate means of cleaning, including a working and regularly emptied vacuum cleaner.

• **Heating**: An effective heating system, covering the whole house, is essential even in warmer regions – weather is unpredictable, and you may well want to attract winter lets.

• **Air-conditioning**: While it is a substantial asset, air-conditioning is not yet considered obligatory except in the most expensive lettings, and can be expensive both to run and to maintain. In more basic lets it's probably best avoided.

• **Swimming pool**: If you are catering to a British clientele, a pool is always highly desirable, and in just about any area it will significantly increase your letting potential. A pool should be of reasonable size and well maintained, but need not be heated.

# Marketing the Property

Properties do not let themselves, and anyone wishing to let out their Italian home at all regularly will have to do some marketing. In the early years, you will have to do more than later on, because you will have no existing client base. As in any other business, the cheapest type of marketing is catching repeat clients, so a bit of money spent on making sure the property lives up to, or exceeds, their expectations (and so brings them or their friends back next year) is probably the best spend that you will make. Otherwise, there seems to be no correlation between the amount spent on marketing and the results achieved, and this is a field in which much money spent is often wasted.

Something to remember is that any form of marketing of a holiday property is only as good as the quality of the response you give to people making enquiries. Owners often do better spending less money on advertising and paying more attention to following up leads they have already generated.

Key points to remember in relation to marketing any kind of short-term lets are the following.

• **Choose the method of marketing most appropriate to your property and circumstances.**

• **Follow up all enquiries and leads at once.** Contact the people involved again after a couple of weeks to see whether or not they have made up their minds.

• **Send any contacts your details again next year at about the same time,** even if they have not stayed with you, as they may well be planning another holiday.

If you have decided to let your property yourself, there are several well-tried means of publicising your property in the British and Irish markets. If you also wish to tap into the Italian market, you can advertise it in local papers. However, your Italian must be good enough for you to handle all enquiries, and many people in this situation prefer to use a letting agency (*see* pp.244–5).

## Directories and Web Directories

If your property is pretty, then you are likely to get good results from the various directories and joint information and booking services that deal with self-catering properties to let in Italy. Most have moved over partly – or, increasingly, completely – from producing brochures and magazines to being web-based. Some provide a full booking service and take part in managing lettings, while others, which are cheaper to use and give owners more freedom of manoeuvre, just give you space for photographs and a presentation of your property. The travel industry directory websites **www.travelgate.co.uk** and **www.uk-villasabroaddirectory.co.uk** and have lists of the many such companies now operating. Some of the most useful are the monthly magazine *Private Villas* (**t** (020) 8329 0120; **www.privatevillas.co.uk**) for upmarket properties,, though advertising is handled via the sister site **www.daltonsholidays.com**; **Owners Direct, t** (01372) 722708, **www. ownersdirect.co.uk**; and the **Owners' Syndicate, t** (020) 7801 9804, **www. owners syndicate.co.uk**, all joint 'noticeboard' services for independent owners looking for tenants.

Advertising in this way only really works if the services are inexpensive, because a private owner with only one property to let has only one opportunity of letting each week, and so a directory that produces, say, 50 enquiries for the first week in July is not particularly helpful.

## Press Advertising

The problems with traditional advertising are its scattergun approach and, usually, its cost. As mentioned above, if you have just one property you only need a very small number of responses, and you cannot afford to pay a large amount in advertising fees for each week's let. Except for very upmarket properties, traditional advertising is too expensive, and is mainly used by property companies and agencies. For individual owners, better places to advertise are the small-ad pages in newspaper travel sections such as that of the *Sunday Times*, and the specialist Italian property press. Good results have been reported from *Dalton's Weekly*, too. According to your target market, apparently unconnected special interest magazines – literary, historical, *Private Eye* – can be a good idea, because your ad doesn't get swamped by 20 others.

On the other hand, you can also get very good results very cheaply by putting a card on your local supermarket noticeboard.

## Personal Website and E-mail

The Internet offers tremendous opportunities for bringing a specialist niche product – such as an isolated villa – to the attention of a vast audience at very little cost. For no extra effort, it can allow people to find out about your Italian home not just in Britain and Italy but in Scandinavia, Germany, the USA and other places that will surprise you. For independent owners offering property for holiday lets, it is strongly recommended that they set up their own website. For many, it quickly becomes their primary means of finding new tenants.

Your website will be your principal brochure, with space to show lots of pictures and other information about the house and the area around it. It is much cheaper to have someone print off a copy of this brochure from their own computer than it is for you to have it printed and sent by post. If you don't know enough about the web to design a site yourself, it is now quite easy to find web designers around Italy, as it is everywhere else, who will create the site for you at low cost.

Your property should also be listed on some of the many Italian property websites that can be found around the Internet, links to which are either free or quite cheap. You will soon find out which ones work for you and which ones don't; some of the best are those that are regionally based, since people find it easy to get to what they want with fewer irrelevancies.

As well as a publicity medium, the website can also be a means of taking bookings. You will have to decide how sophisticated an electronic booking system you want or whether you are happy just to use the Internet to make initial contacts. Actually taking money via the web by credit card is far too expensive an option for most independent property-owners, so you will have to receive payments by more traditional means. Your website will, of course, have your e-mail address on it. Even if you do not set up a website, anyone letting out property with any consistency really should have e-mail, which is more and more people's preferred means of making such bookings. And remember to check it at least once a day.

# Doing Deals

There are two kinds of 'mutual aid' deals that can be helpful to independent owners, both of which work best in slightly out-of-the-way areas. If your property, for example, is in a rural area where there is somebody offering a very local tourist service, it can be a good idea to make contact with them and try to arrange for the people starting their hikes or attending their cookery, painting or meditation courses to stay over in your property. This can significantly increase your lettings, particularly off-peak. If you agree to pay the tour organisers a commission of around 20 per cent you will still be well ahead.

The second type of 'deal' involves co-operating with other people in the area who let properties, assuming there are any. One of the frustrations of marketing your property is when you have four lots of people who all want to rent it for the same week. Getting together with others in a mutual assistance group will allow you to pass excess lettings to each other.

# Your Own Contacts

All these methods aside, personal, direct contacts are still among the best means you have of marketing a property in Italy. If you want to use a second home for a fair amount of time yourselves, you will perhaps only want to let it for, say, 20 weeks each year. Given that many people will take it for two weeks or more, you will probably therefore only be looking for around 10 to 15 lettings, and if you put the word out these should not be hard to put together from friends and from friends of friends.

Among the people who have an advantage in 'marketing' a holiday home in this way are those who work for large organisations, and can publicise it internally. Even without people from work, most owners will be able to find enough friends, neighbours and relatives to rent a nice property in Italy for 10 weeks each year, which will leave only a relatively small number of tenants to be found by other means. With most of your lettings you will have the additional advantage of knowing the people who are going to rent the property, which reduces the risk that they will damage it or fail to pay you.

When letting to family and friends, or indeed work colleagues, you will have to learn how to raise the delicate issue of payment. Given that you are not going to be running up any marketing costs and, probably, not much in the way of property management costs, you should be able to offer them a bargain price and still generate as much income as you would have done by letting through an agency. Make sure that you address this issue when you accept the booking, as doing so later can be very embarrassing.

# Management Agencies

On the whole, the people who are most successful over time in letting their second homes are those who find their tenants themselves. This, however, requires a level of commitment that many people simply cannot afford. For non-resident owners who cannot dedicate much time to keeping track of their property, it is far simpler to use a local letting agency. Agencies – or at least good ones – will be able to attract local, Italian clients as well as foreigners of different nationalities. You will have to pay them a sizeable commission (typically 17.5 to 20 per cent of your letting income, plus VAT), but they will argue that this will be recovered by the extra lettings they make during the holiday season. This may or may not be true. Larger agencies, those who publish glossy brochures, are best contacted well in advance, such as early autumn in the previous year, if you want a property to be advertised for the summer season; smaller agencies will take on properties at any time.

In all the desirable areas you will find agencies that manage and let holiday properties, many of them local estate agents, and there are also many that operate from Britain. If you decide to use one of them, the choice of agency is critical. Some are excellent, both in Italy and in Britain, and some are crooks, and between the two there are some that are just bumbling and inefficient. At worst, agencies may hold on to rents for long periods of time, or let your house while telling you it is empty and pocket the rent themselves; others may just charge a 'signing-on fee' to agree to put your property on your books and then do nothing to let it. In the past, many have assumed that foreign owners thousands of miles away will never find out about anything they do. This is a field where it is important for owners to be cautious and demanding with any agents they engage.

## Selecting an Agency

When selecting a letting agency there are various checks to make.

- **If it is an Italian agency, check whether or not they are professionally qualified and experienced. Many such services are offered as an adjunct to estate agents, who should have qualified staff.**

- **Check their premises, and make an initial judgement about whether or not they seem welcoming and efficient, and if there's evidence of significant letting activity.**

- **Ask for references, preferably from other overseas clients, and follow them up. Phone other owners if you can, and ask if they are happy with the overall performance of the agency and the financial projections given to them have been met.**

• Check how capable they seem to be, especially if you're making contact before actually buying your property. Ask what type of property they think would be best for letting purposes in this area, how many weeks' rental they think you will be able to obtain and how much they think they would generate for you after deduction of expenses and their own fees.

• Take a look at what marketing they do. If they are reliant only on passing trade then, except in the most popular areas, they will not get good results.

• Ask to see a sample information pack sent to a potential client. You will be able to judge a lot from this; think about whether or not this is the image you want to give of your property.

• Ask to inspect two or three properties that they are already managing. If they are dirty or badly cared for, then so will yours be, and it will not let.

• Check carefully what kind of contract they offer you; unless you are familiar with Italian law it is sensible also to get it checked by your lawyer before you sign, as some give you far more rights than others. Make sure that the contract entitles you to full reports showing when the property was let and for what money; these must give a breakdown week by week, not by quarter- or half-year. You should also insist on a full breakdown of all expenses incurred in connection with the property, and ensure the contract gives you the right to dismiss the agency at fairly short notice.

## Controlling the Agency

After you have appointed a letting agency, you need to keep a check on what they are doing. You may not wish to seem so suspicious, but there are too many horror stories around to allow anyone to be complacent.

• Check the reports you receive from the agency and that the money you receive corresponds to the amounts shown in them.

• Let the agency know, in the nicest possible way, that you and all your friends in the area check each other's properties every time you are there, and compare notes about which are occupied and the performance of your letting agencies. If they believe you, this is a good deterrent to unauthorised lettings.

• Telephone the property every week. If someone answers the phone make a note, and make sure that there is income shown for the week of the phone call.

• From time to time, have a friend pose as a prospective customer and send for an enquiry pack.

• If you get the chance, call to see the property without warning to check its condition.

# Formalising the Letting

If you let through an agency, they will draw up fairly standardised rental contracts for you and your tenants to sign. If you handle all your lettings yourself, unless you rent only to family and close friends, it is still advisable for you to give tenants a written contract in line with Italian law, the 'model' for which should preferably be drawn up, with the advice of your lawyer, when you first begin letting.

From the point of view of landlords, the safest type of letting is a short holiday let of furnished property. To be classified as furnished the property must have all of the basic items required to live in a home, such as, at least, a bed, a cooker, a table, a refrigerator and some chairs. A place without these things could be treated as an unfurnished property, in which case, from a legal point of view, the tenant could claim that there was a permanent rental contract, potentially giving them the right to an extension after the contract's first term. Otherwise, a holiday let is one that takes place in a recognised holiday season, which obviously means something different in a ski resort from in Rimini.

## The Letting Agreement

A properly drafted tenancy agreement will take all these factors into account and protect you in the event of a dispute with your tenants and, in particular, if any of them wish to stay on at the end of the tenancy. If your property forms part of a *condominio* (*see* pp.129–30) your tenants will also have to agree to abide by the rules of the community, and this should be indicated in the rental agreement. Tenants should be supplied with a copy of these rules, or at least of the part of them that is relevant. In the rental contract you should also stipulate what things are going to be covered by your insurance and what are not – typically, for example, tenants' personal possessions would not be covered under your policy.

# References

# Dictionary of Useful and Technical Terms

| | |
|---|---|
| Abitabile | Habitable |
| Abitazione | Housing |
| Abusivo | House or part of a building that is illegally built, or without the proper permit |
| ACI (Automobile Club d'Italia) | Italy's driving association |
| Acqua | Water |
| Acquedotto | Aqueduct, or state-supplied water |
| Acquistare su carte | Purchase of a property before it has been built, based on blueprints ('off plan') |
| Affittacamere | Rooms to let |
| Affittasi | To rent; to let |
| Affresco | Frescoes |
| Agente immobiliare | Estate agent |
| Agenzia immobiliare | Estate agency |
| Agriturismo | Farm with rooms to rent |
| Albo degli artigiani | Professional order of artisans |
| Albergo | Hotel |
| Alimentari | Food shop selling cheese, cold meats, tinned goods |
| Aliscafo | High-speed boat or hydrofoil |
| Alloggio | Lodging |
| Amministratore del condominio | Paid official representing an apartment building, condominium administrator |
| Ammobiliato | Furnished |
| Ammortizzare | Reducing debts, like a mortgage, in smaller payments |
| Ampia metratura | Large in size or metres |
| Anagrafe | Bureau of vital statistics or census office |
| Anagrafe canina | Registration office for dogs |
| Angolo cottura | Small construction in kitchen, or kitchen corner |
| Annessi | Attachments or building extensions |
| ANSA | Italy's news or information agency |
| Anticamera | Entranceway |
| Antico | Old or antique |
| Anticipo di pagamento | Deposit |
| Appartamento | Flat or apartment |
| Appartamento ammobiliato | Furnished apartment |
| Appartamento in affitto | Flat for rent |
| Appartamento di lusso | Exclusive apartment |
| Appartamento su due paini | Duplex |
| Appartamento vacanze | Holiday apartment |
| Arcate | Covered walkway or arcade |
| Archivio | Archive |
| Architetto | Architect |
| Arco | Archway |
| Aria condizionamento | Air-conditioning |

| | |
|---|---|
| Arredamento | Interior furnishings |
| Arredato | Furnished |
| Artigiano | Artisan, craftsman |
| Ascensore | Lift |
| Assicurazione | Insurance |
| Assicurazione contro i terzi | Third-party insurance |
| Attaccato | Joined, as in two properties, or next door |
| Attico | Top-floor apartment with terrace; penthouse |
| Atto di compravendita | Conveyance document |
| Attrezzata | Equipped |
| Autobus | Public bus |
| Autonoleggio | Car rental |
| Autorimessa | Car park |
| Autostrada | Motorway; highway |
| Avvocato | Lawyer or solicitor |
| Azienda agricola | Working farm |
| | |
| Bagno | Bathroom or toilet |
| Balcone | Balcony |
| Banca | Bank |
| Bancomat | Bank card or automatic teller machine (ATM) |
| Bar | Where you get breakfast and (if it is a *bartabacchi*) phone cards, cigarettes and stamps |
| Bella figura/bella presenza | Something that creates a good impression |
| Belli arti | Governed by the Ministry of Culture to preserve Italy's cultural heritage. The *belli arti* can block your plans to restore or build a house |
| Ben conservata | Well preserved |
| Ben tenuto | Benefits from good upkeep |
| Benzinaio | Petrol station |
| Biblioteca | Library |
| Bifamiliare | Semi-detached building |
| Biglietti | Tickets |
| Biglietti timbrati | Validated tickets, like on a bus |
| Bilocale | Two-room apartment. Usually a studio apartment with a main room and kitchen |
| Bolletta | Bill or invoice |
| Bollo | Tax stamp |
| Bombola | Gas storage tank; compressed gas |
| Bombolone | Storage tank for compressed or liquid gas |
| Bonifico | Wire transfer used for paying bills from a bank account |
| Borgo | A hamlet or small town. Can also mean 'neighbourhood' |
| Borsa | Stock exchange |
| Borsa di Milano | Main stock exchange; see also *nuovo mercato* |
| Bosco | Forest |

| | |
|---|---|
| Box | Parking for a single car |
| Breve periodo | Short term |
| Buon entrata/buon uscita | 'Key money' or illegal payment made to buy off previous tenants' rent |
| Buona posizione | Good location |
| Buono stato | Good condition |
| BUSARL | Official registry of companies |
| Cabina | Cabin |
| Calce | Limescale |
| Caldaia | Water heater, boiler |
| Camera | Room |
| Camera di commercio | Chamber of commerce |
| Camera doppia | Double room (twin beds) |
| Camera matrimoniale | Room with queen-size bed |
| Camera singola | Single room |
| Cameretta | Small room |
| Camino | Fireplace |
| Cantina | Storage cellar or wine cellar |
| Capannone | Outdoor barn |
| Caparra | Deposit |
| Carabinieri | Police force governed by the Defence Ministry |
| Caratteristico | Picturesque, quaint, charming |
| Carta bollata | Document with tax stamp included |
| Carta d'identità | Identification documents |
| Carta da parati | Wallpaper |
| Carta Verde | Proof of insurance for cars |
| Cartoleria | Stationery supplier |
| Casa | House, home |
| Casa d'epoca | Old house, period home |
| Casa padronale | Landowner's house in the country; main house |
| Casa popolare | Low-income housing |
| Casa di ringhiera | Apartments in Milan on an interior courtyard |
| Casa rurale | Rural house |
| Casa signorile | Exclusive house or property |
| Casa urbana | Urban property |
| Casale | Farmhouse |
| Cascina | Another word for farmhouse |
| Casetta | Small house |
| Cassa | Cash register, till |
| Cassone | Water storage tank |
| Castello | Castle |
| Catasto | Land registry |
| Catasti | Zoning maps |
| Centro | Centre of a city |
| Centro storico | Historic centre, most expensive area |
| Ceramica | Ceramics |
| Certificato di matrimonio | Marriage certificate |

| | |
|---|---|
| Certificato di morte | Death certificate |
| Certificato di nascita | Birth certificate |
| Certificato di residenza | Residence permit |
| Chiave | Key |
| Circoscrizione | A subdivision of the *comune* or municipality |
| Cittadinanza | Citizenship |
| Clausola condizionale | Conditional clause |
| Codice fiscale | Personal taxpayer number |
| Colonna | Column |
| Colonnato | Row of columns |
| Coltivatore diretto | Farmer |
| Commercialista | Accountant, also prepares tax returns |
| Complesso residenziale | Residential or housing complex |
| Compromesso di vendita | Preliminary sales agreement in buying property |
| Comune | Municipality or town hall |
| Concessione edilizia | Planning permission |
| Condizione | Condition |
| Condominio | Condominium |
| Condono | A government 'pardon' for illegal building, usually issued when the state is short of funds |
| Contatti | Contacts |
| Convivere | Living together, sharing an apartment |
| Conguaglio | Adjustment. The electricity company uses this term when they bill based on estimated consumption |
| Contatore | Meter for utilities |
| Contenuto dell'abitazione | Inventory of furnishings |
| Conto | Bill |
| Conto corrente | Bank account |
| Conto estero | A bank account in foreign currency |
| Contraente | Contracting party |
| Contratto | Contract |
| Contratto di affitto | Lease agreement |
| Contratto preliminaria di vendita | Preliminary sales contract |
| Corridoio | Corridor or hallway |
| *Corriere della Sera* | The nation's biggest-circulation newspaper |
| Corso | Main street |
| Cortile | Courtyard |
| Costruttore | Builder |
| Costruzione | Building |
| Cotto | Terracotta |
| Cucina | Kitchen |
| Cucina abitabile | Kitchen-diner |
| Cucina a gas | Gas cooker |
| Cupola | Dome |
| Dammusi | Cube houses, only on the island of Pantelleria |
| Decoratore | Interior decorator |

| | |
|---|---|
| Denuncia | Police report |
| Deposito | Deposit |
| Diritto del coltivatore | Farmers' rights. If a neighbour earns 70 per cent or more of his or her income through agriculture, they have first refusal on adjoining property for sale |
| Disdire/disdetta | To cancel |
| Disponibile | Available |
| Ditta Individuale | Sole proprietorship business |
| DOC | Wine region controlled by geographic origin |
| DOCG | Wine region that is not only controlled but also guarantees geographic origin |
| Doccia | Shower |
| Dogana | Customs |
| Domicilio | Address |
| Doppi servizi | Two bathrooms |
| Doppi vetri | Double-glazing for windows |
| Doppio garage | Car parking for two vehicles |
| Due piani | Two floors |
| | |
| Edicola | Newspaper kiosk |
| Edificio | Building |
| Edilizia | Construction yard |
| Elettricista | Electrician |
| Elettrodomestici | Appliances |
| ENEL (Ente Nazionale per l'Energia Electtrica) | National electricity company |
| ENIT (Ente Nazionale Italiano del Turismo) | State tourism office |
| Enoteca | Wine merchant |
| Entroterra | Hinterland |
| Equo canone | Rent control |
| Escursionisti Esteri (EE) | Car licence plates for foreigners who did not pay IVA tax when they bought their car |
| Ettaro | Hectare |
| EUR | Modern neighbourhood south of Rome, built by Mussolini, that exemplifies Fascist architecture |
| Euro | As of 1 January 2002, Italy's currency: €1 = 1,936 lire according to the fixed exchange rate |
| | |
| Fabbro | Blacksmith; locksmith |
| Facciata | Façade |
| Fai-da-te | Do-it-yourself |
| Falegname | Carpenter |
| Farmacia | Pharmacy |
| Fascia blu | Ordinance banning traffic from the centre of a city |
| Fattoria | Farm |

| | |
|---|---|
| Fattura | Invoice, bill |
| Ferragosto | 15 August holiday (Assumption) |
| Ferramenta | Hardware shop |
| Ferrovia dello Stato (FS) | Railway system |
| Finestra | Window |
| Fienile | Storage area for hay |
| Fisco | Tax authorities |
| Fiume | River |
| Fontana | Fountain |
| Fornaio | Bakery |
| Fornello | Cooker |
| Forno | Oven |
| Forno a legna | Wood-burning oven |
| Fossa settica | Septic tank |
| Francobollo | Stamp |
| Frigorifero | Refrigerator |
| Fronte mare | Facing the sea |
| Fruttivendolo | Greengrocer |
| | |
| Gabinetto | Toilet |
| Gazzetta Ufficiale | Published document with all new legislation |
| Geometra | A combination of an architect and a surveyor. This very important figure exists only in Italy |
| Giardiniere | Gardener |
| Giardino | Garden |
| Giorno | Day |
| Giorno di riposo | Rest day; day off |
| Granaio | Barn; hay storage |
| Grande | Large |
| Grattacielo | Skyscraper |
| Guardia di Finanza | Tax police (also perform coastguard duties) |
| | |
| ICI (Imposta Comunale sugli Immobili) | Property tax |
| Idraulico | Plumber |
| Imbianchino | Painter |
| Immatricolare | To register a car with the Italian state |
| Impianto | Fixtures |
| Imposta | Tax |
| Imposta di registro | Stamp duty |
| Indipendente | Detached |
| Indirizzo | Address |
| Ingegnere | Engineer |
| Ingresso | Entrance |
| Inquilino | Tenant |
| Interrato | Basement; underground |
| Intonaco | Plaster |

| | |
|---|---|
| Ipoteca | Mortgage |
| ISTAT | The national statistics institute |
| IVA (Imposta sul Valore Aggiunto) | Value Added Tax (20 per cent) |
| | |
| Kasher | Kosher food, also spelled *cosher* and *casher* |
| | |
| Lago | Lake |
| Lampadina | Light bulb |
| Largo | Square |
| Latteria | Dairy shop |
| Laurea | University degree |
| Lavabo | Wash basin |
| Lavanderia | Launderette; dry cleaners |
| Lavastoviglie | Dishwasher |
| Lavatrice | Washing machine |
| Lavoro | Work |
| Lavoro al nero | Illegal (black market) work |
| Legname | Timber |
| Legno | Wood |
| Libretto di circolazione | Car registration papers |
| Libero | Unoccupied |
| Libreria | Bookshop |
| Lira | Italy's old currency, phased out after the euro's introduction on 1 January 2002: €1 = 1,936 lire according to the fixed exchange rate |
| Locanda | Inn |
| Loggia | Covered space on building |
| Luce | Light |
| Lungomare | Boardwalk, road near beach |
| Lusso | Luxury |
| | |
| Macchina | Car |
| Macelleria | Butcher's shop |
| Mammismo | The tendency of adult 'children' to live at home with their parents |
| Mansarda | Top-floor apartment under eaves, with sloped ceilings |
| Manutenzione | Maintenance |
| Marca da bollo | Tax stamp |
| Mare | Sea |
| Marmo | Marble |
| Marmo di Carrara | White marble from Carrara |
| Mas | From old Celtic word for 'house', a type of home found in the Alpine north |
| Maso | Same as a *Mas* |
| Masseria | From old Celtic word for 'house', a type of palace found in the south |

| | |
|---|---|
| Mattone | Bricks |
| Mediatore | Another word for an estate agent |
| Medico | Doctor |
| Medico Mutualistico | Doctor under health insurance plan |
| Mensile | Monthly |
| Mercato | Market |
| Metrature | Size as measured in square metres |
| Metri quadri | Square metres |
| Metro | Ruler (measure) |
| Metropolitane | Metro or underground service |
| Mezza pensione | Half-board, just room and breakfast |
| Mezzogiorno | The name for the collective south of Italy |
| Misura | Size, measure |
| Modernizzare | Refurbish, restore |
| Monolocale | One-room apartment, studio apartment |
| Motorino | Moped or scooter |
| Moquette | Carpet |
| Municipio | Town hall |
| Multe | Traffic violations or parking tickets |
| Muratore | Carpenter, bricklayer, handyman or mason |
| Mura | Walls of a city |
| Muro | Walls of a house |
| Mutuo | Mortgage or medical coverage |
| Mutuo compreso | Mortgage included |
| Mutuo per ristrutturazione | Loan for reconstruction |
| | |
| Non-residente | Non-resident of Italy (better as a tenant for your property) |
| Notaio | Notary. Very important when buying property because he or she conducts basic investigations |
| Nulla osta | 'No obstacle' permit |
| Numero di polizza | Insurance policy number |
| Numero di telaio | Serial number, as on a moped |
| Nuova | New |
| Nuovo Mercato | Milan's index for high-growth companies |
| | |
| Occasione | Bargain |
| Officina | Workshop |
| Oliveto | Olive grove |
| Orario | Business hours, schedule |
| Orario non-stop/continuato | Non-stop business hours, no lunch break |
| Originale | Original |
| Ospedale | Hospital |
| Ottima posizione | Prime location |
| Ottima condizione | Prime condition |

| | |
|---|---|
| Padrone/a | Landlord/landlady |
| Paese | Town |
| Pagamento | Payment |
| Palazzo | Building or palace |
| Panetteria | Bread shop |
| Parco | Park |
| Partita IVA | VAT registration number for businesses and freelancers |
| Parzialmente arredato | Partially furnished |
| Passaggio di proprietà | Ownership change, such as when you sell a car |
| Pasticceria | Pastry shop |
| Patente | Driver's licence |
| Pavimento in cotto | Terracotta floor |
| Pavimento | Floor |
| Pensione | Small hotel |
| Periferie | Suburbs |
| Perito agronomo | Land surveyor |
| Permessi comunali | Planning permits from the town hall |
| Permesso di lavoro | Work permit |
| Permesso di soggiorno | Permit to stay in Italy for tourism, work, study or living |
| Piano | Floor |
| Piano nobile | Considered the best floor of a building, the first floor up with the highest ceilings |
| Piano regolatore | Zoning plan |
| Piano terra | Ground floor ('first' floor in the USA) |
| Piastrelle | Tiles |
| Piazza | Town square |
| Piazzale | Larger square |
| Piccolo | Small |
| Pietra | Stone |
| Pineto | Pine forest |
| Piscina | Swimming pool |
| Pitture | Painting |
| Più spese | Expenses, such as utilities, not included |
| Polizia | Police regulated by the Interior Ministry |
| Ponte | Bridge |
| Portico | Covered walkway |
| Portiere | Porter, doorman or woman |
| Portinaio/portineria | Porter and porter's quarters at the entrance of a building |
| Porta | Door |
| Porta blindata | Armoured door with steel beams that extend on to the wall |
| Porta Portese | Rome's biggest Sunday flea market |
| Porto | Sea port |
| Portone | The main door of a building |

| | |
|---|---|
| Posto macchina | Car park |
| Pozzo | Well |
| Pratica | Bureaucratic file |
| Prato | Lawn |
| Prefettura | Courthouse |
| Premio | Insurance premium |
| Prenotazione | Reservation, such as for a train or in a restaurant |
| Prestito | Loan |
| Preventivo | Estimate of work costs, quotation |
| Prezzo | Price |
| Prima casa | First house or primary residence |
| Primo piano | First floor |
| Procura | Tribunal; power of attorney |
| Progetto | Project |
| Pronta consegna | Ready to be lived in, or moved into |
| Proposta d'acquisto | Initial offer made on a property |
| Proprietà | Property |
| | |
| Quadro | Painting |
| Questura | Police station where you apply for a permit to stay |
| Quotazione | Quotation (*preventivo* is better) |
| | |
| Radiatori | Radiators |
| Ragioniere | Accountant |
| Rate | Instalments, as when paying bills |
| Referenziati | References required |
| Regolamento di condominio | Condominium conditions or rules |
| Rendita catastale | Value of a property |
| Residence | A room or flat for rent on a weekly/monthly basis |
| Residente | Resident of Italy |
| Residenza | Official residency as registered at the *anagrafe* |
| Restaurare | To restore |
| Restaurato | Restored |
| Ricostruire | To be reconstructed, re-built |
| Rilevamento | Land survey |
| Rinnovamento | Modernisation, renovation |
| Riparazione | Repair |
| Ripostiglio | Storage room or broom cupboard |
| Riscaldamento | Heating |
| Riscaldamento autonomo | Means a house has its own boiler and the owner can turn the heat off or on as desired. Owner pays for his/her individual use |
| Riscaldamento centrale | One main boiler heats a building and the apartment owner does not decide when it is turned on or off. Cost is divided equally between all inhabitants |
| Ristrutturare | To restore, refurbish |

| | |
|---|---|
| Ritenuta d'acconto | When the 20 per cent IVA tax is withheld from pay |
| Rocca | Fortress |
| Rogito | Act or final deed signed in front of a *notaio* |
| Rovina | Ruins |
| Rudere | Ruins, or pile of rocks of historic significance |
| Rustico | Rustic |
| | |
| Sala | Room |
| Sala da pranzo | Dining room |
| Saldo | Sale |
| Salone | Sitting room |
| Salotto | Hallway or sitting room |
| Scala | Stairs |
| Scalinata | Stairway |
| Scaldabagno | Same as *caldaio* or boiler, water heater |
| Scatti | Phone units or segments of time used to calculate phone bills |
| Scatti di anzianità | Pay increase based on length of employment |
| Sconto | Discount |
| Scontrino | Receipt |
| Semi arredato | Partially furnished |
| Semicentro | The area of a city just outside the centre |
| Seminterrato | Apartment at basement level |
| Serrande | Shutters or metal curtains |
| Servizi | Kitchen and bathroom, excluded from the number of rooms listed for a home |
| Sfratto | Eviction |
| Sindaco | Mayor |
| Sistemare | To fix |
| Società | Company |
| Società di capitali | Corporation |
| Società di persone | Partnership |
| Società in accomandita semplice (S.a.s.) | Limited partnership in which liability is determined by the original investment |
| Società in nome collettivo (S.n.c.) | General business partnership. All partners are liable without limit of debt. |
| Società per Azioni (S.p.A.) | Joint stock corporation |
| Società a responsabilità limitata (S.r.l.) | Limited liability company |
| Soffitta | Attic |
| Soffitti a volta | Vaulted ceilings |
| Soffitto | Ceiling |
| Soggiorno | Room, sitting room |
| Soggiorno pranzo | Dining room |
| Sorgente | Spring source of water |
| Sottodichiarazione | Common practice of under-declaring a property's value for tax reasons |

| | |
|---|---|
| Spese | Expenses |
| Spese agenzia | Agent's fee |
| Spese del condominio | Building, maintenance or condominium fees |
| Spese condominiali comprese | Maintenance fee included |
| Spiaggia | Beach |
| Spiaggia libera | Public beach |
| Spiaggia privata | Private beach |
| Stanza | Room |
| Stanza da letto | Bedroom |
| Stato | Condition, state |
| Stato di famiglia | Family status document (single, married with children, etc.) |
| Stazione | Train station |
| Stima | Estimate |
| Strada | Street |
| Struttura | Structure |
| Stucco | Plaster or stucco |
| Studio | Office or laboratory, den |
| Suolo | Ground |
| Supermercato | Supermarket |
| Supplemento | Surplus to pay, extra charge |
| Supplemento rapido | Extra fee to pay on fast trains |
| Tabacchi | State-licensed tobacco store where you buy cigarettes, bus tickets, phone cards, postage stamps and tax stamps (*marca da bollo*) |
| Tabelle professionali | Salary classifications regulated by the state |
| Tangenziale | The ring roads around major cities like Milan. In Rome it is called the Grand Raccordo Anulare |
| Tappeto | Carpet |
| Targhe | Licence plates for a car |
| Targhe alterne | Used at times of high smog levels. On alternate days, city authorities allow into the centre cars with an odd number at the end of their licence plate or those with an even number |
| Tassa comunale dei rifiuti | Refuse (rubbish) tax |
| Telecom Italia | Once had monopoly on phone service. Now faces competition from other companies |
| Telefono | Land-line phone |
| Telefonino | 'Little phone', meaning mobile phone |
| Terra | Ground floor |
| Terrazza | Terrace |
| Terreno | Land |
| Terreno alberato | Land with trees |
| Terreno coltivato | Cultivated land |
| Tessera | A subscription, such as for a month's worth of bus tickets |
| Testamento | Will, or last testament |

| | |
|---|---|
| Tetto | Roof |
| Tintoria | Dry cleaners |
| Titolo di proprietà | Deed of property |
| Torre | Tower |
| Torrente | Stream |
| Traghetto | Ferry boat |
| Trattabile | Negotiable |
| Trattazione riservata | Closed session negotiation, reserved |
| Travertino | Porous marble from Lazio |
| Travi di legno | Wooden ceiling-beam |
| Trulli | Cone-shaped stone houses found only in Puglia |
| Tutto città | The road atlas published for every town and city |
| | |
| Ufficio delle Imposte Dirette | Tax office where you get your *codice fiscale* |
| Ufficio di Stato Civile | Same as *anagrafe*, or census office |
| Ufficio postale | Post office |
| Ultimo piano | Top floor |
| Umidità | Humidity/damp, a common problem in old homes |
| | |
| Valore | Value |
| Valore catastale | Value of property for tax purposes |
| Vano | Room |
| Vaporetto | Water transport in Venice; a boat |
| Vasca | Bath |
| Vecchio | Old |
| Vendesi | For sale |
| Veranda | Porch |
| Vetro | Glass |
| Via | Street |
| Viale | Wider street |
| Vicolo | Little street |
| Vicoletto | Even smaller street |
| Vigili urbani | Traffic police, street police |
| Vigneto | Vineyard |
| Villa | House |
| Villetta (villino) | A smaller house, often modern |
| Villaggio | Village |
| Vista | View |
| Visto | Visa for travel to Italy or for studying, working or living in Italy |
| Vista sul mare | Sea views |
| Vista sul monte | Mountain views |
| | |
| Zona | Zone |
| Zona censuaria | Parts into which a town is divided for tax purposes |
| Zona tranquilla | Quiet area |

# Internet Vocabulary

| | |
|---|---|
| Banche dati | Database |
| Cancellare | Delete |
| Chiocciolina | @ |
| Decifrare | Decode |
| Doppia barra; doppia slash | // |
| Due punti | : (colon) |
| In rete | Online |
| Indirrizo elettonico | E-mail address |
| Linetta in basso | _ (underline) |
| Posta elettronica | E-mail |
| Punto | . (dot) |
| Rete | Network |
| Riavviare | Re-start |
| Selezionare | To select |
| Sfogliare | To browse |
| Slash; barra che parte da destra | / (forward slash) |
| Smetti | Shut down |
| Trattino | – (hyphen) |
| Utente | User |
| Vu, vu, vu; doppia vu tre volte | www |

# Directory of Contacts

## Major Resources in Britain

### Embassy of Italy in the United Kingdom
14 Three Kings' Yard, London W1K 4EH
t (020) 7312 2200
f (020) 7312 2230
ambasciata.londra@esteri.it
www.amblondra.esteri.it

### Italian Consulate General
38 Eaton Place, London SW1X 8AN
t (020) 7235 9371 (Mon–Fri 3–4:30pm)
f (020) 7823 1609
consolato.londra@esteri.it
www.itconlond.org.uk

# British Resources in Italy

## British Chamber of Commerce for Italy
(Camera di Commercio Italo-Britannica)
Via Dante 12
20121 Milano MI
t 02 877798/t 02 805 6094/ELCS t 02 876981
f 02 8646 1885
bcci@britchamitaly.com

## Consolato Britannico, Bari
Via Dalmazia 127, 70121 Bari
t 080 554 3668
f 080 554 2977
gavan@tin.it

## Consolato Britannico, Cagliari
Viale Colombo 160, 90129 Quartu S.E., Cagliari
t 070 828628
f 070 862293
agraham@iol.it

## Consolato Britannico, Catania
Via Verdi 53, 95100 Catania
t 095 715 1864
f 095 715 1503
consular@omnilog.com

## Consolato Britannico, Florence
Lungarno Corsini 2, 50123 Firenze
t 055 284133/t 055 289556
f 055 219112
florenceconsular@florence.mail.fco.gov.uk

## Consolato Britannico, Genoa
Via G. Verdi 6/a, 16121 Genova
t 010 574 0071
f 010 530 4096

## Consolato Generale Britannico, Milan
Via S. Paolo 7, 20121 Milano
t 02 723001
f 02 864 65081
commercialmilano@milan.mail.fco.gov.uk

## Consolato Britannico, Naples
Via dei Mille 40, 80121 Napoli
t 081 423 8911
f 081 422 434
naplesinformation@feo.gov.uk

## Consolato Britannico, Palermo
Via Cavour 117, 90133 Palermo
t 091 326412
f 091 584240

## Consolato Britannico, Rome
Via XX Settembre 80/a, 00187 Roma
t 06 4220 0001
f 06 4220 2334
ConsularEnquiries@rome.mail.fco.gov.uk

## Consolato Britannico, Trieste
Via Roma 15, 34122 Trieste
t/f 040 3478303

## Consolato Britannico, Turin
Via Saluzzo 60, 10125 Torino
t 011 650 9202
f 011 669 5982
bcturin@yahoo.com

## Consolato Britannico, Venice
Accademia Dorsoduro 1051, 30123 Venezia
t 041 522 7207/t 041 522 7408
f 041 522 2617
britconvenice@tin.it

# Foreign Embassies in Italy

## Australia
Via Antonio Bosio 5, 00161 Roma
t 06 85 2721
f 06 85 272300
consular-rome@dfat.gov.au
www.italy.embassy.gov.au

## Great Britain
Via XX Settembre 80, 00187 Roma
t 06 4220 0001
f 06 4220 2333
RomePoliticalSection@fco.gov.uk
www.britain.it

## India
Via XX Settembre 5/2, 00187 Roma
t 06 4201 4072/t 06 4201 3078
f 06 4201 3078
admin.wing@indianembassy.it
www.indianembassy.it

### Ireland
Piazza Campitelli 3, 00186 Roma
t 06 6979 1211
f 06 6979 1231
**irish.embassy@esteri.it**

### New Zealand
Via Zara 28, 00198 Roma
t 06 441 7171
f 06 440 2984
**Nzemb.rom@flashnet.it**

### United States of America
Via Veneto 121, 00187 Roma
t 06 46741
f 06 488 2672

# Removal Companies

## UK

Bishop's Move Group
t (020) 7498 0300
**www.bishopsmove.com**

Bradshaw International, Manchester
t (0161) 877 5555
**www.bradshawinternational.com**

Burke Brothers, Wolverhampton
t (01902) 714555
**www.burkebros.co.uk**

International Removals SC
t (00 34) 952 235 054
**www.internationalremovals-sc.com**

Roy Trevor, Cheshire-based company.
t (01925) 630441
**www.roy-trevor.com**

Moving Solutions, London-based, and offering particularly personal service.
t (020) 8871 4466
**www.moving-solutions.com**

Union Jack Removals
t 0800 036 1011
**www.union-jack-removals.co.uk**

# Italy

Bolliger International Movers, Via Fosso della Magliana 12, 00148 Roma
t 06 656 6881
f 06 655 7133
www.bolliger.net

Bolliger International Movers, Via Palmieri  46, 20141 Milano
t 02 844721
f 02 8950 1233
milano@bolliger.it

Florence International Movers s.r.l., Via S. Pertini 51/53, 50019 Sesto Fiorentino, Firenze
t 055 425 1086
f 055 420 6176
firenze@bolliger.it

C. Stein di A. Righetti, Via di Rebibbia 119/121, 00156 Roma
t 06 407 3522
f 06 407 2521
info@cstein.org
www.cstein.org

IFC Worldwide Cargo, Via Lucrezia Romana 95/b, 00043 Ciampino (Roma)
t 06 790 851
f 06 7932 1113
ifc@ifcwwcargo.com
www.ifcwwcargo.com

Italian Moving Network , Via Oreste Ranelletti 61, 00166 Roma
t 06 6618 1888
f 06 6618 2111
italianmovingnetwork@tin.it
www.italianmovingnetwork.com

Milano Multiservis s.r.l., Milan Office, Via E. Cialdini 111, 20161 Milano
t 02 6622 1588/t 02 6622 1592
f 02 646 0183
info@milanomultiservis.it

Nessi, Via dei Valtorta, 41, 20127 Milano
t 02 261 3168
f 02 289 0876
nessi@nessi.it
www.nessi.it

World Cargo, Via  Valderoa 60, 00054 Fiumicino (Roma)
t 06 650 29134
f 06 658 4594
information@worldcargo.it
www.worldcargo.it

# Resources and Reference

## English-language Resources

### English *Yellow Pages*
Via Belisario 4/B, 00187 Roma
t 06 474 0861/t 06 9761 7528, f 06 9761 7529
info@englishyellowpages.it
www.intoitaly.it or www.englishyellowpages.it

### *Informer*
Via dei Tigli 2, 20020 Arese (Milano)
t 02 9358 1477, f 02 9358 0280
informer@informer.it
www.informer.it

### *Italy Daily*
ADV S.r.l., Via Leinì 19, 10036 Settimo Torinese (Torino)
info@italydaily.com
www.italydaily.com

### *Wanted in Rome*
(An English-language fortnightly publication.)
Via dei Delfini 17, Roma 00186
t 06 679 0190, f 06 678 3798
info@wantedinrome.com
www.wantedinrome.com

## Bookmark These

| | |
|---|---|
| www.accomodationsrome.com | If you want to rent in Rome, try here |
| www.ariassrl.it | Estate agency services specialising in law and planning permissions |
| www.asteimmobili.it | Online legal auctions of properties in Italy |
| www.bingocasa.it | Property-consulting directory |
| www.casa.it | Has an excellent database of property |
| www.casait.it | Properties for sale in Umbria and Tuscany |
| www.casainchianti.it | Tavernelle agency markets properties in Chianti, from apartments to prestigious villas |
| www.casa4you.net | Balducci properties in Umbria and Tuscany |
| www.casa-toscana.com | Villas for sale in Tuscany, and general information |
| www.eurom.com/fumagalli | Good selection of off-the-beaten-track properties in Pistoia and Tuscany |
| www.fiaip.it | Italian Federation of Professional Real Estate Agents. The only association composed solely of estate agents was founded in 1976 and now has about 3,000 members. |

| | |
|---|---|
| www.gabetti.com | Estate agency network with 300 branches |
| www.grimaldi.net | Estate agency franchising network across Italy with headquarters in Turin |
| www.groundsforliving.com | Full in-house service with architects and surveyors |
| www.immobiliarefumagalli.it | Good selection of off-the-beaten-track properties |
| www.immobilnet.com | Homes for sale and rental and holidays in Italy. Direct contact with the seller |
| www.italian-villas.com | In the USA, a vast selection of villas/apartments and Sardinia |
| www.italimmo.ch | Based in Switzerland, offers houses, farms, condominiums and villas for sale |
| www.italrentals.com | Offers hundreds of properties in Tuscany, Umbria |
| www.netimmobiliare.com | Estate agent in Venice specialising in businesses and commercial properties |
| www.rentitalianvillas.com | Although it only handles rentals, this US-based site is great for those looking for temporary accommodation in Tuscany and Rome |
| www.sitidoltremare.it | Property company for architectural restoration of ancient buildings in Puglia |
| www.spazioimmobiliare.com | Florentine agency with property across the country nationwide |
| www.venicerealestate.it | Specalising in homes in Venice. |

# Other Italian Internet Property Resources

| | |
|---|---|
| 100 Case – Immobiliare | www.100case.it |
| Agenzia Toscana Immobiliare | www.agenziatoscana.com |
| Babele Case | www.babelecase.net |
| Bene Habitare | www.benehabitare.it |
| Borsa Immobiliare di Roma | www.borsaimmobiliare.roma.it |
| Bravo Casa | www.bravocasa.it |
| CasaClick | www.casaclick.it |
| Casa & Mare | www.casaemare.com |
| Case Online | www.case-online.com |
| Caseaffari | www.caseaffari.it |
| Cas@OnLine | www.casaonline.it |
| Casa per me | www.casaperme.it |
| Casa per casa | www.casapercasa.it |
| CercaCasa.it | www.cercacasa.it |
| CercarCasa | www.cercarcasa.it |
| Corriere Immobiliare | www.corriereimmobiliare.it |
| DomusClick | www.domusclick.com |
| Ecasa | www.ecasa.it |
| Essegi Immobiliare | www.essegi.lucca.it |
| InCasa | www.incasa.it |
| Laila | www.laila.it |
| Mercato Immobiliare | www.mercato-immobiliare.com |
| Punto Partenza | www.casa.puntopartenza.it |

| | |
|---|---|
| Quattromura | **www.quattromura.it** |
| SoloCase | **www.solocase.it** |
| Studio I.M.P. | **www.studioimp.it** |
| Tecnocasa | **www.tecnocasa.it** |
| Toscana Immobiliare | **www.toscanaimmobiliare.net** |
| Trova Casa | **www.trova-casa.it** |
| Zio Tom | **www.ziotom.it** |

# Italian Holidays and Celebrations

## Days Celebrated Nationwide

| | |
|---|---|
| 1 January | 15 August |
| 6 January | 1 November |
| Easter | 2 November |
| Easter Monday | 8 December |
| 25 April | 25 December |
| 1 May | 26 December |
| 2 June | |

## Major Celebrations

**1 January**  *Capodanno* or *San Silvestro*. New Year's Day is celebrated with fireworks and champagne. Not too long ago people threw their old furniture out of their windows to celebrate a new beginning.

**6 January**  *Befana* or *Epifania*. On the day of the Epiphany a good witch flies into children's rooms and gives them gifts if they've been good or coal if they've been bad.

**January–March**  *Carnivale*. Carnival celebrations are taken very seriously in Venice (with a masquerade parade), in Ivrea (where townsfolk pummel each other with oranges), and in Viareggio (where floats resembling popular and unpopular politicians are paraded through town).

**February**  *Festival della Canzona Italiana*. The seaside town of San Remo is transformed by Italy's biggest music festival.

**8 March**  *Festa delle Donne*. On Women's Day yellow mimosa flowers are given to favourite females and the women head out to dinner together.

**March or April**  *Pasqua*. On Easter Sunday, Italians eat lamb and a dove-shaped cake. It's a day that the extended family spends together.

*Pasquetta*. Easter Monday is a national holiday and time for more eating.

**25 April**  *Anniversario della Liberazione*. On Liberation Day, parades and parties to celebrate Italy's freedom from Germany in 1945.

**1 May**  *Primo Maggio*. Labour Day is celebrated with parades and a massive outdoor concert in Rome.

| | |
|---|---|
| June–September | *Biennale di Venezia.* In even-numbered years, this international art event is held through the summer. |
| 2 June | *Festa della Repubblica.* The Celebration of the Italian Republic is honoured with military parades. |
| July and August | *Palio di Siena.* This Tuscan town holds its famous horse race once in July and then again the following month. |
| July or August | *La Festa di Noantri.* Rome's Trastevere celebrates with food, games and music. |
| | *Festival dei Due Mondi.* In Spoleto, Umbria, the 'Festival of Two Worlds', has music and performing arts. |
| 15 August | *Ferragosto.* The Festival of the Assumption is one day when which you can count on every Italian being on holiday. |
| September | *Regatta Storica.* A boat race in Venice on the Grand Canal. |
| | *Mostra Internazionale d'Arte Cinematografica.* During the first two weeks of the month, Venice puts on Italy's most important film festival. |
| 1 November | *Ognissanti.* All Saints' Day. |
| 2 November | *Tutti i Morti.* All Soul's Day is when people bring flowers to the tombs of their relatives. |
| 8 December | *L'Immacolata Concezione.* Immaculate Conception. |
| 25 December | *Natale.* Christmas is celebrated with gifts and, more recently, a tree, but tradition calls for a *percepio*, a Nativity scene with hand-made figurines. |
| 26 December | *Santo Stefano.* The day after Christmas, or Saint Steven's Day, is the time for a big family lunch. |

## Saint's Days

In addition to public holidays, each town has its saint's day off as a public holiday. These are celebrated with fervour and match an individual's *onomastico*, or name day.

| Date | Saint | Place Celebrated |
|---|---|---|
| 25 April | San Marco | Venice |
| 1 May | Sant'Elisio | Cágliari |
| 13 June | Sant'Antonio | Padua |
| 24 June | San Giovanni | Turin, Genoa, Florence |
| 29 June | San Pietro | Rome |
| 10–15 July | Santa Rosalia | Palermo |
| 26 July | Santa Anna | Ischia |
| 19 September | San Gennaro | Naples |
| 4 October | San Petronio | Bologna |
| 4 October | San Francesco | Assisi |
| 7 December | Sant'Ambrogio | Milan |

# Further Reading

Barzini, Luigi, *The Italians* (Hamish Hamilton)
Clark, Martin, *Modern Italy, 1871–1982*
Dickens, Charles, *Pictures From Italy*
Duggan, Christopher, *A Concise History of Italy*
Forster, E. M., *A Room With a View; Where Angels Fear to Tread*
Ginsborg, Paul, *A History of Contemporary Italy; Society and Politics 1943–1988* (Penguin)
Goethe, J. W., *Italian Journey* (Penguin Classics)
James, Henry, *The Portrait of a Lady; Italian Hours; Henry James on Italy*
Larner, Monica and Travis Neighbor, *Living, Studying and Working in Italy* (Henry Holt)
Lawrence, D. H., *Twilight in Italy; Sea and Sardinia; Etruscan Places*
Mann, Thomas, *Death in Venice*
McCarthy, Mary, *The Stones of Florence and Venice Observed* (Penguin)
Morton, H. V., *A Traveller in Rome; A Traveller in Southern Italy* (Methuen)
Stowe, Harriet Beecher, *Agnes of Sorrento*
Wharton, Edith, *Italian Backgrounds, Italian Villas and Their Gardens, Roman Fever*

# Climate Charts

## Average Seasonal Temperatures °Fahrenheit/°Celsius

|          | Jan   | Feb   | Mar   | Apr   | May   | June  | July  | Aug   | Sept  | Oct   | Nov   | Dec   |
|----------|-------|-------|-------|-------|-------|-------|-------|-------|-------|-------|-------|-------|
| Amalfi   | 55/13 | 52/11 | 53/12 | 57/14 | 64/18 | 78/26 | 78/26 | 77/25 | 73/23 | 70/21 | 55/13 | 56/13 |
| Bologna  | 35/2  | 40/4  | 48/9  | 55/13 | 63/17 | 74/23 | 77/35 | 75/24 | 68/20 | 61/16 | 46/8  | 36/2  |
| Florence | 42/6  | 45/7  | 50/10 | 55/13 | 63/17 | 74/23 | 78/26 | 75/24 | 68/20 | 60/16 | 50/10 | 43/6  |
| Genoa    | 46/8  | 48/9  | 52/11 | 57/14 | 63/17 | 69/21 | 75/24 | 74/23 | 69/20 | 63/17 | 54/12 | 48/9  |
| Milan    | 34/2  | 37/3  | 44/7  | 50/10 | 59/15 | 70/21 | 78/26 | 75/24 | 64/18 | 54/12 | 42/6  | 35/2  |
| Naples   | 46/8  | 47/8  | 51/10 | 55/13 | 63/17 | 70/21 | 79/26 | 77/25 | 69/20 | 61/16 | 54/12 | 49/9  |
| Palermo  | 54/12 | 55/13 | 56/13 | 60/16 | 65/18 | 67/19 | 78/26 | 79/26 | 75/24 | 69/21 | 62/17 | 56/13 |
| Rome     | 46/8  | 48/9  | 51/10 | 55/13 | 62/17 | 69/21 | 77/25 | 75/24 | 69/20 | 62/17 | 55/13 | 49/9  |
| Venice   | 36/2  | 40/4  | 46/8  | 54/12 | 62/17 | 68/20 | 75/25 | 73/23 | 66/19 | 56/13 | 45/7  | 38/3  |

## Average Precipitation in Inches

|          | Jan | Feb | Mar | Apr | May | June | July | Aug | Sept | Oct | Nov | Dec |
|----------|-----|-----|-----|-----|-----|------|------|-----|------|-----|-----|-----|
| Bologna  | 1.7 | 1.8 | 2.4 | 2.6 | 2.6 | 2.1  | 1.7  | 2.3 | 2.4  | 2.8 | 3.2 | 2.4 |
| Como     | 2.4 | 2.2 | 3.2 | 5.0 | 6.9 | 6.4  | 4.7  | 6.3 | 5.6  | 5.6 | 3.7 | 2.1 |
| Florence | 2.9 | 2.7 | 3.2 | 3.1 | 2.9 | 2.2  | 1.6  | 3.0 | 3.1  | 3.5 | 4.4 | 3.6 |
| Genoa    | 4.2 | 3.7 | 4.2 | 3.4 | 3.0 | 2.1  | 1.1  | 3.2 | 3.9  | 6.0 | 4.4 | 3.2 |
| Milan    | 2.7 | 3.0 | 3.9 | 4.2 | 5.2 | 3.7  | 2.6  | 3.8 | 2.9  | 4.2 | 4.2 | 2.2 |
| Naples   | 4.1 | 3.9 | 3.4 | 3.0 | 2.0 | 1.3  | 1.0  | 1.6 | 3.2  | 5.1 | 6.4 | 4.8 |
| Palermo  | 2.8 | 2.6 | 2.3 | 1.7 | 1.0 | 0.5  | 0.2  | 0.5 | 1.6  | 3.9 | 3.7 | 3.2 |
| Rome     | 3.2 | 3.0 | 2.6 | 2.2 | 1.3 | 0.6  | 0.6  | 1.3 | 2.7  | 3.7 | 4.4 | 3.5 |
| Venice   | 2.3 | 2.1 | 2.3 | 2.5 | 2.7 | 3.0  | 2.5  | 3.3 | 2.6  | 2.7 | 3.4 | 2.1 |

# Appendix

## Checklist – Do-it-yourself Inspection of Property
Task ✓

**Title** – check that the property corresponds with its description:
Number of rooms
Plot size

**Plot**
Identify the physical boundaries of the plot
Is there any dispute with anyone over these boundaries?
Are there any obvious foreign elements on your plot such as pipes,
cables, drainage ditches, water tanks, etc.?
Are there any signs of anyone else having rights over the property –
footpaths, access ways, cartridges from hunting, etc.?

**Garden/terrace**
Are any plants, ornaments, etc. on site not being sold with the property?

**Pool** – is there a pool? If so:
What size is it?
Is it clean and algae-free?
Do the pumps work?
How old is the machinery?
Who maintains it?
What is the annual cost of maintenance?
Does it appear to be in good condition?

**Walls** – stand back from property and inspect from outside:
Any signs of subsidence?
Walls vertical?
Any obvious cracks in walls?
Are walls well pointed?
Any obvious damp patches?
Any new repairs to walls or repointing?

**Roof** – inspect from outside property:
Does roof sag?
Are there missing/slipped tiles?
Do all faces of roof join squarely?
Lead present and in good order?

**Guttering and downpipes** – inspect from outside property:
All present?
Securely attached?
Fall of guttering constant?
Any obvious leaks?
Any recent repairs?

# Checklist – Do-it-yourself Inspection of Property (*cont.*)
## Task ✓

**Enter property**
Does it smell of damp?
Does it smell musty?
Does it smell of dry rot?
Any other strange smells?

**Doors**
Signs of rot?
Close properly – without catching?
Provide proper seal?
Locks work?

**Windows**
Signs of rot?
Close properly – without catching?
Provide proper seal?
Locks work?
Excessive condensation?

**Floor**
Can you see it all?
Does it appear in good condition?
Any sign of cracked or rotten boards?

**Under floor**
Can you get access under the floor?
If so, is it ventilated?
Is there any sign of rot?
How close are joists?
Are joist ends in good condition where they go into walls?
What is maximum unsupported length of joist run?
Is there any sign of damp or standing water?

**Roof void**
Is it accessible?
Is there sign of water entry?
Can you see daylight through the roof?
Is there an underlining between the tiles and the void?
Is there any sign of rot in timbers?
Horizontal distance between roof timbers
Size of roof timbers (section)
Maximum unsupported length of roof timbers
Is roof insulated – if so, what depth and type of insulation?

# Checklist – Do-it-yourself Inspection of Property (*cont.*)
## Task ✓

**Woodwork**

    Any sign of rot?

    Any sign of wood-boring insects?

    Is it dry?

**Interior walls**

    Any significant cracks?

    Any obvious damp problems?

    Any sign of recent repair/redecoration?

**Electricity**

    Check electricity meter:

        How old is it?

        What is its rated capacity?

    Check all visible wiring:

        What type is it?

        Does it appear in good physical condition?

    Check all plugs:

        Is there power to plug?

        Does plug tester show good earth and show 'OK'?

        Are there enough plugs?

    Lighting:

        Do all lights work?

        Which light fittings are included in sale?

**Water**

    Do all hot and cold taps work?

    Is flow adequate?

    Do taps drip?

    Is there a security cut-off on all taps between mains and tap?

    Do they seem in good condition?

    Hot water:

        Is hot water 'on'? If so, does it work at all taps, showers, etc.?

        What type of hot water system is fitted?

        Age?

**Gas**

    Is the property fitted with city (piped) gas? If so:

        Age of meter?

        Does installation appear in good order?

        Is there any smell of gas?

    Is the property fitted with bottled gas? If so:

        Where are bottles stored?

        Is it ventilated to outside of premises?

# Checklist – Do-it-yourself Inspection of Property (*cont.*)
## Task ✓

**Central heating**
Is the property fitted with central heating? If so:
Is it on?
Will it turn on?
What type is it?
Is there heat at all radiators/outlets?
Do any thermostats appear to work?
Are there any signs of leaks?

**Fireplaces**
Is the property fitted with any solid fuel heaters? If so:
Any sign of blow-back from chimneys?
Do chimneys (outside) show stains from leakage?
Do chimneys seem in good order?

**Air-conditioning**
Which rooms are air-conditioned?
Are units included in the sale?
Do the units work (deliver cold air)?
What type of air-conditioning is it?
How old is it?

**Phone**
Does it work?
Number?

**Satellite TV**
Does it work?
Is it included in the sale?

**Drainage**
What type of drainage does property have?
If septic tank, how old?
Who maintains it?
When was it last serviced?
Any smell of drainage problems in bathrooms and toilets?
Does water drain away rapidly from all sinks, showers and toilets?
Is there any inspection access through which you can see
drainage taking place?
Is there any sign of plant ingress to drains?
Do drains appear to be in good condition and well pointed?

## Checklist – Do-it-yourself Inspection of Property (*cont.*)
Task ✓

**Kitchen**
    Do all cupboards open/close properly?
    Any sign of rot?
    Tiling secure and in good order?
    Enough plugs?
    What appliances are included in sale?
    Do they work?
    Age of appliances included?

**Bathroom**
    Security and condition of tiling?
    Ventilation?

**Appliances**
    What appliances generally are included in sale?
    What is *not* included in sale?

**Furniture**
    What furniture is included in sale?
    What is *not* included in sale?

**Repairs/Improvements/Additions**
    What repairs have been carried out in last two years?
    What improvements have been carried out in last two years/ ten years?
    What additions have been made to the property in last two years/ten years?
    Are there builders' receipts'/guarantees?
    Is there building consent/planning permission for any additions or alterations?

**Defects**
    Is seller aware of any defects in the property?

# Index

# Italy touring atlas

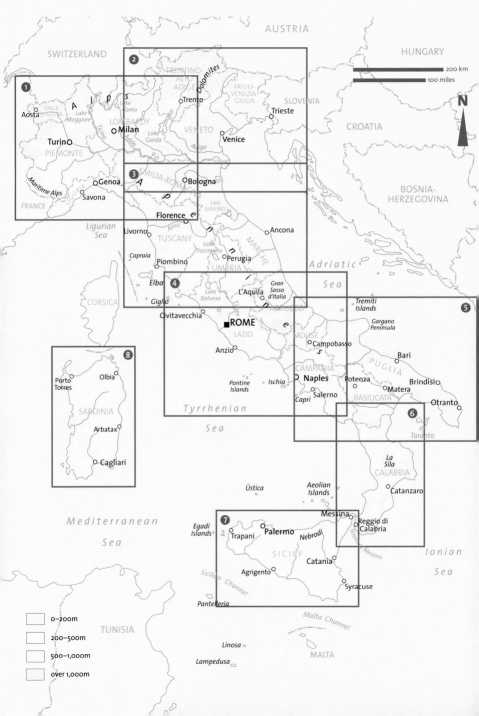

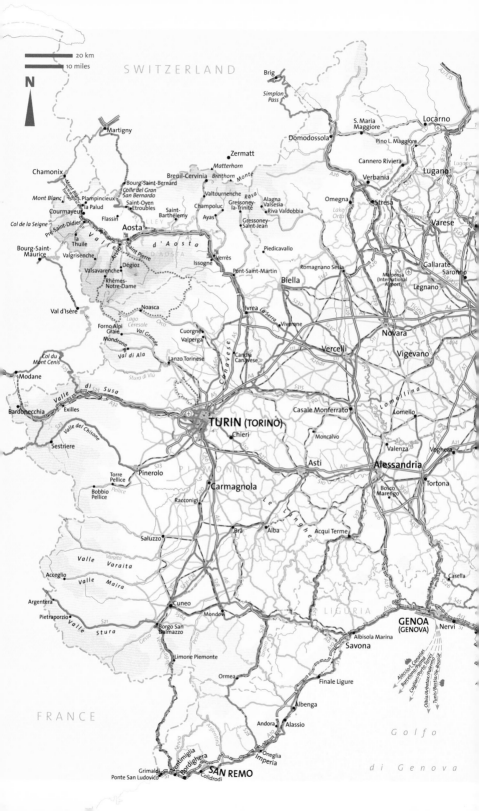

AUSTRIA

20 km
10 miles

N

Comelico
Superiore
Sto Stefano
di Cadore
Comeglians
Tarvisio
Calalzo di Cadore
Pieve di Cadore
Lago di
Sauris
Ampezzo
Tolmezzo
Lago del Predil
Forni di
Sotto
Sella Nevea
Belluno
Clauzetto
Gemona di Friuli
FRIULI-VENEZIA-
GIULIA
Cividale del Friuli
SLOVENIA
Udine
Vittorio
Veneto
Pordenone
Codroipo
Palmanova
Gorizia
Sacile
Conegliano
Sesto al
Reghena
Monfalcone
Oderzo
Portogruaro
Treviso
Lignano
Sabbiadoro
Lignano Riviera
Grado
Trieste
Muggia
Caorle
Mestre
Lido di Jesolo
Venice

Golfo di

Chioggia
Sottomarina
Venezia

CROATIA

Rosolina Mare
Isola di Albarella

Po

Delta

Adriatic

Lido di
Volano
Lido delle Nazioni
Lidi di Comacchio
Comacchio

Sea

Ravenna

I. Strómboli
I. di Ùstica
I. Panarea
I. Filicudi
I. Salina
I. Alicudi
Aeolian Islands
I. Lipari
Tyrrhenian Sea
I. Vulcano
Capo di Milazzo
Lido Mortelle
Milazzo
Villa S. Giovanni
Capo Tindari
MESSINA
Capo d'Orlando
Barcellona
REGGIO DI CALABRIA
Capo S. Vito
Punta Raisi Airport
PALERMO
Capo Zafferano
Golfo di Castellammare
S. Agata di Militello
Monti Peloritani
Itála
Monreale
Cefalù
Egadi Islands
Tràpani
Erice
Castellammare del Golfo
Termini Imerese
Monti Nebrodi
I. di Levanzo
Alcamo
Capo Sant'Alessio
Gola di Alcàntara
Cáccamo
Castelbuono
Taormina
I. Maréttimo
Segesta
Randazzo
Monti Madonie
Giardini-Naxos
I. Favignana
Caltavuturo
Corleone
Monte Etna
Marsala
Gibellina
Nicosia
Giarre
Prizzi
Sta. Margherita di Bélice
Resultano
Adrano
Castelvetrano
Acireale
Monti Sicani
Cammarata
Vilalba
Mazara del Vallo
Catenanuova
Paternò
Selinunte
Enna
CATANIA
Ribera
Fontana Rossa Airport
Sciacca
Caltanissetta
Piana di Catania
Golfo di Catania
Montallegro
Piazza Armerina
Capo Bianco
Canicattì
Siculiana
Siculiana Marina
Lentini
Agrigento
Mediterranean Sea
Caltagirone
Augusta
To the Pelagie Islands
Grammichele
Butera
N
Licata
SYRACUSE
Palazzolo Acréide
Gela
I. di Linosa
Ognina
Golfo di Gela
Vittòria
Cómiso
Pelagie Islands
Ragusa
Noto
Avola
20 km
Módica
10 miles
Ionian Sea
I. di Pantelleria
7
Ispica
10 km
Marina di Ragusa
I. di Lampedusa
5 miles
Capo Pássero

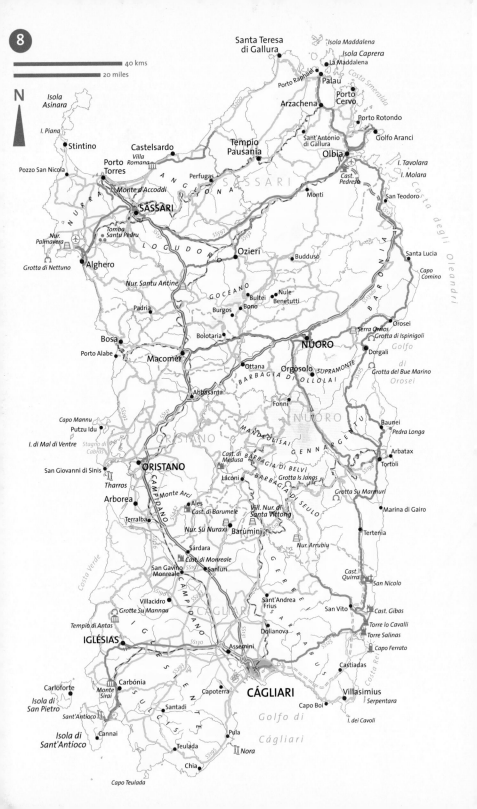

**CADOGAN**guides  **ITALY**

'Erudite, informed, irreverent and indulgent'

*The Sunday Times*

# Titles available in the *Buying a Property* series

*Buying a Property: France*
*Buying a Property: Spain*
*Buying a Property: Portugal*
*Buying a Property: Ireland*
*Buying a Property: Florida*
*Buying a Property: Greece*
*Buying a Property: Turkey*
*Buying a Property: Cyprus*
*Buying a Property: Eastern Europe*
*Buying a Property: Abroad*
*Buying a Property: Retiring Abroad*

# Related titles: *Working and Living*

*Working and Living: France*
*Working and Living: Spain*
*Working and Living: Italy*
*Working and Living: Portugal*
*Working and Living: Australia*
*Working and Living: New Zealand*
*Working and Living: Canada*
*Working and Living: USA*

# Related titles: *Starting a Business*

*Starting a Business: France*
*Starting a Business: Spain*